ENRICHETTA
WOMAN OF GOD

ENRICHETTA WOMAN OF GOD

The life of Mother Enrichetta Dominici, Superior of the Institute of the Sisters of St Ann

by

Fernando Bea

BURNS & OATES
London

This translation first published in Great Britain and
associated territories in 1977 by Burns & Oates
Limited, 2-10 Jerdan Place, London SW6 5PT.
Translated from the original *Enrichetta Donna di Dio*,
first published in Italian by Gribaudi of Turin, Italy,
and copyright © 1977 Piero Gribaudi Editore, 10128
Torine — C.so Galileo Ferraris 67. This translation and
arrangement copyright © 1977 Search Press Limited.
All rights reserved. No part of this book may be
reproduced, stored in an information retrieval system
of any kind, transmitted, performed in any form or
any way, or translated, without the previous written
permission of the publishers, Burns & Oates, 2-10
Jerdan Place, London SW6 5PT, Great Britain.
The translation was made by V. Green with the
assistance and advice of Barbara Wall, Sarah Twohig,
Sarah Fawcett, Helen Douglas-Cooper, Dinah
Livingstone, Sir Alec Randall and Paul Burns.

ISBN 086012 059 7

Set IBM by Tek-Art, Croydon, Surrey

Printed and bound in Great Britian by
Billing & Sons Limited,
Guildford, London and Worcester.

Contents

Preface

Mother Enrichetta is a unique 'case', yet her life —
recounted here with clarity and precision — is marked
by nothing peculiar or bizarre. The actions of her
outward existence hardly differed, in fact, from those
of other figures of her time. Her spirituality seems at
first rather like that typical of the nineteenth century.
Yet Mother Enrichetta demands our attention. The
picture we have of her, in spite of its apparent
ordinariness, has an insistently enigmatic quality that
nags at the mind. Her message asks to be decyphered;
it seems at first obvious and clear-cut, yet in the end
it faces any averagely sensitive and sympathetic reader
with a lasting paradox.

We have tried, in the relatively small space of this
book and, in the few introductory lines that follow, to
suggest an approach that will go some way to resolving
the problem. It is not an easy task, for there are some
beings whom God hides under the protection of his
mantle in a quite special way. He seems particularly
jealous of their welfare and their reputation. They are
people in whom the ordinary and the sublime, simplicity
and complexity, the visible and the invisible, are so
intimately joined and perfectly integrated as to be

strangely irksome in a world as shattered and lacking in integration as our own. Mother Enrichetta is a problem personality: a scandal in the best sense even in these days when tribulation and hope both still have their parts to play. Any real attempt to penetrate the mystery of this woman must be more than a mere theoretical exercise. It must be an attempt to discover God's presence in our mundane world.

Essentially, Mother Enrichetta appears to us as a woman like no other, as a true woman of God. She was of course a woman in the deepest sense of the word — complete and fulfilled. She is in fact an extraordinary up-to-date figure in these days when women are taking their place at the very heart of the revolutionary transformation of mankind.

Nowadays, while subjecting their own identity to unrelenting scrutiny, women are trying to give the world itself a new character. Mother Enrichetta, on a simple human level, embodied the most typical feminine characteristics that are now the object of study and investigation. She was a woman who did not prize possessions; a woman of deep sympathies; a woman of sure control and right practice. She was a woman who practised her humanity in the true sense, and one well able to respond appropriately to others and to live to the full the life to which she was called. And she did not dissimulate or disguise what she knew to be the truth about herself.

She was a woman of direct human appeal who offers us now an essentially consistent life-story deserving of the respect we owe a great woman of religion, but also the robust admiration a fine human achievement and a rounded character should call forth from any sane and sympathetic person.

Another way of approaching the figure of Mother Enrichetta as we meet it in the pages that follow is her special variety of spiritual example: the way in which she turned spiritual dryness to good ends and never rendered arid, let alone destroyed, the precious essence of spirit. In a time of listlessness of faith and vagueness of resolution she was and remains truly alive, able to sense and encourage the breath of the Spirit in the wastelands of the soul.

Her kind of belief is valuable indeed and perhaps the most attractive to us now of the qualities that draw people to her. She thought of living the faith as living Christ himself. She did not as it were 'cultivate' her faith, seeking in some way to analyze its peculiarities; instead, her life was her faith. The absoluteness, the radical nature, of her belief combined daring mystical intensity with exemplary gospel simplicity in following the will of God.

Mother Enrichetta was open to God. She lived in unceasing communion with the voice of his Spirit; she was a window through which the countenance of God could shine into this weary, dusty world. The language she used to address her Lord is unusual and even, some might think, infantile. That is far from the truth. It is the language of a dialogue with God that is always trusting, gentle and loving, tender and ardent in its way, but always frank and straightforward. For Mother Enrichetta prayer fed faith and faith sustained life; but life even more was prayer, and therefore faith.

Mother Enrichetta possessed yet another quality: the ability to stimulate and maintain the spirit of community, of human co-operation. Hence the astonishing growth and spread of her Institute in response to the encouragement of her genius for guidance and organization. Her inspiration was and remains the unusual capacity of her followers to come together and unite in the common endeavour and freedom of the Spirit. An Order is so impelled and inspired only when it is constantly visited and sustained by the Spirit of God. In that inspiration we may abandon historical precision and opt for the essential truth in seeing Mother Enrichetta as the cofounder of the Institute of the Sisters of St Ann. The intuition — the idea — came from Giulia di Barolo, but the finishing touch,the spiritual actuality, was the work of Mother Enrichetta.

The astounding harmony of Mother Enrichetta's spiritual character was the fruit of the mystery of the Cross. The young Caterina's longing to live the passion of Christ became one with the intensely lived and effective existence of a woman dedicated to the service of others.

Mother Enrichetta's life was a fusion of action and contemplation, of love and inwardness, of objective life and mysticism. She took the Cross of Christ into lived existence. For her it was the Cross of suffering and triumph at one and the same time. It was liberation through the Cross. The love of God and the love of humankind are appropiately intermixed in her life and devotion.

Seen thus, the true modernity of Mother Enrichetta shines forth as an inward intensity of unmistakable outward relevance. She was a woman of deep humility and at the same time profound Christian daring; a wholly mature and balanced counsellor in the ways and instructions of the Lord and his demand on us. Her message is one of truly resolute faith even when all earthly supports seem insecure; of belief in divine goodness when all reason for hope seems lost or unfounded; of love in a world of paradoxes and crises. She is a figure who moves from her own times into our post-conciliar world to offer a modern example of loving faithfulness to all that really matters. She is a living sign not only to religious of any kind but to all Christians moving along the ways of the world as it is.

Mother Enrichetta's message has spread and continues to spread far beyond the confines of the body she founded. Whoever is open to the Spirit can learn from her example of comfort and consolation, advice and

the Spirit will find in her an example of the Christian
mentor who offers sure guidance in a time of uncertainty
and mere will-o'the-wisp ventures. This great woman
of God gives us a vital example of assurance and courage.
She does so across the years from the sound basis of
trust in God and knowledge of his unfailing goodness
and continuing presence at our side.

THE PUBLISHERS

I Life is life only where there is love

The starlit sky
At that time – in 1829 – the starlit sky was the most beautiful sight the humble people of Borgo Salsasio[1] had to enjoy in the summer, on their doorsteps late into the evening, in the freshness that followed the burning heat of the day, which even the water from the well failed to relieve.

The silence was conducive to sleep and fatigue was very real, especially for anyone who had worked all day in the fields.

Turin, the capital of the Kingdom of Sardinia, was about thirty kilometres away, though even further away from the concerns and the many needs of these people, accustomed to work from morning till night. They were a robust, simple people, sunburnt, with roughened hands.

He was rich in these parts who had a pair of oxen for his plough. Some of the land still needed to be tilled: nothing was cultivated but hemp and willow. It was from the presence of the willows in this once marshy area, that the name Salsasio, which is that of one of the four *borghi* or districts of the busy township of Carmagnola, derived.

Many families were involved in the production of

hemp, from the time in March when it was sown in close furrows so as to obtain a longer stem, to the time of the harvest at the beginning of August.

In this part of Piedmont, the art of carding the hemp was traditional. Carmagnolese hemp was famous: it was made into cloth, rope, fuses and ship's rigging. Every year, when the work was finished, from the port on the river in the outskirts of Carmagnola barges sailed off down the Po. They were taking the product to Turin, and even as far as Lombardy and the Veneto.

The hemp industry was an important one, in spite of the fluctuations caused by the harvest itself, which was not always abundant, by unfavourable political events, and by the demand on the market. Many were the rope-makers who emigrated to nearby France, where they could find work, especially in the port of Marseilles. These were the emigrants who, at the time of the French Revolution, as they came together of an evening to drink a glass of wine and sing the popular songs of their far off country, composed 'La Carmagnole', which became famous for the protest element it contained; and 'Carmagnoles' was the name given to the songs intoned on feast days by the people who danced beneath the tree of liberty.[2] 'Carmagnole', too, was the name given to the jacket worn by the Piedmontese workers and adopted by the people of Marseilles when they entered Paris in 1792, a symbol of the ideal of equality proclaimed by the revolution.

The rope-makers who stayed at home joined together, under the protection of St Bartholemew, in a society[3] the origins of which were lost in the mists of time, as indeed was the art of working with hemp. There were numerous confraternities of rope-makers, true 'universities' in which the older and more experienced members had the coveted title of 'master' and all enjoyed particular benefits: the services of a doctor, free hospital accommodation, a basic pension – which at that time was a great deal, above all in a poor district like Salsasio.

Another and far less profitable form of industry came from the cultivation of the willow. From the slender twigs of this plant, which flourished along the river, wicker baskets were made and then sold at fairs in different parts of the country. The leftovers, the more intractable shoots which stayed red and were known as 'venghet', were used to make panniers, covered baskets and objects for use in the country. Nothing was wasted, and at home during the long winter evenings by the fire, the younger members of the family learnt from their elders how to work the wicker. It was a craft practised by both men and women, and the agile hands moved quickly, tracing long shadows against the light shed by the warming flame.

At Salsasio, as in the neighbouring *borghi* — with the exception of the celebrated printing press of Barbie di Carmagnola,[4] where in 1821 the historical proclamation of Santorre di Santarosa was printed — there were no other activities. Apart, of course, from the age-old activity of the fields, which in every age demands much and gives little in return.

There was great poverty in Salsasio. The village was still feeling the effects of the great fire of 13 May 1799, for which the Napoleonic forces under General Fraissinet were responsible. The terrible incident left lasting marks everywhere. The village was laid waste in response to the rebellion of a normally peaceful people who were stirred to action for reasons which, in the last analysis, were not and never will be known.[5] They had been told of a holy war, of a struggle against the heretics who were intending to import the sinister ideas of the Revolution: to their innate distrust of the French was joined a determination to fight in defence of their threatened land, and of their religion. And so, armed with hayforks and pruning hooks and a handful of shotguns, they found themselves engaged in battle against a full blown army.

3

The result? The parish church was stripped and burned, houses were destroyed, stables and fields plundered. This useless action ended with an immense funeral pyre, and the four hundred or so dead remained unburied for four days because there was no one left in the devastated village.[6]

It may be that the financial difficulties of the Dominici family, who at one time must have enjoyed a certain wealth, however modest and in proportion to their rural surroundings, can be traced to this event.[7]

Even today there are Dominici living in the area, and their nickname has always been *Capala,* which is the dialect word for a sheaf, a bundle of hay or wheat. The nickname suggests that the Dominici can be traced back to a time when they worked the land, probably as tenant farmers, given that small land-holdings were rare in those days. What is certain is that in the list of villagers who lost their lives in the fire, the name Dominici appears at least twice: 'Sebastiano Dominici, son of the late Peter, husband of Bobba Margherita, aged forty-three years, and Giuseppe Dominici, son of the late Peter, aged thirty-seven years'.[8]

In 1829, the Dominicis lived almost opposite the parish church in a straight-fronted house, longer than it was high, with an outside staircase and porch leading to the upper floor. On the ground floor was the living room, with the fireplace and narrow cooking range. Upstairs there were three bedrooms with beamed ceilings; the windows overlooked the courtyard; on one side the green fields could be seen; on the other was the road that led to Carmagnola. Beyond the threshing floor there was the stable for the animals.

Giuseppe Dominici, son of Giovanni Battista,[9] and Anna Pipino, daughter of Luigi, were married on 10 January 1820.[10] According to those who knew them, it was a case of love at first sight: he was twenty-one and had scarcely attained his majority; she was twenty.

They lived from their work in 'average' conditions:[11] neither great poverty nor great wealth. They did not want for necessities, which was already a great deal; but from the first days of the marriage an element of friction was created between husband and wife. It is impossible to diagnose the real reasons for the disagreement which went on growing until it became irreparable: misunderstandings perhaps, questions of personal interest or, quite simply, the development in Guiseppe of an intolerance for the demands of family life.

Certainly, before making the definitive break which was to take place in 1833,[12] they made repeated efforts to start all over again, in harmony. Most of the efforts were made on the part of the wife, who was a sensitive and profoundly religious person. But the situation was not resolved.[13]

It is easy to imagine the young girl, waiting alone late into the evening for the return of her husband. In the darkness — the lamp remained unlit to save oil — by the light of the dying fire, she said the rosary. Faith could be and often was a support, but it was hard to go on like this. Every slightest sound outside — a hen moving in the chicken run or the dog barking at some rare passer by — made her jump. Between one Hail Mary and the next she waited patiently. Moment after moment, she would listen for his step near the door, his key going into the lock. But then she would almost be afraid that the moment had come: she would have to face her husband in an ugly mood, and drunk, as he was every evening.

As far as possible she kept her sorrow to herself. She was reserved, and it was difficult to find people who understood her. When she could bear it no longer, she would go to her brother, don Andrea, parish priest of neighbouring Borgo San Bernardo,[14] for advice. She was not a woman to conceal things, however. In the district she was highly regarded, and yet, when she went to church for Mass on Sundays, or on other days for the evening benediction, she used to feel everyone was reading her bitterness and disappointment in her face.

It all called for strength. Virtue demands endurance and patience, and love for one's children makes suffering in silence less hard to bear.

In 1821 Lucia was born, in 1824 Teresa, and in 1826 Giovanni Battista.[15] And always there was the same illusion that, with one more child, Giovanni would become more attached to his family, face up to his many difficulties more calmly, and finally realize his responsibilities as a father.

Moments of improvement, when it seemed that everything might return to normal, if indeed it ever had been that, alternated with periods of crisis, which led one to expect the worst.

Borgo San Bernardo

The patronal feast of the Madonna at the end of September was just over. People had come for the occasion from Carmagnola, Borgo San Bernardo, Casanova, and all the surrounding districts. There were street decorations, the multicoloured booths of the travelling salesmen, the shining brass of the highly-acclaimed Accademia Filarmonica of Carmagnola, the band, and the numerous members of the confraternities — such as would have been part of the life of any festival.

September 24 was the great day, and at midday there was not a family that did not sit down to a big dish of 'bagna del pru', a rabbit delicacy which was customarily washed down with a wine that was a joy to drink. In the afternoon there was the solemn procession: long white lines of cottas, priestly vestments, the long flowing habits of the confraternities, conspicuous among which was the scarlet of the Confraternity of the Holy Trinity.[16] The crowd was such that the *borgo* could not contain it. The climax came in the evening: fireworks, climbing high, red yellow and green, against the dark sky, a cascade of colours. It was a feast day like few others in Salsasio, which even today is proud to be known as 'Borgo dalla Madonna.'

On 10 October 1829, a child was born in the Dominici household. The following day she was baptized and given the names Anna Caterina Maria.[17] The godfather was a maternal uncle, Antonia Pipino, the godmother Caterina Strumia. The parish priest at the time was don Carlo Masera.[18]

It is impossible to say whether the birth of the child helped to restore peace to the family, even for a time. What is certain is that a few years later Anna Dominici was once again expecting a child — a boy, who died, according to the records at Borgo San Bernardo, shortly after his birth. Indeed, since there is no name on the birth certificate, he was presumably stillborn and baptised *sub conditione,* perhaps by the midwife herself, one Maria Reynero, on 23 February 1834.[19]

At this time, Anna Dominici, together with her children, was living as the guest of her brother, the parish priest of Borgo San Bernardo. And she was to remain there for some time, determined to live no longer with the man who had brought her so much bitterness. That so grave a decision matured in the woman's mind while she was expecting a child suggests that something particular happened, something very serious. The reasons for the separation remain obscure, open to every hypothesis. Nor is much light thrown on the matter by what Mother Enrichetta had to say on the subject in her autobiography: 'Family misfortunes, together with the unworthy behaviour of my poor father, forced my good and virtuous mother to separate from him, with the approval of the Archbishop of Turin, by a formal divorce.[20] I have nothing to say and no feelings about these disasters, since they happened at a time when my tender age — I was about four years old — meant I was incapable of being involved in the many misfortunes that befell my family'.[21]

The father, too, left Salsasio, most probably starting up another family in Turin or elsewhere.[22] And as far as one can guess from what is said in the autobiography of 1866 he was not to show himself again.[23] 'I have always prayed, and I still pray for my poor father, and I have great confidence that God will be merciful to him, whether he is alive or dead'.[24]

The parish church of Borgo San Bernardo[25] stood on ground that, once marshy, had been reclaimed and rendered fertile by the work of the Cistercian monks of the nearby abbey of Casanova, which was suppressed in 1792. The patron saint was Bernard of Clairvaux, whose historical presence was very alive in this part of the country: witness the pillar erected by the inhabitants — and reconstructed in the valley of the Meletta in 1904 — near the chapel of the Madonnina,[26] called Madonna delle Rollette, after the plants that provide shade there during the summer.

The parish priest's house was no different from any other in the neighbourhood; a modest building beside the church, structurally one with the adjoining girls' school — which like all rural schools was reduced to the essential, with one or two rooms in all, on the ground floor.

In a municipal ordinance of 1690 we read that 'the villages were provided with vice-curates and other assistant priests, who functioned as schoolmasters.' It must, however, be admitted that teaching was imparted exclusively to those who contributed to the upkeep of the teacher. Only in 1846 did the schools come under communal control, and everyone was able to attend free of charge, though in Borgo San Bernardo this provision was anticipated by some years, thanks to the initiative of private individuals.

In 1834, don Andrea was thirty-seven, and he lived

with his elderly father and a twenty-five-year-old sister, Caterina.[27] It was a life regulated by the sound of the bells in the nearby *campanile*,[28] by the services celebrated morning and evening in the parish church, by the births and deaths of the parishioners; a quiet, untroubled life, without surprises or distressing problems. There was no lack of essentials, and whenever possible what there was was shared with the poor.

The arrival of his sister with her children, and her unhappy story of her husband's desertion, must have caused quite an upset in the parish priest's household: where there had been peace and quiet — perhaps even too much of it — suddenly there were the laughter, the tears, and the thousand and one games of small children who never keep still. Don Andrea was involved in the demands of his ministry, but for Aunt Caterina, even though her sister helped her, the weight of household duties was suddenly doubled. Before, when they were few, everything went well, and they were happy together. Now there was a large family to care for. The pattern of life, and its perspective, changed. Needs acquired different dimensions. It was enough to see the line of washing hung out to dry in the sun: dresses, woollen garments and shirts in all sizes, from the smallest (belonging to Anna, who at home was known as Caterina), to the medium-sized ones of Giovanni Battista and the larger ones of Teresa and Lucia.

Every difficulty was overcome through love, through great affection for this family, which had been left without support. The welcome was generous and spontaneous, and with time don Andrea became less of an uncle and much more of a father to the children.

The first thing learned by the last-born, Caterina, was the daily recital, in common, of the rosary,[29] after supper, while they still sat at table in the tenuous light of the oil lamp: the slow rhythmic response scarcely audible, as the children were overcome by sleep. When the rosary was finished, they all went to bed — to the big room on the upper floor, and the enormous double bed that was waiting for them. Kneeling down, the children would recite their evening prayers, their voices failing as they struggled against the onset of sleep. Framed on the wall was a faded print of the Holy Trinity — a very popular devotion in the village.

Down below, don Andrea would retire into his study, taking with him the foot-warmer as protection against the damp in the atmosphere. There he would remain at his desk, late into the night, reading and taking notes, alone but for the cat, who purred contentedly in the heat from the grate.

The flower grows and blooms
Season followed season, and the years passed. Caterina went to school — though so near was it,[30] on the side of the garden where the well was, and separated from the rest of the house by a hedge of rambler roses, that you might say school was at home: out of one door and in through another, without even crossing the road. It all consisted of one large room, with a few benches and makeshift tables for writing and arithmetic, the rostrum, and a blackboard hanging from the wall. Girls of all ages found themselves together in the same place. There was no division into classes: that they all had a teacher was already something.

Exactly the same situation prevailed in the boys school opposite, beside the church. Giovanni, who was barely ten, went there, and was lucky enough to be taught by his uncle, don Andrea.

Lucia was fifteen, but because of her delicate constitution she stayed at home to help her mother and aunt, as also did Teresa, who at twelve years old no longer went to school. From time to time they would do a few lessons in the evening, when their uncle had time and was not too tired.

Caterina, who was seven, began to learn to read and write, showing herself to be alert and intelligent. She was friendly, with an easy manner and full of initiative. She was never still for a moment, and scolding was wasted on her. The hours spent in school seemed interminable: it was so difficult to remain quiet and still with folded arms, listening to the teacher, when outside there was a whole world of wonders to discover. It was a small, peaceful world, the limits of which did not go beyond the town of Carmagnola, and the River Po, which flowed nearby; a world from which one could learn about the small, good things of life, which in the end is all that matters.

One day Caterina, scolded by her mother, answered in a way she certainly would not have done had her uncle been there: 'I was rude,' she wrote in 1866, 'to my dearest mother, who loved me and still loves me so much. Poor mother, how I upset her!'[31] The response suggests a none-too-easy temperament, quick to react. Such a character, had it not been trained, could easily have got out of control. There is also evidence of a certain impatience with correction. 'I was small, but my vanity was very great'.[32]

Anna Dominici lived for her children, and her deepest wish was that they should grow up capable of distinguishing good from evil. In their upbringing she combined gentleness with firmness, so that they would not be too conscious of their father's absence — even though don Andrea was more than a father to them. Thus, for the famous 'rude' answer, she immediately made Caterina apologize to those present, which intensified the child's sense of wounded vanity and her feelings of resentment. Then, after the apology, even if given grudgingly, her mother gave her a hug and all was forgotten.

Life in the priest's house went on quietly, though not without anxieties, the greatest of which was Lucia's health. She had been unwell for years. Caterina, who was eight years younger, stayed with her when she could; and Teresa and Giovanni did everything possible to entertain her during the long hours she passed, exhausted with sickness, sitting in the shade of an arbour in the garden. In the general anxiety of those days, don Andrea discovered that every joy, even the most sacred, is bought by suffering.

From the moment his sister had come to live with him, don Andrea was a changed person. He was delighted to have a larger family around him; he grew fond of the nieces and nephew, whom he watched growing up and making progress in their studies, and he sought in all things to be a father. It is not good for a man to be alone: if the heart is not supported by noble ideals, it will become withered, and he will no longer be able to sympathize with others. Living with others, however, and loving them, inevitably brings with it an element of suffering. And the suffering came, indifferent and inexorable, to disturb the peace of this loving family which had already been so sorely tried. On 21 August 1837, Lucia died.[33] It was Caterina's first contact with death: there is no mention of it in the autobiography, but it certainly made an impression that was to contribute to the formation of her character.

The church was two steps from the house; all one had to do was cross the garden. Early each morning, Anna Dominici and her sister attended Mass; then, while the priest was making his thanksgiving, they would go straight back to the kitchen to prepare the breakfast, which they all then took together.

During the summer holidays, when there was no school, the children went to Mass daily as well. Giovanni, as altar-boy, would put on the black cassock, which had to be turned up because it was too long, and the starched white cotta, and assist his uncle in the liturgical ceremonies. Caterina admired her brother,[34] for the seriousness of his manner, for his fluent, faultless reading, for his obedience. She was well aware that her own behaviour was far from being like his, always faultless, always correct. Even Teresa made herself useful, helping her mother about the house, while she herself just drove everyone mad. Not always, it is true, but it did happen and she regretted it — which was a start and an incentive to try to do better. Besides, not everything she was blamed for was her fault: she was only a child, barely nine years old, whatever might be said by her elders, who were quick to forget her age and make too heavy demands on her.

In church they used to sit together in the front pew, and Caterina would look thoughtfully at her brother and sister, as they went reverently up to communion, with joined hands and bowed head. She had been told that Jesus was really and truly present on the altar. In their innocence children fully grasp the mystery and assent to it wholeheartedly, without reserve. Jesus was no stranger in her family, indeed, he was a real person, known and loved for as long as she could remember. Her education and her world, the presbytery and the parish church, narrow perhaps from a superficial point of view, took on new life in the spiritual dimension. God was love, providence, and he could change her character, which was at times too excitable, impatient of restraints and easily distracted. She was convinced of this, and she dearly hoped that when she met Jesus in the Eucharist she would at last change for the better.[35]

This conviction was the introduction to an alternating pattern of stimulus and progress, which, with the passage of time, was to become an ascesis. Caterina recognized her own defects, and tried to correct them even though she did not always succeed. Her desire was to prepare herself in the best way possible for her first communion.

At last the time came, and the long-awaited day was not far off. With the other children of the parish she attended catechism classes, applying herself with determination, and in so far as she could she made various modest but nonetheless costing sacrifices in order to be worthy of the extraordinary encounter she was anxiously awaiting. 'I had a great desire to receive my beloved Jesus,' she was to write, 'and I set about preparing myself with certain mortifications, but it could be that I practised those that were the least wounding to my self love'.[36]

On 26 March 1839, in the parish church of Borgo San Bernardo, she received her first communion from the hands of her priest uncle.

'After I had approached the holy table for the first time, I do not recollect that there was any notable change in my manner of life, and I continued to be frivolous and unpredictable, as I had been in the past.'[37] The extreme sincerity of these lines betrays an element of exaggeration in her judgment, after a lapse of many years, of common childhood failings. She goes quickly on to say what the frivolity and unpredictability consisted of: 'On several occasions, out of greed, I took fruit without permission'; and again: 'I liked to make a good impression, and I minded very much if I saw that one of my companions was better dressed than I.'[38] To all of this was added a certain instability in her life of prayer: 'One day I would give myself up entirely to prayer, and the next I would be thinking of nothing but my favourite pastimes'[39] — all of which is quite logical: she was a normal child, in no way different from others except through the inner call which, confused as yet, was beginning to make itself heard.

Caterina spent her free time with her brother: they were inseparable and got on very well with each other. Together they would set up little altars[40] — a freshly laundered napkin spread out on a bench, with a statue of our Lady, two candles, and flowers picked from the garden — at which Giovanni carried out real true-to-life ceremonies before the admiring eyes of his sister. For the altar, as for the church, Caterina made an exception and allowed flowers to be picked, giving considerable care to the matter, spending all her savings on vases, bulbs and seeds. On the other hand, she was always at loggerheads with Teresa, who, as soon as she saw a flower, would pick it for the house without giving the matter a moment's thought.

They spent entire afternoons around the little altar, decorating it and redecorating it, always trying to make it more beautiful. At sunset, when everything had been prepared, they would summon the willing faithful to the sound of a little bell. Kneeling down, a solemn-faced Giovanni would intone the prayers, imitating even the rhythmic cadences of his uncle as he did so. His sister, hands joined and with a veil on her head, would respond with conviction. Nor were they alone: they would frequently be joined by friends from the neighbourhood, and it was a great joy to them when their uncle and mother took part too. Sometimes, when the ceremony was already in full swing, don Andrea passing hurriedly by, would pause for a moment with satisfaction, inwardly uniting himself to that prayer which was not meant to be, and indeed was not, a mere game.

Caterina's oneness of mind and heart with her brother, who was two years older than herself, was complete, which is why, if something happened to disturb the harmony between the two of them, it was impossible to sustain the quarrel for long. Caterina was sensitive: she could take offence at a trifle, and she always wanted to be in the right.[41] One day Giovanni was tired and made it quite clear that he did not want to have anything to do with her. The effect was immediate: touched to the quick, Caterina decided to change in order to be worthy of the company of her brother, who was thoughtful beyond his years. 'Moved by this, I gave up a little more time to prayer and recollection. But it didn't last long, and I soon relapsed into my usual childish ways'.[42] Among these 'childish ways', she lists in the first place her passion for flowers and her attachment to a pair of canaries entrusted to her by her brother.

Sometimes she found it troublesome to go to Mass in the morning, and in the autobiography she refers to this almost as to a fault: 'In spite of the fact that I never omitted to perform my Christian duties morning and evening, it was only on rare occasions that I attended Mass on weekdays — regardless of the fact that this was against the wishes of my mother, and that, because we lived with our uncle in the presbytery and had the church next to our own home, it was easy enough for me to do so'.[43]

Nevertheless, there were days when she longed to belong entirely to God. She would spend longer in church, and, alone in her room, would kneel down in front of the picture of the Madonna, to whom, impelled by feelings of generosity, she would make promises and resolutions which she subsequently failed in part to keep.[44]

Once she fell ill and was forced to spend a few days in bed. She became convinced that the sickness was a warning from God that she should lose no time in taking the way that leads to good: 'I thought the pain was perhaps a warning and a chastisement from God, and without saying anything to anyone, as I usually did, I promised God that if I was cured I would go to Mass every day and make sure that my passion for flowers did not prejudice the passionate concern I should have had for my soul.'[45]

Once she was better she kept her promise, even though she did not go to church every day with the same enthusiasm.

When she was eleven years old, she received the sacrament of confirmation in the parish church of Borgo

Cornalese, together with her brother, her sister, and a group of children from Borgo San Bernardo.[46] It was 11 June 1840, a day of mixed rejoicing, expectation and anxiety for all concerned. The celebrant was Archbishop Vicenzo Massi, apostolic nuncio to the court of the King of Sardinia.

There was little that was wanting to the ceremony. Relatives were there waiting, some inside the church, others outside talking; the children, overcome by the solemnity of the occasion, were waiting in their places. The candles had been lit, and the altar was covered with white linen. Don Andrea, in cotta and stole, took turns with the local parish priest to lead the singing and the prayers: the silvery, solemn, shrill and sonorous voices; then a prolonged and barely repressed whisper announced the arrival of the archbishop, who entered the church, followed by the clergy and the altar boys in order, to a powerful welcome from the organ.

Deeply moved, Caterina received the light of the Holy Spirit. Beside her, acting as godmother, was the noble Francesca Ottavia dei Conti de Maistre.

The flowers spoke to Caterina of God: 'The things around me lifted my spirit to the author of all good, who alone preserves us with his omnipotence, and in his fatherly goodness fills us with joy at the wonders of nature. At the sight of so much goodness, the desire to be good myself grew ever greater within my heart'.[47]

From the day of her confirmation, gradually but with deep lasting effect, a change began to take place in her soul. She was more reflective, more obedient, more disposed to prayer. Prayer became the food of her soul, and the young girl found in it a joy and support in her daily struggle to improve. All the same she still spent a great deal of time in the garden with the flowers, digging, removing dead leaves, pruning and watering for hours on end. Of all the plants, her favourite was the climbing jasmine, and in order to annoy her, one of her cousins, the seminarian Domenico Taverna,[48] would amuse himself, each time he passed, by shaking the plant in such a way as to tangle its twisted branches. Caterina would patiently let him carry on, without showing her anger. In the past she would have protested in a loud voice; now she accepted the teasing and, when her cousin had gone off she would resignedly sort out the maltreated plant as best she could. These were her first steps in the conquest of self — a long and difficult way that was to take her far.

The uncle, don Andrea, was a man of few words, but he had a great affection for his nieces and nephew, especially the youngest. One day he came across her while she was completely absorbed in tending her flowers. He had no objection to her spending her time in the garden, but he did point out to her that she could possibly occupy herself elsewhere with greater profit. The remark did not fall on deaf ears. We read in the autobiography the words of her uncle on this occasion, 'the decisive moment in my conversion to the service of God,' and the incident is described: 'Tell me, Caterina, what is the advantage of spending as much time as you do with the flowers?'[49] From that moment she was less to be found in the garden, and her passion for flowers was replaced by a passion for reading the lives of the saints. 'All the money from my meagre purse, which I had previously spent in the purchase of vases for flowers, I now spent in acquiring meditation books and lives of the saints, which reading I preferred above every other'. Her reading of the achievements of the saints, and of the great works of charity they performed in the name of an ideal, fired her enthusiasm, and gave her a burning desire to imitate them. And with an insight that came from God, she was virtually certain that if she wanted to imitate them she could.

She became aware of a strong, new feeling growing within her, a spontaneous attraction to the good and the true. What began as an indistinct glimmering became light, conviction, a principle of existence. Her soul was created for the light, and it surrendered to the light of grace.

Prayer, and the Eucharist which, with the permission of her confessor she received twice a week — no mean concession for those times — led her to discover God as love. She understood that love cannot be reduced to words and external manifestations, to good resolutions that often remain unfulfilled. Something more is needed, and with love all things are possible.

Love is a presence
The way of love calls for self-conquest through a complete gift of self which never looks back or claims rewards. Caterina had learned, from family conversations, of her brother's intention to follow the religious life — he would probably enter the novitiate of the Somaschi Fathers. The vocation, that great mystery, is not to be identified with this or that habit, this or that congregation, however worthy, but uniquely with the habit of love.

Although Caterina remained within the restricted environment of the presbytery, her horizon broadened out under the influence of love. Her life acquired a new meaning. She began to discover a thread running through every section, even the most trivial: the master-thread of love, that wonderful reality which is revealed to the simple.

The love of God for men, the beauties of nature that proclaim it, the flowers — these bear witness to love. And that is not all: love has become incarnate and lives among us. And yet we do not recognize it, we do not want to recognize it, slaves as we are to our own uninspired love which wants everything and offers nothing in exchange.

From the life of Aloysius Gonzaga she learned the

love of purity, and began to recite three Hail Marys each night to obtain this virtue. From the life of Catherine of Siena she learned fortitude and the love of sacrifice; from that of Vincent de Paul compassionate generosity towards the poor. Her one aspiration was to perform great deeds like the saints. She wanted to imitate them, and having made this decision, she set out gradually, with a determination beyond her years, on the narrow path of asceticism. 'It is true that I only went in for small acts of mortification: for example, I would leave something unsaid, or speak, as circumstances required; I would put off having a drink, even though I felt very thirsty; or I would perform some task when I could quite easily have left it without failing in my duties'.[50]

One step at a time, the 'little mortifications' grew into the first chord of a concerto. Once the instruments were tuned, the notes became a symphony, powerful music which she alone understood because only her heart and ear were attuned to it.

To say no to even the most innocent things, 'to remain in an uncomfortable position,' to go 'in the company of others to see some unusual sight,' that of the 'illuminations in the township on the occasion of some feast'; to say no, too, to every less than legitimate feeling or movement of the soul; to accept irritations; to smile and respond courteously when she wanted to protest: it was a school in which she said no in order that her yes to the principle of all things might be louder, more convinced, more compelling.

Caterina's fear, during these years, was that she might appear 'singular'. The adjective 'singular' implies strange, different from one's peers. In order not to appear so, she would sometimes accept the invitation to go to the piazza to see the lights. Yet when she found herself in the thick of the noisy crowd, which was caught up in admiration for the dazzling multi-coloured lights, she would avert her eyes. She played, talked, and laughed in amusement, but her spirit was far away, gathered up in the silence of the most hidden recesses of her soul.

'I would often join in,' she wrote, 'in order not to look singular, but then the Lord gave me inwardly to understand that he was asking me to sacrifice even this innocent form of satisfaction, at the same time giving me the grace to do so by keeping guard over my eyes in such a way that no one was aware of my mortification.'[51]

All the same, and in spite of all her best intentions, at times her self-love and earlier characteristics surfaced again, which proves that virtue is not something static, a habit to be put on on feast days; it is something dynamic, a point of arrival and at the same time of departure, a continually renewed act of conquest.

One day her mother asked her to give a hand in cleaning the church: the woman who normally saw to it was ill. Her immediate reaction, though controlled, indicated not so much fatigue as human respect at the thought of being seen in so humble a role. 'My mother noticed my repugnance, but she pretended not to, and I had to resign myself'.[52] And she set to work against her will.

Many years later she was to remember the incident with regret and to add in conclusion: 'After that I went spontaneously on many other occasions to do the same thing; indeed I later counted it a privilege, and it was a consolation to me to be able to contribute in some way to the upkeep of the house of God',[53] Even in such circumstances as these love was to conquer.

The way of renunciation

Caterina was now fifteen years old: friendly, spontaneous, intelligent. To the marked sensitivity of her character were united strength of mind and considerable will power. What is surprising, above all from a reading of the autobiography, is her constant dedication to the way of asceticism. She wanted to be holy, but in a strong, original way.

Through renunciation she was making her way towards holiness, without however, making any claim to do so. Even if it meant sacrifice, holiness for her was as natural as life — indeed, was identified with life which, supernaturally speaking, gained breadth and depth. It was a way of loving, and she could not help loving and responding to the great love which is the beginning and end of all things.

After the example of Catherine of Siena, she decided not to drink another drop of wine, and when her mother asked her the reason for this decision, she replied simply: 'Since I cannot imitate her in other things, at least I will try and imitate her in this'.[54] From this reply, and from her daughter's manner, Anna Dominici recognized the presence of the Lord.

Love suggested to her that she should do penance and make reparation for the many sins committed particularly at carnival time.

'In the morning I used to take some soup and raw fruit, though not of the kind I liked, otherwise there would have been little mortification in my depriving myself of the main course. In the evening I would have three breadsticks of the sort normally eaten in the Turin region, which certainly did not weigh as much as three ounces; and something light to go with them. Without anyone in the house realizing it, I used to live like this throughout almost the entire carnival.' And she adds with a touch of humour: 'I felt the pangs of hunger continually'.[55]

This fasting for love's sake, as a token of reparation and spiritual perfection, may look like extravagence, but it is not, as is proved by the great pains Caterina took to see that her spiritual progress was not ostentatious. Penance became a need she could not suppress, the means by which she got rid of everything that was a hindrance to her. This was love's foolishness, driving her to complete renunciation in silence, without anyone being aware of it.

During the day, when she was fasting, not only at carnival time but also during Lent and on the vigils of the major feasts, she used to feel quite hungry. 'But in order to stifle it, a little reflection on the many offences that were being done to God in the way of intemperance and greed was enough to rekindle within me the desire to make reparation, at least in some measure, for such great offences, and if it had been possible to me in my weakness, I would have even liked to increase my mortifications.'[56]

Through her reading she discovered an attraction for meditation that was unusual in a girl of her age, which inclines more to outward display, high spirits and fun. Meditation was not simply a question of reading, but of pausing at every thought; of reflecting, and waiting patiently in a state or recollection, almost of waiting; of listening in silence to the voice of her soul. And the louder, the more insistent, the more compelling and sweeter this became, the more she followed it, with the enthusiasm of youth.

It is like going through a narrow door: one enters with difficulty, but having passed the threshold one discovers new horizons stretching further and further into the distance. And then one continues to meditate in the certainty that, even further on, the extreme edge of the horizon coincides with infinity: God who is goodness, love and providence, the goal and centre of every thought which elevates, educates and strengthens. The particular becomes universal, the limited limitless; love expands in a generosity never before experienced. One is alone in the presence of the mystery, and the mystery makes itself known.

In the context of meditation, reflection means prayer, dialogue, inner searching, and in order not to let anyone, not even her own family, know how much time she spent in recollection, Caterina used to deprive herself of hours of her sleep at night.

When she had helped her mother in the kitchen, and the rosary was over, she would go straight to bed. Lying under the covers she would listen hard, waiting until everyone was asleep. Ever since her brother Giovanni had left home to join the novitiate of the Somaschi Fathers in Genoa[57] she had had a room to herself, and her sister Teresa, in the other room, was a heavy sleeper. Even her uncle would have gone up to his room: she had heard him climb the stairs and shut the door. Then, taking care not to make any noise, she would get out of bed and move gropingly on tip-toe through the darkness to the oil lamp on the night table. She would light it and then go quick to make sure that the shutters on the windows were closed fast, so that no one could see the light from the street. Then, making the sign of the cross, she would kneel down beside the bed, still in her nightdress, and begin to pray. The silence of the night gave wings to her prayer, and her intentions were so many, so pressing: her absent father, who had left for another part of the country without giving so much as a nod; her mother, so wise and prudent, who worked hard from morning till night; her patient, understanding uncle, truly a heart of gold; Giovanni, whom she so much admired, and all the more so since he had had the courage to follow his own way. At the thought of her brother's vocation another thought would push itself forward, one that for some time now had seemed rather persistent. Teresa was already making plans for the future: she would get married and would be a good mother to her family.[58] And herself? It was a difficult question, but in heart of hearts she already knew the answer. Love was to be her life.

She would then take up something to read. Her favourite theme was the passion of Christ.[59] She was often deeply moved by those pages, old and yet ever new, which told of the tragedy that through love brought new life to the world: a love which became flesh for the salvation of many, sublime even in martyrdom. Here was the ideal of love as a complete, absolute gift of self for others, in the name of the Lord.

Her decision was made — and had been for some time, even though she did not tell anyone: she would consecrate herself to the Lord. She would enter a convent, which she imagined as a highly congenial place, so much so that from then on she wanted to live as though she were a novice — a novitiate of the spirit where, at once novice mistress and novice, she was alone and impelled by love to grow in the life of the spirit. Her one obstacle was her love for her family. However, when the time was ripe a way would open if this was the will of God.

'I greatly feared the pull of my poor heart, which was so very sensitive to the affection of those who merited my most tender affection. I therefore made a resolution to be silent with all but God and to try meanwhile to do a bit of novitiate at home, under my own guidance. This novitiate, in which I was myself the novice mistress, was extremely strict, and even, I must admit, somewhat indiscreet. I had learned to imitate the lives of the saints, and because sensible fervour carried me away, I fell into excess'.[60]

It is easy to guess what those excesses were. Her prolonged fasting and nocturnal vigils, her work in the house helping her mother, the continuous spiritual tension in which she lived as she sought to dominate her character, which would otherwise have been moody and obstinate, reduced her to a disturbing state of exhaustion.

'However much I tried to conceal from those at home the privations to which I was subjecting myself, they realized from my pallor and the loss of weight which became increasingly more obvious in my appearance. I was no more than skin and bones, and if my spiritual fervour had not carried me forward, I would certainly have succumbed to the heavy strain.'[61]

At the end of a few months her health gave way. To the persistent weakness was suddenly added 'the coughing of blood,' which was repeated 'on three consecutive days, several times a day.'[62] This worried her, and she prayed that it would all pass.

Forced to rest and to adopt a gentler pattern of life, she soon recovered. From this experience, which was the result of her enthusiasm for renunciation, she drew one lesson: 'The Lord, in his great mercy, gave me the light to realize that virtue did not consist only in prayer and a sterile desire for mortification, but that it was necessary to arrive at the practice of it by over-coming myself and my laziness in order, as far as I could, to relieve my dear mother and sister of their household tasks'.[63] The decision reflects the maturity she had achieved in the arduous path of the spiritual life.

To her prayer and meditation, and to the fasts which she continued, although in an attenuated form, she added action. Action stems from within, from an intense spiritual life. Caterina looked around and assessed the conditions in which she found herself. Then, although she remained firm in her as yet unspoken vocation, continuing to live as a novice, she set about doing her duty in the modest occasions that presented themselves each day. 'I resolved . . . as far as possible to take on myself the household tasks, so as to begin thus to serve God a little more through works, without ever losing sight of him in the process, and it seemed to me that I was always in his presence, and succeeded purely through his goodness and mercy'.[64]

At this time, seeing how earnest his niece was, and admiring her for the spiritual maturity she had achieved, don Andrea entrusted to her the task of explaining the catechism to the children of the parish, a duty she was to discharge for six years.[65]

On the afternoons of feast days, the catechism class was held in the church, or in a ground-floor room adjacent to the presbytery.[66] The children liked her because she made the highest truths of the faith accessible to them. 'It was a great joy to me to be able to teach those poor creatures to love God, and I delighted in hearing them repeat: "We were created to love and serve God in this life, in order then to enjoy him for all eternity!" '[67]

This was Caterina's first experience of the apostolate, and the joy she experienced confirmed her in her vocation. Each time she prepared herself with great care, leaving nothing to chance, to improvization. She meditated on the concepts she would have to explain, studying the material beforehand; and she tried to make sure that her language was suited to the occasion, free from error, simple and familiar, according to the mentality of the children who listened to her. Their number increased, and those who lived a long way off walked for miles to arrive in time for the class.

Sometimes Caterina would go with the youngest, accompanying them on their way home. On the way they talked, played, sang, and competed with one another to see who could be the first to reach this or that willow tree along the dusty road. Carts would pass them on their way, most of them waggons taking fodder to the stables for the winter. Whenever they recognized the driver they would call out a greeting, with a wave of the hand. And if they knew him well they would jump onto the waggon, settle on the prickly hay and laughed delightedly at this unexpected meeting. They would get off in front of the Madonnina, the ancient cemetery chapel, and recite a heartfelt Hail Mary. Then they would take up the journey again on foot until they got home. There was not a single family that did not have its troubles, and the opportunities to do good multiplied. Caterina did not miss one of them and discovered in the practice of charity a joy she had never experienced before. To make oneself useful to others, and available to all in the name of the Lord, means living for love.

She went to visit the sick in hospital and stopped to chat 'with those who, because they had contagious diseases, were kept in separate rooms'.[68] She became the dispenser of the bounty of her uncle, the parish priest, often adding to it her own small savings. She obliged readily whenever some service was asked of her: always prompt to say yes, she never held back, but with a good grace tackled any task, however difficult.

Notes

1.   'Borgo Salsasio, one of the four that form the nucleus of the town of Carmagnola, is situated at about 27 kilometres from Turin; it stands in a broad and pleasant plain on the right bank of the Po; the land is highly suited to agriculture. The name Salsasio is said to be derived from the fact that the area was once known for the abundance of its willow trees. In the past Salsasio used to enjoy a certain importance on account of its natural position, being as it was a more or less obligatory route to and from Monferrato, or to and from the Alpine passes. Stretches of the old roads still exist today. The Roman legions once passed through the region, leaving behind them no uncertain traces of their stay. Here the Roman settlers got a foothold before the coming of Christ — a fact to which the gold and bronze coins from the reigns of the emperors Augustus and Claudius discovered near the Grua region, bear witness; in the same way, the material of rediscovered early brickwork provides evidence of very ancient buildings. It is generally maintained by historians that the first to proclaim the Christian faith in this region was St Dalmazzo, who subsequently suffered martyrdom at Monferrato. Some claim that St Barnabas was the first to preach the Gospel here, but the only plausible evidence for this is that of his cult who had a chapel dedicated to him in the ancient one-time castle of Fortepasso. However, the sporadic cult of the apostle Barnabas is not sufficient proof of the authenticity of his apostolate among us' (from *Memorie Storiche del Borgo Salsasio di Carmagnola*, Carmagnola, 1930, pp. 8-9).
2.   In the Museo Civico of Carmagnola can still be seen the

'Phrygian cap', which was raised up on the tree of liberty as the people danced round it to the sound of the ballad, 'La Carmagnole'. 'La Carmagnole' was so well known that it was chosen by Niccolò Paganini for his concert début, which took place in Genoa in 1795.
3.   The Società dei Cordari originated in the neighbouring Borgo San Bernardo, and had many members in Salsasio. It is impossible to say exactly when it was founded, in spite of Canon Pietro Cortassa, historian of the *borgo* where he was born, who dates the society back to the beginning of the 16th century. What is certain is that it already existed in 1600, that is, before the destruction of Borgo Viurso, which was succeeded by present-day Borgo San Bernardo. The tradition of hemp cultivation is very ancient in the Carmagnolese region, and it is mentioned in documents of 1235. It is known, furthermore, that from 1617 to 1640, the government granted a local entrepreneur, with about 20 workers in his service, the right to supply fuses and threads for handguns and artillery. The principal task of the corporation, according to the documents, was to watch over the art of rope-making, which was abused by some and exercised badly, and with mutual help to re-establish peace and brotherhood. Thus it was that the first rope makers felt the need to join together to defend their interests against the profiteers, who, cashing in on such competitive divisions as existed, sought to reduce the price of hemp to the minimum. The patron of the society was St Bartholemew, and in the parish church of Borgo San Bernardo until a short while ago — it has since been stolen — a sixteenth-century portrait of St Bartholemew was preserved. Why was St Bartholemew chosen? Cortassa sees in the martyrdom of the saint a link with certain aspects of work with hemp. As the saint, steeped in a life of continuous sacrifice, came after he had been skinned alive to bear witness to his faith, so the hemp is steeped and the fibre separated from the stalk and put aside for use.
4.   The Carmagnola press is among the oldest and most illustrious in Italy. The first book to come from it, although it does not carry the name of the printer, dates from 1497. Next door to the press there was a wood-engraving workshop, which is remembered by an *Ecce Homo,* with halo and cross, and the legend: *Ieronimus Texis faciebat Carmagnolae 1561....,* the oldest wood-engraving known in Piedmont (R. Menochio, *Memorie Storicher della Città di Carmagnola,* Carmagnola, 1963, pp. 250-251). As for the celebrated Proclama, printed during the night of 10 March 1821, it should be mentioned that the old wooden press used to print it is in the museum of Carmagnola, which houses evidence of a centuries-old tradition of printing.
5.   R. Menochio, *op. cit.,* pp. 213-220.
6.   Recalling the tragic consequences of the devastation of

1799, Salsasio is still known today, in dialect, as 'bourg d'la lecca' or 'bourg d'la patela'.

7.   This may be deduced from the fact that, at a time when we find in the margin of many death certificates a note to the effect that the burial was carried out wholly or in part without payment, such a note is not found by the name Dominici. Another proof comes to us indirectly, as well as through popular tradition, in the pages of the baptismal registers from 1750 to 1800. Here we discover that every now and then the baptism was not performed by the local parish priest but by don Uglio. This priest was also a teacher during the period when schools were left to private initiative, and it may be assumed that don Uglio administered the sacrament of baptism to those who had time and money enough to go to school. It is not by chance that among those baptized by don Uglio the register featured the names of the better off families of Salsasio: Miletto, Pipino, Raineri (Rine).

8.   'The village has just been set fire to. They burnt 135 houses according to an inquiry ordered by the municipality at the end of that year; with an estimated total loss of 141,390 lire. The bodies of about 134 dead were discovered there, and about 250 in the surrounding country. The French dead amounted to 50'. (R. Menochi, *op. cit.*, p. 217).

9.   From the Salsasio parish register it is possible to trace the ancestry of the Dominici: *Tomaso Dominici,* born in about 1640; *Giuseppe* married his second wife, Maria Bernardina Casale on 1 June 1700; *Giovanbattista* married Anna Mileto on 8 February 1733; *Giuseppe* married Agnese Caterina Maina on 25 February 1756; *Giovanbattista* married Lucia Anna Albertino on 23 March 1795; *Giuseppe* (born 1 June 1799) married Anna Pipino (born 10 November 1800).

10.   The witnesses to the marriage were Giovanni Albertino, uncle of the bridegroom's mother, and Bartolomeo Pipino, uncle of the bride.

11.   'My parents were of modest status' (Autobiography of M. Enrichetta Dominici, *Vigilia Eroica,* 1951, p. 73).

12.   The date 1833 is deduced from the following passage in the autobiography: 'Family misfortunes, together with the shameful behaviour of my poor father, led my dear and virtuous mother to separate from him by means of a formal divorce, approved by the Archbishop of Turin. I can say nothing about these disasters; I was unaware of them, because they happened at a time when, because of my tender years – I was only four – I was incapable of being involved in the many misfortunes that befell our family' (p. 73).

13.   This painful situation can also be deduced from a fact that appears in the Salsasio parish records. Relations between

Guiseppe Dominici and the parents of his wife, Luigi Pipino and Teresa Angonoa, deteriorated continuously, until the time of the separation. In fact, the baptismal register indicates that although Anna's brother, don Andrea, baptized Anna Maria Teresa on 19 April 1824, he did not come in 1826 and 1829 to baptise Luciana and Caterina, although he was only a stone's throw away in Borgo San Bernardo, and in spite of the fact that he came on other occasions to baptise the children of relatives.

14.   Giovanni Andrea Pipino, son of Luigi and of Teresa Angonoa, born at Borgo Salsasio on 11 November 1797. Parish priest of Borgo San Bernardo from April 1845 to April 1848, the year he gave up his parish for a canonry in the collegiate church of Carmagnola. He died on 11 February 1860. The latter dates are confirmed in a list of canons, starting in 1400, which still exists in Carmagnola, and which was compiled by don Lorenzo Pegolo. Here we read: *'Andreas Pipino Carm. S.T.D. Curatus sub. S. Bernardi poss. Adpe. 8 aprilis 1848 – Obiit 11 febbr. 1860.'*

15.   The dates of birth can be gleaned from the Salsasio baptismal registers: Lucia Maria Anna, 15 October 1821; Anna Maria Teresa, 19 April 1824; Giovanni Battista, 21 December 1826.

16.   The original of the Confraternity of the Holy Trinity in Borgo San Bernardo can be traced back to very early times. There were in fact those who remembered that the confraternity members with the characteristic scarlet sash, which they alone of all the parish, still put on for burials and processions, were already numerous when the parish was still centred on Borgo di Viurso. Popes Paul V (on 27 December 1604) and Urban VIII (on 27 February 1624) issued briefs in which they granted the confraternity – which was commonly known as the 'Batu russ' on account of its dress – special indulgences, graces and privileges.

17.   The baptismal certificate, as found in the parish archives at Borgo Salsasio, reads as follows: *'Dominisci (sic) Anna Catherina, Maria filia Josephi at Annae Pipino filiae Aloysii jugalium Dominisci, nata die decima, et undecima octobris anni millesmi octingentesimi vigesimi noni baptizata ab Adm, Rev. D. Bartholomeo Albertino Vicecurato. Patrino Pipino Antonius filius Aloysii, et Catharina Strumia filia Johannis Baptistae et vidua quondam Nicolai Milett'.* In the original of the above document one observes the name Dominisci, not Dominici. It cannot be regarded as an orthographical error of the compiler of the manuscript, because it appears several times on the same page. A reasonable inference might be that it reflects the French influence on pronunciation.

18.   At that time the parish priests in the *borghi* had the title of 'rector'. It is written thus at the foot of Caterina's birth certificate, where the name of the theologian Carlo Masera appears.

19.   The death certificate comes from the register of the parish

church of San Bernardo: *'Dominici N. filius Josephi et Annae Mariae Pipino vix natus et domi (periculo) baptizatus a Maria Reynero obiit die vigesima tertia et vigesima quarta februarii anni millesimi octingentesimi trigesimi quarti sepultus'* (Th. Andreas Pipino, Rector).

20. The term 'divorce' should be understood as separation by mutual consent. Very probably, according to the practice of the archdiocese, it was don Andrea who presented the case to the archbishop who agreed immediately to the separation, which had in fact already taken place. No reference to the case is to be found, however, in the archives of the curial offices in Turin.

21. Autobiography, p. 73.

22. In the civil registers of Salsasio, written after 1861, which include information provided by the parishes from their registers, the death of Giuseppe Dominici is not registered, from which it is assumed that he emigrated without leaving any trace of his whereabouts.

23. The autobiography was written from 1866 to 8 March 1867, and covers her life from her birth until the end of 1865. It was written at the request of her spiritual director, don Pellegrino Tofoni, who was for years secretary to Cardinal de Angelis, Archbishop of Fermo.

24. Autobiography, p. 74.

25. The construction of the parish church began in 1640 and it was solemnly opened in 1642. It stood on a piece of slightly elevated ground; on the east and south sides it bordered on the street; on the west side was the presbytery garden, and to the north the plot that formerly served as a cemetery. In 1859 it was necessary to enlarge and redecorate the church as a whole. The vaulted ceiling of the sacristy was redone and provision was made for the silver plating of the sacred vessels and the processional cross. The expense, which amounted to 6700 francs, was met thanks to 1600 francs from the proceeds of hemp combed and spun especially for the church; 600 francs from performances of mystery plays; 672 francs received from the Confraternity of the Holy Trinity; 240 francs offered at the Annunciation altar; 50 francs from the Company of San Luigi. The remainder came from the offerings of the people. The church building, in Piedmontese baroque style, has been subjected to many alterations, not always in accordance with artistic criteria. It has three naves, closed off at the end by the lofty tribune for the choir where members of the Confraternity of the Holy Trinity still come each Sunday to recite the Office.

26. In about 1640 reconstruction work began after the destruction by the French of Borgo Viurso, and the inhabitants split up into two groups, the one constructing Borgo San Bernardo and the other Borgo San Michele. Both were attached to an

ancient wooden statue of the Madonna, which they had succeeded in salvaging from the ruins of the church, and a dispute arose as to which of them should have it. The controversy was settled in the following strange way: after the statue had been attached to a cart drawn by two heifers, these were left unattended at a point where the roads leading to the sites destined for the new *borghi* crossed. The heifers took the road to San Michele, and the statue of the Madonna is still honoured in the church there, in a niche alongside the high altar. Both parishes, however, retain the title 'Santa Maria del Viurso'.

The inhabitants of San Bernardo erected in honour of the Virgin, as patroness of the parish, the Cappella della Madonnina, originally known also as the Madonna delle Rollette. The chapel still exists today, adorned with a painting of the Madonna di Viurso, executed in 1887 by the Carmagnolese artist Turletti. Underneath this work, still visible and in good condition, is the old fresco by an unknown artist. Numerous *ex voto* bear witness to the age-old devotion. In 1946, on the initiative of the inhabitants of the region, the chapel was restored. From 1780 to 1857, the cemetery of the *borgo* was opposite the little church.
27.   Don Andrea's father (his mother had died much earlier) came from Salsasio and died in Borgo San Bernardo, the home of his wife Teresa Angonoa, on 12 September 1834 at the age of seventy-four. His sister Caterina, born in Salsasio on 16 April 1809, died in Borgo San Bernardo on 27 June 1838.
28.   The massive bell tower, which rises to a height of twenty-eight metres, did not share the fate of the church, and retains its original structure. Tradition has it that the damage done to one corner of the campanile can be attributed to cannon shot fired by the artillery under General Fraissinet during the uprising of 1799.
29.   In the autobiography we read: '. . . I learned early the habit of reciting my prayers as a Christian morning and evening' (p.74).
30.   The old building of the boys' school was situated behind the parish church, which is now given over to the use of the Scuola Cantorum: that of the girls' school, a little house beside the church itself, is now the seat of the parish council of San Vincenzo. The first master to teach at San Bernardo (1728) was one don Gio Battista Fontana, from the Nice area, whose stipend was 160 lire *per annum*.
31.   Autobiography, p. 75.
32.   *Op. cit.*, p. 75.
33.   From the death certificate in the San Bernardo parish register: '*Dominici Lucianna filia Josephi et Annae Mariae Pipino annorum sexdecim Sacramentis munita obiit die vigesima prima et vigesima secunda Augusti anni millesimi octingentesimi trigesimi septimi sepulta. Th. Jo. es Andreas Pipino Rector.*'

34. 'My brother, who was two-and-a-half years older than I, was very good, and his seriousness frequently served as a corrective to my frivolity. . . . Together we spurred each other on to be good and virtuous. However, he did far better than I, being both more persistent and more sensible' (Autobiography, p.78).

35. 'I thought that after I had made my first communion I would be more docile and obedient, as I had promised the Lord with all my heart on that day that I would be' (*Op. cit.*, p.76).

36. *Op. cit.*, p.75.

37. *Op. cit.*, p.77.

38. *Op. cit.*, p.77.

39. *Op. cit.*, p.79.

40. 'I willingly passed my time with this dear brother of mine, and we took great pleasure in setting up little altars and adorning them as best we could. We enjoyed spending on them the time we had free from school.' (Autobiography, p.78).

41. 'At that time I took offence easily, even at the smallest things. . .' (*Op. cit.*, p.78).

42. *Op. cit.*, p.79.

43. *Op. cit.*, p.80

44. 'Sometimes the fervour lasted only for a moment, but on other occasions it lasted for days on end, and then I forgot my usual amusements and gave myself up to that sweetness in the things of God which he permitted me to experience. At such a time I would spend longer in church after Mass, and often I would take myself, too, to my good mother, Mary, whose image I had in my room, and there I would make her the most beautiful promises — that I wanted to belong entirely to her son forever, and that with her help I would lead a more devout, recollected life. But I never kept my promises' (Autobiography, p.82).

45. *Op. cit.*, pp. 80-81.

46. From documents in the parish archives, we learn that on that day one hundred and thirty-seven children received the sacrament of confirmation, seventy-five girls and sixty-two boys.

47. *Op. cit.*, pp. 82-83.

48. Son of Francesco and Maria Dominici, born at San Bernardo on 10 January 1828.

49. Autobiography, pp. 83-84.

50. *Op. cit.*, p.87.

51. *Op. cit.*, p.87.

52. *Op. cit.*, p.89.

53. *Op. cit.*, p.89.

54. *Op. cit.*, p.90.

55. *Op. cit.*, p.100.

56. *Op. cit.*, pp. 100-101.

57. The house in question is La Maddalena, that of the Padri

Somaschi of Genoa, where he did his novitiate under the master, P. Ottavio Laura. He was clothed on 12 September 1845, and made his profession on 13 September 1846 at the hands of the provincial, P. Giuseppe Ferreri.

58. She was in fact to marry Giuseppe Osella, and one of her daughters became a religious with the Sisters of St Ann.

59. 'I can't say what the method of my prayer was, in fact I don't think I had one; but I do know that as I meditated the eternal truth, the passion of Christ, which so inflamed me with love for God, the hours passed quickly for me, and my soul acquired great strength to endure' (Autobiography, p.101).

60. *Op. cit.*, p.98.

61. *Op. cit.*, p.102.

62. *Op. cit.*, p.102.

63. *Op. cit.*, p.91.

64. *Op. cit.*, p.92.

65. '. . . At about this time I was entrusted with the task of teaching the catechism to little girls, which I did in the church on Sundays, during Lent, and on holy days of obligation. I retained this office for six years, to the great consolation and profit of my soul' (Autobiography, p.85).

66. At Borgo San Bernardo, beside the presbytery, where the Conferenza di San Vincenzo has its headquarters, the following can be read on a plaque on the wall:
'The Conferenza di San Vincenzo
in pious memory of the servant of God Madre Enrichetta Dominici
who in this place
which was formerly the headquarters of the Compagnia della Christiana
stopped to teach the catechism to the girls of the *borgo.*'

67. *Op. cit.*, pp. 85-86.

68. *Op. cit.*, p.114.

II A waggon hitched to a star

'The divine will is my own'

Aunt Caterina died in 1838.[1] Don Andrea never recovered from that day. He lost his customary gaiety, which showed itself, albeit with a certain reserve as befitted a good Piedmontese, by a thorough frankness, completely genuine. A kind of gloom settled on him, he could take an interest in nothing, he was tired of seeming to be idle. It was a kind of depression. In the autobiography of Mother Enrichetta it was described as 'a mental sickness'[2] although the present day meaning could not be applied to it; then it meant a state which could last a long time, and ended with being shut up in a lunatic asylum.[3] That is to say that in those times it was easy to get confined to a home for mental patients; the remedies prescribed by modern progress did not exist.

The unavoidable absence of her uncle was a sore trial.[4] Anna Dominici felt lonely again. Her son having left, her two daughters still to be settled in life and Caterina was dreaming of life in a convent, her one desire being to devote herself to her vocation. She soon began to speak of it. To follow what seemed an inner voice, a desire of perfection, might be a way of escape from the responsibilities of life. Her mother hoped that it was only a passing infatuation.

The limitations, the needs and problems were many, above all in a family which had not known the support of a father and lived on the hospitality of an uncle in poor health. Caterina was aware of all these troubles, and was worried by them. She did not underrate the difficulties, but left them all to the Lord. Prayer was the surest way to overcome obstacles. 'Many times I went behind the altar where Jesus dwelt in the Blessed Sacrament, and prayed to Him.'[5] In the evening, when the church was closed, and her household tasks in the kitchen were finished, she went and knelt by the altar. In the darkness there was only a gleam from the lamp that burned, giving a sign of a presence which would not deceive. Her speech was intensified, it took on a confidence that was above prayer; though prayer was beautiful it seemed to grow faint, in a spontaneous abandonment. The Lord was near, so near that she felt at one with him, with his love, sympathy and hope. Hope would become a certainty, which consoled and frightened at the same time, with the thought that she would find a way of following her vocation.

'I was repelled by the idea of doing my own will; I wanted to do the Lord's will above everything else. But I prayed that the divine will would conform with mine, because I wanted to be a religious at all costs.'[6] In these few words, which at this distance of time still keep the fragrance of youth, the fragrance of those years of prayer, was held the secret of her vocation. May the will of God be made plain to her, seen and embraced by her: human will identified with God's.

In such conditions and with her uncle far away and in ill health it was absurd to think of leaving the family. And yet Caterina was convinced that a glimmer of light would appear. She had to look beyond all the changes of daily life. Such conditions prompted her to write of her uncle's malady. 'How good is the Lord, to bring good out of evil. This misfortune should rather be called a special grace for my soul; it serves to convince me of the emptiness and fallibility of the things of this world and I conceived a contempt for everything, even the most attractive'.[7]

One day when she was alone in the house, she felt inspired to pray in a very special way for her uncle. She interrupted her household tasks, knelt down on the floor and with her whole heart declared herself ready to suffer anything if only don Andrea could come back. She got up, and felt an abounding inner certainty. Notwithstanding the doctor's opinion the Borgo San Bernardo would get back their parish priest within a year.

When her mother came back from her shopping she was still on her knees. Hearing her mother going upstairs she hastily got up and tidied her dark brown hair. She looked in the mirror to make sure that she did not seem too disturbed, and went to embrace her mother. She was happy. She would have liked to tell everyone of her new sense of confidence; she wanted especially to tell her mother, 'who would be greatly consoled by her news.'[8] Yet she remained silent, and did not speak to anyone. It was her secret.

For the poor

The priest in charge during don Andrea's absence, don Sola, told the parishioners at the Sunday Mass that their parish priest would be back with them on the next Sunday. It was August of 1846.

The news surprised the congregation and was the subject of conversation as they came out and stood in the churchyard. Many were the opinions expressed, even if in whispers, accompanied by long and meaningful glances at the priest's house nearby. It was a subject of gossip for days. There was even talk of organizing a reception. Many plans were discussed, but all agreed on a ceremony of thanksgiving in which only the most faithful should take part.

At home all were busy with preparations, and no effort was spared. Teresa and Caterina were busy with their mother tidying things up, and cleaning. It seemed as if the week would never end. Then the evening before the return arrived. All were seated at table and thinking of the details of the dinner to come. A neighbour had brought a hen for the soup, don Sola had brought some bottles of the best wine, and the dough for the bread, already made, was rising in the tin.

Caterina's confidence in her prayers was finally justified. Early in the morning people went in a cab to meet the good don Andrea. People were waiting in the piazza. Caterina was putting flowers in a vase standing in the entrance and arranging them as well as she could, all the time thinking of the Lord's goodness.

The parish priest at length arrived. The boys and young men who were waiting for him in the street now surrounded the cab, which slowed down. The more eager of the reception committee climbed up on a ledge, one by one. Notwithstanding the Jacobin ideas professed at the time by many, the reception was warmhearted, festive and spontaneous, beyond all expectation.

Don Andrea had not expected such a welcome and as he got down from the cab and met his parishioners, there was a lump in his throat. He wanted to embrace them all, shake hands with them, thank them for the affection they showed for him. But he could hardly speak. He was overcome by emotion and weak perhaps with the illness which he had suffered and from which he had only just recovered. He was not yet fifty years old and yet he had come to look like an old man.

Day by day life began to return to normal, as it always does. Caterina did not forget the grace she had received, and the sign which she thought admitted of no doubt, concerning the way she was to follow and wished to follow at all costs.

She plucked up courage and after much prayer went to speak to her confessor. It was the first occasion on which she had openly spoken of her vocation. The priest listened to her. He knew her very well and decided to speak as soon as possible to her uncle; that would surely be the simplest way.[9]

From that moment anxiety grew over the outcome of this meeting. She could hardly sleep and in the house when she saw her mother's glances she almost felt a sense of guilt. She was overcome by the thought that she would not be able to resist but end up leaving all she knew.[10] She wished to follow her vocation but she feared being unable to do so; the bonds of affection seemed as if they would overcome all her intentions.

Her uncle's reply was not long in coming. It was negative and left no way of escape. His reasons were her delicate constitution, his niece's timid and sensitive temperament, which he considered made it impossible for her to adapt herself to living in a convent.[11] If he thought like this he was not unjust, as she had said she wanted to go into a cloister.[12] In fact Caterina's ideas from the first had been that she wanted to live in an enclosed order, in the strictest sense of the word. 'The idea of being a religious and yet concerned with the affairs of the world was contrary to my ideas, and it seemed preferable to the life I could have lived at home, withdrawn from all worldly concerns.'[13]

On all this a discussion began and went on for a considerable time. On one side the enthusiasm and generosity of youth; on the other the calm firmness of experience and age. In reality don Andrea was not opposed to his niece's vocation.[14] His intention was to test her to make sure that it was not a case of passing infatuation. There was also the opinion that she was not fitted to the rigour of an enclosed convent. Above all, there was the question of her health. On this point he was not to be moved. He would not listen when she spoke of such an arduous undertaking. 'Without giving me time to explain my feelings he closed my mouth with the words: You are not called; don't resist'.[15]

As she could not speak to her uncle about what was nearest to her heart she wrote to him. Words were written down secretly, in her room before she went to bed, and carefully left the next day, in full view on the desk of the parish priest. They were spontaneous expressions of her deep affection and hopes that she would not have to go back on the decision she had made. Patiently she waited for the answer. She redoubled her prayers, looking eagerly for his reaction in the hope that something would change. But every time the reply was the same.

Having read that St Teresa 'offered herself fifty times a day to God'[16] she took to the shorter prayer: 'O God, do with me what pleases you most; let me know what you wish of me, that I can do it all the time'.[17] When she was busy in the kitchen or explaining the catechism to the young girls of the parish, when she had to go out on errands or, tired at the end of the day, she could at last sit and rest in the open air, she said 'Do with me what pleases you'.

It is not easy to perceive the Lord's will, especially when it does not correspond with ours. It is still harder to understand it, to love it, to follow it. And when she looked at the face of the moon, when she considered the mystery of the heavens, everything became easier to understand. The law of the universe is love, and God is love. To abandon oneself, to conform and to become an integral part of that love is to do God's will. Not to rebel, to be patient and trusting, it cannot be doubted that this is the divine will. Her thoughts were the same as her confessor's advice. To wait and prepare herself for the great day when a solution would surely come. Meanwhile she said the Office of Our Lady, made a daily examination of her conscience, and never missed the Eucharist.

In the meantime she grew in charity. At the Borgo San Bernardo it was customary, as in all the lower valley of the Po, to accompany the dead to the burial place, carrying the coffin on the shoulders. On the death of a poor person it was not always easy to find anyone to do this duty, above all at harvest time.

One day Caterina met a funeral procession. It was of a poor woman who lived in the depth of the country. A few people followed; it was summer time and people were busy in the fields. She had known her. Often she had been to take her something when her uncle gave her something and she managed to bring something from the kitchen which she knew would give her special pleasure. At the carrying of the bier there was one person missing who should share the burden. There were only three women all friends of the deceased who lived close by. She wanted to offer to share in this charitable action. 'But human respect, a kind of excessive shyness, in a word pride'[18] overcame her. She struggled against it but another woman, old and feeble, in fact hardly able to walk, took up the sorrowful burden. But after getting into the church and finishing the funeral service it was obvious that someone must give a hand to lift up the coffin. She didn't resist but helped carry the coffin to the cemetery. 'I felt almost pushed to do it, and I was powerless to hold back any more.'[19] At the contact with the rough wood she felt herself transformed. Step by step the effort brought a new joy which moved her very much. With the poor, using one's strength to serve them out of love reveals the greatness of one's vocation. Until then she had acted by intuition; now she was fully conscious of it.

That evening, returning to her housework still perspiring from the effort, she was happy. 'I was satisfied at the thought that I had done a good deed, and had obeyed, though somewhat tardily the call I had received'.[20]

In the family she was forced to defend her own position. Her mother did not conceal her grief that, in spite of everything, she persisted in wishing for the life of a religious. Her sister rebuked her for not wishing to go with her to Carmagnola. There one could meet young people of the same age; there perhaps it might be possible to give up the idea which had become an obsession with her. She wanted amusement, wished to give more attention to her dress, keep up with the fashion as far as possible.[21] One is young only once, she kept telling her. But Caterina paid no attention. Perhaps it was because of her vocation, a plan which seemed absurd, that she found a way of keeping young with no fear of time.

The opposing points of view of the two sisters were made clear in the autobiography by one detail. Teresa had joined the Children of Mary. In this she was partly influenced by the costume they wore; white with a blue sash. Caterina, 'wishing to overcome her natural inclination to vanity'[22] chose the 'Umiliate'[23] with a dress of sackcloth kept in place by a belt; with bare feet and thus clad, she went with the dead to the place of burial. It was one more victory over herself.

The power of clasped hands
The year 1848 was a prophetic one, for Piedmont as well as for Europe. A thrill of social and political reform aroused the people. In Paris the Revolution gave rise to the Second Republic. In Germany, Austria, and Hungary, there was serious disorder. In Venice Daniel Manin and Nicholas Tommaseo proclaimed a republic and drove out the Austrians.

On 8 February there was jubilation in Turin. That evening in the Piazza Castello there was not enough room for the crowd that gathered, applauding, under the windows of the royal palace. Many of them left Carmagnola for a demonstration in the Borgo San

Bernardo where they wanted the parish priest to ring the bells for such a festive occasion. Carlo Alberto had announced the grant of a new constitution. The Savoy dynasty became completely constitutional.

They were days of great euphoria and in such clamour, confusion of ideas was unavoidable. In the provinces a good number of the clergy took part in the liberal movement. Some of them, unable to observe ecclesiastical discipline, thought the time had come to shake off the authority of the bishops. Others were infatuated by a reading of the works of Gioberti who expected the arrival of a liberal pope. Most of the people shared the illusion and showed their ingenuousness; they were carried away by all the exaggerated shouting, by all the enthusiasm, by the exaltation of the day.

At home don Andrea was not carried away by such overwhelming events. He had never taken much interest in politics. He knew of the miserable life of the poor people in the town, with their calloused hands, and the difficulty many of them had in carrying on a life so full of drudgery. And that was enough. To tell the truth, at this time he had other things to worry about. His health seemed to be failing and at his last meeting with the bishop he had spoken of his wish to leave the parish. In the curia they understood. He could leave the borgo, settle at Carmagnola and become the canon of the Collegiata.[24]

The transfer was fixed for the end of March and arrived in a condition of general patriotic fervour. The twenty-third of that month Carlo Alberto had declared war against Austria, and, putting on the tricolour, had gone to the defence of the rebels in Lombardy and Venetia, bringing that 'help which brothers expect from brothers, friends from friends'.[25]

The move from the Borgo to Carmagnola was short. But to follow a cart laden with the furniture, the books, all the contents of the house which seemed to get bigger as they were moved, was quite an undertaking, especially in those days of festivity — and one could not describe them otherwise, though war is never a festival. Everywhere white, red and green were the predominating colours. Those who did not put on the cockade were regarded with suspicion. People stood about in the streets and stayed up late talking, making comments, waiting for news of the troops who had crossed the Ticino. There was singing and shouting; the most applauded were the military convoys leaving for Turin. The young men who went to take up arms were embraced by the crowd and accompanied in triumph up to the recruiting centres. The King and Pius IX were applauded and as far as the latter was concerned don Andrea was happy. The dream of Gioberti and Balbo was turning into reality. That is, the federal union of all the Italian states under the guidance of the Pope, and in defence of the house of Savoy. And it was this dream which on 29 April was shattered beyond all hope. On that day Pius IX, in his allocution to the Cardinals, declared the supremacy of the missionary spirit of the Holy See and the incompatability between its mandate and the support of any of the belligerents.

The new house was next to the façade of the College of St Peter and St Paul in its original simplicity, before alteration had changed its appearance.[26]

Caterina's disappointment was great at leaving her flowers, the orchard, her corner of the garden in the shade of the bell tower. But she soon got used to it. But it was a compensation that the church was worthy to be a cathedral. The choir was splendid, the high altar richly adorned with marble, the pulpit with inlaid wood from which St Francis de Sales had preached. Incomparable was the chapel of the Immaculate Conception, erected by the unanimous vow of the citizens in thanksgiving for their escape from a plague.[27]

Every morning after Mass and during the day when

she could, Caterina went to pray at the feet of the
Madonna, an old painted wooden statue made by the
sculptor Michaele Enaten of Asti; two years before it
had been covered by a royal mantle given by Maria
Christina of Sardinia.[28]

Things had been tidied up, the tiring days of the move
were past and ordinary life began. The uncle stayed at
home more. Mamma was still fussy. Teresa was happy
at last to stay in the city. There everything was different.
There was the covered market, the strolling about the
piazza, the shops, the festivals which brought such
pleasure to the people; the flower festival in May, the
archery festival at Pentecost, the students at the
Annunciation.[29] Provincial it might be, but it was
lively and warmhearted. Catherine found conditions very
satisfactory, especially because her confessor lived nearby; he was an Oratorian, and he lived at the monastery
of St Philip, only a few steps away.

A change in surroundings did not, as many hoped,
influence her ideas for the future. Even if she never
spoke of it, because she did not wish to make her
mother unhappy, the thought of her vocation was still
with her, always in her mind and as strong as ever. In
the convent, notwithstanding her sister's opinion, she
was convinced that she would find 'inestimable
happiness.'[30] Her view of the religious life was a lofty
one, perhaps too lofty to correspond to the reality.
'I imagined that becoming a religious, I could live as in
heaven;'[31] 'I believed that religious were angels on
earth.'

She did not know which Order to enter. About her
twentieth year, she wrote in her autobiography, she had
a sudden intuition. She had read the life of a religious
who had suffered much in trying to bring the original
spirit of charity to the community in which she lived.
She was warned that she could meet with fears, even
the certainty[32] of suffering the same distress. She would

46

enter a convent. Her vocation would not end in nothing. She would reach her goal: she would be first of all 'the instrument of God in reforming my convent and then become the object of censure, of calumnies and persecution by men'.[33] It was a vision of the future which was very different from the serene view she had had of the life of a religious. But it didn't alarm her; on the contrary it strengthened her decision.

'Far from lessening the warmth of my dream, it confirmed me all the more in what I had proposed for myself; it almost gave me the certitude that only by this way could I accomplish the designs God had in store for me. They said I should never be able to adapt myself to the life of the cloister, and that even when I had embraced it I would soon abandon it. I felt that God was calling me and in calling me would give me hope and certainty, and the necessary strength to overcome all difficulties for the sake of his love'.[34]

During these years, as throughout her life, God's presence was almost tangible. The supernatural intervened, in different forms, but constantly according to the varied experiences of everyday. It may have been fine to go on in the full light of day, but it was painful to advance in the darkness when that interior joy that illuminated her path, that certainty which sustained her and gave her assurance, seemed to grow dim. It was the dark night of the soul. Instead of light which gave comfort there was the darkness which oppressed and distressed her. 'Little by little the good God withdrew all his gifts, and I became cold, dry and devoid of feeling'.[35]

If now is the hour of darkness, it is also the hour of the greatest splendour. The darkness is necessary because the day that follows it can be all the more radiant. Her confessor confirmed this and she did not despair. Just because the darkness was wearisome then greater would be the desire to seek the light. The night will be followed by the dawn and the sun will return high up in the heaven of the soul. This is not only hope, but certainty and certainty is life. In this state which may be prolonged by years and is defined as 'excessively painful',[36] one chooses the only remedy, to go forward in prayer, as if nothing had changed. 'I persevered in all the usual exercises and practices of piety, although there was no feeling of rapture at first. In my devotions I felt no satisfaction, but nevertheless I felt a certain refreshment of spirit which helped me and gave me the courage to bear calmly the loss of that interior sweetness which I had found so attractive in the past'.[37]

Prayer became an act of the will. No longer was it dependent on love. The object of love seemed to be seeking obscurity. And yet only a sublime love can stimulate more love, prayer when thoughts, even the most fervent ones, seem to fade away. One joins one's hands in prayer, wearily, almost as if unwilling, and clasps them with faith, still more with greater faith. The darkness which arose within the soul will have no effect. Despite all, the light is present and it cannot grow dim. One may be unable to perceive it, to respond to all its blessings and impetuously yield to the generous promptings of the reason, the will, the aspiration to continue to make progress at all costs. It would be folly to admit that one has failed and deny the existence of the light because the shades of night have for a time obscured it.

'Even with the worst of my inner distress, it seemed that my heart was not lacking in that childlike trust which God in his infinite mercy had granted me'.[38] This trust in the Lord's goodness was the thread which led her through all the distress of her soul.

However dedicated she might be to carrying out a plan which encountered such obstacles, there were days when she was overcome by the most profound discouragement. 'When I was completely at a loss of knowing what I should do, and when I felt abandoned by all and in the deepest darkness, I sometimes stood before the crucifix, unable to speak, and looked and thought, Jesus died for me. This thought lasted some time and I decided that if Jesus had died for me it was not possible that he should wish me to fail when I had the conviction that with the help of his grace I would do everything on my part to serve and love him in the way he wished and asked of me'.[39]

'God has called me and I must obey'

In November 1849 something happened in don Andrea's house which gave him much happiness. His nephew Giovanni, who had joined the Somaschi Fathers, had received holy orders. On 22 December, at the convent of St Catherine at Casale, he received the tonsure. It brought much encouragement to Caterina; she had a great affection for her brother and she now felt all the more cheerful at trying to achieve what stood closest to her heart.

She confided in a childhood friend, her cousin Domenico Taverna, recently ordained. She asked him to intervene with her uncle. To these new requests don Andrea seemed more receptive than at other times. He listened to the niece's arguments given him by her cousin. He explained that his attitude was dictated by prudence and by the necessity he felt that she should test her vocation. He was not totally opposed; he was even ready to give his consent. But he was still opposed to her choice of an enclosed convent. At that time the convents of contemplative sisters took perpetual vows. This was not so with the sisters who led active lives.[40] It was this fear that his niece would have second thoughts that determined his attitude.

However, in November 1850 it seemed that his consent might be obtained. The uncle called Caterina and talked to her at length. He was like a father, a priest who appreciated what a treasure a vocation could be, but knew what difficulties could arise day by day even in his own experience. It was not the question of a moment's illumination, but of a light which had to be kept constantly bright, in spite of everything. The enthusiasm of youth is understandable especially in a generous character, but it had to be remembered that enthusiasm could fail. Life in a community is not easy; it calls for sacrifices. In the course of years, often frustrated by bitter experience, one has to learn to rediscover one's enthusiasm, find again that zeal which could prompt one to persevere in such an important undertaking. The way one was called to follow was arduous and the higher the vocation, the deeper was the loneliness which one was called to endure. To live in a community and yet feel lonely seemed contrary to nature and yet it was the culmination of every vocation.

Caterina listened in silence. As soon as she could reply it was to confirm her vocation, simply and frankly. As things were, high qualities and faults together, she had been caught up in a marvellous undertaking which rose superior to herself, to which no explanation could be given but that of love.

Don Andrea looked at the young woman with deep affection. He wished her well and in her eyes he glimpsed the light of God, the same light as had aroused all the girl's enthusiasm and seemed likely to persist. All this notwithstanding, he wished to remove one last doubt. It was not a question of a mere human purpose.[41] He took from his desk an envelope containing the will he had secretly drawn up years before. His niece read the document carefully. She understood that the will was in her favour and would allow her, if she remained in the world, to live in comfort. For a time she stayed thinking it over; she was much impressed by this proof of his affection,[42] then she thanked him but confirmed her own decision. In her autobiography she was to write: 'God called me and I felt I must obey'.[43]

Having obtained consent, the choice agreed between them was the Sisters of St Ann and of Providence, who at that time had houses at Turin, Moncalieri, Altessano and Santena. The choice was due to the uncle's acquaintance with, and appreciation of the recently established convent and the spirit which, in the field of education, inspired it.

The Congregation had been founded in 1834 by the Marchese and Marchesa Falletti di Barolo, Tancredi[44] and Giulia Colbert,[45] great-nephew of Louis XIV's minister. Its object was to give a suitable education to the daughters of families of slender means, and at the same time to finance those young women, lacking in that support, who wished to enter the religious life. Institutions like these, for educating young girls, did not exist at that time in Piedmont, or were only just at the point of being formed.

The Barolos had also in France the Sisters of Providence, established at St Diez, and, on the pattern of their constitution, drew up the rules of the new community. Later, to distinguish them from other congregations with the same name, the new body called themselves 'Sisters of Saint Ann and of Providence.' Their present title is 'Congregation of the Sisters of St Ann.

After one year of training under some of the Sisters of St Joseph of Chambery, called for this purpose from Savoy, the religious started their apostolate with assistance to baby girls whose parents had left them orphans in the cholera epidemic of 1835.

In 1838 the Marchese Tancredi died, and his widow was faithful to the wishes given in her husband's will, 'I think with the greatest satisfaction that my wife will certainly make good use of my wealth to further the aims which for a long time past we have had in common'.

51

The Marchesa Giulia, although she was the founder and supporter of the Institute, remained apart from it and respected the superiors who were elected in accordance with canon law. This did not prevent her from having a great influence on the religious, especially in the choice of novices.

In 1839, at the first Chapter for the election of the first Superior of the Congregation, Sister Mary of the Angels was chosen for a period of six years according to the rule laid down by the Holy See. In 1845 the same Mother was re-elected, and in 1847 was the first Mother General. Meanwhile on 3 April, twelve years from its foundation, the Institute was given Papal approval.

Notes

1. The documents in the archives of the parish of San Bernardo records that she died on 28 June, 1838.
2. Autobiography, p.95.
3. *Ibid.*
4. The uncle's absence really lasted eleven years, as is stated in the autobiography; in fact the documents in the parish archives of Borgo San Bernardo show that the absence was from January 1845 until August 1846. The signature of the parish priest is missing. In its place there is the signature of don Andrea Sola, first as assistant curate then, from September 1845, as administrator.
5. Autobiography, p.97.
6. *Ibid.*
7. *Op. cit.*, p.95.
8. *Op. cit.*, p.96.
9. 'Up to this point I have kept my resolve not to reveal my decision, but after discussion with a close friend, who was kind to me and of sound judgment, I told her part of my intentions. This dear good friend, hearing that I had not revealed anything to anyone on this subject, advised me to open my heart to my confessor. I followed this advice on the first occasion of going to confession and that excellent priest counselled me to remain constant to my proposals, and to be ready to overcome whatever hindrance there might be, and to respond to the divine vocation. And since I dared not get consent from my uncle, I asked my confessor to speak to him himself, and thus I was persuaded that I should soon reach the fulfilment of my aims. How wrong

I was! I had to wait five years' (*Op. cit.,* pp. 104-105).
10. 'My natural affection for my mother, my uncle and my sister had a powerful influence on my mind' (*Op. cit.,* p.105).
11. 'When my confessor informed my uncle he replied by a decided refusal, and denied that he had done anything or offered any money in this connexion. My natural frailty and my sensitivity were for him strong motives for concluding that the cloistered life was not for me' (*Op. cit.,* p.107).
12. *Ibid.*
13. *Ibid.*
14. 'My uncle was firm in his decision. Though he was far from interfering with my free will and a wish to put obstacles in the way of my vocation he argued that, seeing my feebleness he thought that God would not call me to the sort of life which I could not follow for long without breaking under the weight of weariness and austerity. "With your character," he said, "with its tendency to self-reproach, you would be overcome within three months' (*Op. cit.,* pp. 107-108).
15. *Op. cit.,* p. 108.
16. *Op. cit.,* p. 109.
17. *Ibid.*
18. *Op. cit.,* p.113.
19. *Ibid.*
20. *Ibid.*
21. 'Decided as I was to quit the world and having shown all the signs of such a resolve, I loved to dress in a humble fashion, though always clean and respectable. My good sister, though by God's grace not given to vanity, in some ways did not quite approve of me and for a time reproved me, though always politely' (*Op. cit.,* p.111).
22. *Op. cit.,* p.112.
23. The so-called Umiliate formed part of the Confraternity of Mercy — as we are informed by don Lorenzao Pelego in his History of the city of Carmagnola — and was founded in 1597, and had an oratory in the church of St Augustine. The chief aim of the Confraternity was that its members, dressed in sackcloth with a hood, later abolished to avoid abuses, was to assist prisoners who were condemned to death and accompany the body to the cemetery. At the time Caterina lived, death sentences were not often given. The members, wearing a hood, went in procession with the dead persons to the cemetery.
24. The College of Carmagnola still possesses a list, written in Indian ink, drawn up by don Pegola, which shows the succession of canons, from 1400 onwards. On the Canon Andrea Pipino see 'Andrea Pipino, Carm. S.T.D. Sub. S. Bernardo poss. dep 8 April 1848. Died 11 February 1860.
25. From Carlo Alberto's proclamation on the occasion of the first War of Independence, Turin. 23 March 1848.

26. The present facade, by Alessio Ragazzoni of Turin, is superimposed on the old one, and was begun in 1894.

27. *Chapel of the Immaculate Conception.* Collegiata of Carmagnola. A monument expressing the faith, the love and the gratitude of the whole city to its patron. It was decided to build it in accordance with a vow in 1522, and it was completed in 1894. It had a wealth of marble, of stucco and gold, and its splendid decoration was by Professor Angelo Moia of Turin and the painter Francesco Gonin. On the right hand wall is a picture illustrating the vow of 1522, on the left a picture illustrating the vow of 1630, painted by Luigi Vacca (1810). The altar and the floor are of precious marble, made in 1796.

28. The royal gift was donated on 5 December, 1846.

29. Lorenzo Pegolo, *History of the city of Carmagnola,* (1925), p.162.

30. Autobiography, p.118.

31. *Op. cit.,* p.122.

32. *Op. cit.,* p.123.

33. *Ibid.*

34. *Ibid.*

35. *Op. cit.,* p.119.

36. *Ibid.*

37. *Ibid.*

38. *Op. cit.,* p.120.

39. *Ibid.*

40. During the life of Mother Enrichetta it was only the cloistered orders that took perpetual vows; the active orders took only temporary vows. But in the latter, vows could be perpetual, after a period of temporary vows, which could last more or less for one, two or three three year periods dating from the first profession. There could also be simple vows, from which a dispensation could be granted by the Ecclesiastical authority for serious reasons, even when they were perpetual. In the Institute of the Sisters of St Ann, to which Mother Enrichetta belonged, perpetual vows began to be taken only in 1898, four years after her death, when there was a revision of the Constitution of the Institute modified by Pope Leo XIII, dated 12 March, 1897. This allowed perpetual vows to be taken by any sister who had served three three year periods under temporary vows. The three year periods were reduced to two, after another revision of the constitution in 1929.

41. Autobiography, p.124.

42. *Op. cit.,* p.129.

43. *Ibid.*

44. The Marchese Carlo Tancredi Falletti di Barolo was born on 26 October 1782. He was the last survivor of a brilliant ancient feudal family. He was deeply religious and cultured; he studied

especially state economics, and was especially interested in social problems and the demands of the age in which he lived, following the French Revolution, above all in relation to the lower classes of society. He gave all his energies and his great wealth to studying, promoting and putting into practice those plans which he thought best suited to meet the needs of his time.

In 1832, while he was Secretary of the Deputation of the General Council of Public Instruction, he entrusted all primary schools to the Brothers of the Christian Schools. He died suddenly at Chiari (Brescia) while he was on a journey, on 4 September, 1838.

45.   Giulia Viturnia Francesca, Marchesa di Barolo, was born in the Vendée, into the Colbert family, on their property of Maulevrier, on 27 June, 1785, and died at Turin on 19 January 1864. She lived in exile in Germany and Holland with her father under Napoleon, who called her to serve at his court. There she met the Marchese Carlo Tancredi Falletti di Barolo and married him in 1807. After the Restoration she settled with him at Turin, and lived in the Barolo family palace there. Inspired by the Servant of God, Pio Brunone Lanteri and by St Giuseppe Cafasso, she showed heroic devotion and was lavish with her wealth, with which she carried out wonderful works of charity.

III Life is never an everyday affair

Meeting 'Maman'

The village of Valdocco, beyond the River Dora is green with orchards and vineyards. It is outside the city but not really open country. The village has a place in the history of charity which has given it the name 'village of good deeds'.[1] The most fervent strivings in the extraordinary flowering of sanctity in nineteenth century Turin began and grew up here. Its ancient name was *vallis occisorum* in memory of the tradition that soldiers of the Thebean Legion were martyred here. Hence — as Pellico explains[2] — the abbreviation Val d'Oc, which became Valdocco. And the blood of the martyrs who refused to burn incense to the gods seems to have fertilized the land and brought forth the seed of human and Christian solidarity. The foundations of the marchesses of Barolo, the Small House of the Divine Providence of Cottolengo, the Oratory of St Francis de Sales with the boys of Don Bosco are all huddled together in Valdocco, almost within the palm of your hand.

The first of the family to found one such charitable institution was Giulia di Barolo who endowed the Refuge[3] in 1822. This was a house of hospitality for women who had lived lives of ill-fame, often in prison;

here they could recuperate and learn a trade.[4] The foundation was a continuation and fulfilment of this generous and saintly lady's work in the city prisons; her name was among the most famous in Piedmontese society. In 1834 the Magdalene convent was built next to the Refuge. The noble lady founded this convent as an enclosed order for girls who wanted to leave the world and enter the religious life. The congregation still exists and continues in the spirit of its foundress: today it is the congregation of the Sisters of St Mary Magdalene. Nearby the Marchesa decided to build St Philomena's Children's Hospital for sick or unfortunate children,[5] and a little further on, a few steps from the Sanctuary of the Consolata, the convent and school of St Ann for 'decent girls of humble means.'[6]

In 1832 the Marchesa Tancredi, with this latter institution in mind, entered into negotiations to acquire the land on which, as well as the convent for the Sisters of St Ann, the first children's home in Italy was to arise.[7] This was 'when the apostolate of the Mantuan Ferrante Aporti had not yet produced the good fruits it was to bear later on'.[8]

On November 12 1850 when don Andrea accompanied his niece to the Convent of St Ann for the first time, the institution was in full swing. The building was finished. Part of it was occupied by the school and the nuns, and another housed the 'Juliets' who were a group of girls orphaned by cholera in 1835 and who had come to the convent after the others.[9]

They were admitted by the portress to the parlour on the ground floor which was a large room opening onto a wide courtyard. It was recreation time and the pupils were enjoying the late autumn sunshine in the open air.

While they were waiting for the Sister Superior, Caterina watched the crowd of 'breathless' children from the window. They were running about, jumping and shouting. The quietest ones were holding hands and dancing round in a ring. They were wearing starched white bonnets. The sisters walked about calmly, sometimes beckoning here or there, enjoying and controlling the exuberance very patiently. Then they called the children to stand in line and they obediently did so. One sister fetched a laggard to join the others.

The convent was not at all as Caterina had imagined it for years. There was no cloistral severity. The atmosphere was lively and the children all-important. There was a family atmosphere suggested by the simple elegance of the parlour. Everything was very simple but pleasant. There was a hand-embroidered table-cloth on the centre table, which had a plant on it, there were cushions with the Barolo monogram, a basket of flowers worked in feathers and beads under a glass bell, and a picture of St Ann on the wall.

The sisters she had seen, apart from their head-dresses, could have been taken for the children's mothers. They talked, smiled, ran about with them and had lots of little ways of making them be good. In these nuns the veil hadn't destroyed their maternal feelings, but brought it out and given it a new value and meaning. Teaching: a vocation born of love and the certain faith that the world can change. If hope for the future was lost — and these children were the future — all teaching would become futile lifeless formulae. But when the aim of the school was not only to instruct but to give enduring principles which would be the salt of life, the teacher's job acquired an incomparable dignity, a work of creation, prevening and sustaining the action of grace.

While she waited excitedly to meet the Sister Superior, Caterina realized all this. Perhaps she thought and felt that her own vocation would be to be a teacher. Thousands of children growing into womanhood would pass through her hands and she could show them the ever-new attraction of the supernatural. She remembered the joy she felt when she taught catechism in the village of San Bernardo.

The arrival of the Superior distracted her from these thoughts that flushed her face with excitement. She was deeply moved; she knew she was taking a decisive step. She trusted but felt afraid, strangely afraid that she might not be able to go through with it. Embarrassed and preoccupied she hardly succeeded in kissing the nun's hand. The Superior welcomed her with words of encouragement.

Her uncle had given notice of Caterina's arrival and as the Marchesa di Barolo — 'Maman' as she was called by the sisters — was at home in the Palazzo, he agreed to the proposal to go and pay their respects to her.

The young postulant had not expected this; she went out through the convent door again, together with her uncle and the Sister Superior, and walked the short distance to the Palazzo Barolo. The Palazzo, which had undergone the extravagances of 'monssu Druent',[10] a popular eighteenth century gentleman who had had it built, could be described as 'the fairest jewel of eighteenth century Piedmontese private architecture'.[11] The entrance was imposing, the hall spacious and elegant, the main staircase was magnificent with its double flight of converging steps.

They were received by a servant in livery who obsequiously preceded them through room after room, all damask, and their walls covered in richly gilded mirrors and pictures by Guercino, Tintoretto, Caravaggio.[12] In every corner it seemed that 'all the arts competed to give proof of their excellence'.[13] But Caterina was too absorbed and shy to take much notice of all this beauty.

The guests waited a little while and the Marchesa came to receive them, in the green study, so called because of its tapestries. Guilia Barolo came towards them. She was sixty five but did not look it, although her life had been full of problems. She was above average height and seemed even taller because of her dignified but not haughty carriage, not at all bent with age. A fringe of lace on her well cared-for hair framed her expressive face which looked as if it often had a smile on it. The veins showed through the delicate skin on her frail hands. Her eyes were light-coloured and lively, under her arched brows. Her forehead was smooth, broad and unwrinkled.

The first words were spoken in French and addressed to the Sister Superior, then she excused herself, changed to Italian and turned to the canon and bent to kiss his hand. Don Andrea tried to find the best words he could to explain the reason for their visit and shyly mentioned his niece's wish — she was like a daughter to him — to enter the Institute of St Ann. The noble lady listened with interest and looked kindly at the girl sitting with her hands in her lap and lowered eyes. It was a meeting of age and youth and two very different social classes. However from that moment they felt they understood each other. They had something in common. The Marchesa wanted to hear more about it, characteristically going straight to the point and questioning the girl.

Caterina, who had overcome her embarrassment, spoke sincerely about her vocation. She spoke about the opposition of her parents, the many difficulties, the long road she had had to travel to reach the certainty that she was truly called to the religious life. Her account was succinct, sometimes she became excited but she felt very timid. She always found it difficult to express what she felt.

The old lady listened, almost without interruption, letting her talk. She was accustomed to meeting people of every class and was rarely mistaken in her judgments of them. The girl's candour moved her profoundly. She was especially pleased by a certain strength of character which came out in the way she told her story. She had certainly made a very good impression. If that was what she wanted she could enter the congregation. From that day on, Caterina like all the other sisters, learnt to call the Marchesa 'Maman'.

Sometimes heaven is deaf

When she got back to Carmagnola, Caterina hastened to get everything ready to enter the novitiate. The Sister Superior had agreed to give her eight days to make necessary preparations and allow her to remain until the Feast of the Immaculate Conception, which was celebrated with great solemnity in her town and Caterina had promised to attend.[14]

Although this motive was plausible, her real one was different and she gave it in her autobiography: 'Those eight days were an excruciating martyrdom for my poor heart, which felt all the love of my parents from whom I had to separate and I felt it would be impossible to live a long time without them'.[15]

As the days went by and the date of her departure grew nearer her anguish became intolerable. She went through a period of spiritual dryness, found no comfort in prayer, even though she continued to kneel before the altar and gaze with her whole soul at the Madonna. She was alone, completely alone in her struggle with her deepest feelings: 'I turned to God but heaven seemed to have become deaf to my pleadings'.[16] Choking back her tears, especially when she met her mother's resigned eyes, she forced herself to be strong and happy to have finally obtained what she wanted. But although it was possible to make others understand, her mother was different. Her uncle understood what she was going through but pretended to believe she was happy so as not to worsen the situation. Her sister said nothing — Caterina could do as she liked but she did not understand her. At last the day of parting came. The human soul is strange, which is why it is so rich, unpredictable and ever new. For years all that Caterina had wanted was to enter the Institute, and now that all the waiting was over, she almost wanted to turn back. Not because she doubted her vocation and no longer wanted to enter the convent of St Ann, but because she couldn't bear to leave her family. When the eight days were up and everything was ready for her to leave, she felt such great anguish she thought she 'must give way'[17] any moment, hopelessly. She could stay at home which would have pleased her parents, particularly her mother. To overcome her inner crisis and the strong temptation to deny her vocation because you can also do good by remaining in the world, she turned to her confessor. 'And I told him plainly that I felt I could no longer leave my family and enter the religious life'.[18] The good monk listened to her and was not surprised to find her so depressed. He knew her well, and because he did, he found the right words to encourage her. Don't be afraid. No great act can be done without pain.

Renunciation is an essential part of a religious vocation. It was natural for her to be attached to her parents and to feel pain at having to leave them. It showed that her feelings were deep, but it was also true that her vocation was too great a treasure to throw away. The Lord loved her. Looking back over the years she could see that her whole life had been a preparation for this decisive moment. Now she was past twenty. She was an adult and ought to be able to choose. If she had already chosen, she should follow where grace led her to the end of the road, courageously.

The confessor spoke firmly which made her reflect. But she was particularly struck by his tone because — as she later confessed — 'he did not usually treat me like this'.[19] She went home feeling better. She had made up her mind to go. 'I was able to master myself, hold back my tears and look happy when I was feeling so sad'.[20]

On 19 November 1850 everything was ready. She had only to leave. The gig was at the door. Her uncle was going with her. Her mother did not feel up to it. She knew she would break down.

'Thus I entered the Convent of St Ann, after five years of waiting and trials, which soon changed into other trials which were new to me and quite unexpected'.[21] She was not surprised at this and gave an explanation for it. 'Considering the agreement I made with my God as soon as I set foot in the convent. While I was in the world I had constantly prayed to God not to allow me to be without suffering. . . In the convent everything changed, but the desire my God had set in my heart to suffer for him, and so I prayed to him and made an agreement. . . that he should always give me something to suffer either internal or external, but that I should still be able to attend to the duties imposed on me by obedience and that I should not be a burden to the community'.[22]

This was a strange outlook for a twenty-year-old girl to face life with: to suffer something every day in the name of love. It was a daunting prospect and common sense would reject it as madness. To want suffering is absurd, and against all human logic. However understanding the meaning of her wish, which is not easy, gives us the secret of her greatness.

The secret of the cross. The Passion is something that both repels and attracts, appals and calls. Caterina had no doubts. She knew clearly that following her vocation meant following the cross. Her Lord, her God made man, died on the cross. Sharing the suffering of the one you love, smiling even when the pain seems overwhelming, is an act of love. Sharing the cross with Christ. Stretch out her arms together with his tortured arms. Open her hands to accept without resistance the hammering in of the nails. Mix her blood with his. Feel all the thorns that pierced his blessed forehead. Alone with him on the cross of shame which became the sign of redemption. 'I am nailed to the cross with Christ' said Paul of Tarsus, and any other Christian can also choose to be. The example of Golgotha is not dead and negative. It is an example which can rouse the heart to fearless heroism, superhuman virtue. This was the road which was to lead her so far, on which the young novice firmly set out. As well as wanting to suffer she was capable of feeling to an extent that might seem excessive but was instead proof of the fineness of her spirit.

On the Sunday after her entry, during Mass the priest spoke about the gospel parable of the fig tree, that did not bear fruit and the farmer ordered it to be uprooted and thrown on the fire. Caterina was moved to tears. 'I cried all through the sermon and thought that I was that unfruitful tree without good works'.[23] The novice mistress saw her crying and went up to her, feeling worried that she was missing her family. After the Mass she called her and asked her kindly what was the matter. When she heard the reason, she was impressed and admired such spontaneous tenderness towards the supernatural.

It was difficult for the novice to settle down. She felt uncomfortable. The impact of reality was hard and more than once during the early months she thought of leaving the convent. She was afraid she could not bear it but she did not mention her feelings to anybody because she was afraid she would be sent home as unfit for the religious life. She suffered a jumble of mixed feelings and the struggle she was going through was well expressed in a sentence she wrote, even though she wrote it several years later: 'To tell the truth, I would have been very glad if the Sister Superior had ordered me to go but I was more afraid of that happening than I was of dying.'[24]

In this suffering state made worse by a continuing dryness of spirit, she also had to cope with the disappointment she felt when she found that the spiritual adviser to the community was someone who could not understand her.

In fact Caterina was already so advanced in the spiritual life that she was difficult to understand. It is not easy to search the secrets of the heart and when this heart in its simplicity has something extraordinary about it judgment may be superficial. Probably, as he did not know her, the confessor did not take what she said very seriously and did not follow her way of expressing her extraordinary experience of God. This saddened her. From what she wrote we gather she was 'disgusted'[25] but she preferred to say nothing: 'I did not speak about it to anyone except my God'.[26] But all her difficulties were poured out in prayer and an intense, confident loving conversation which was life to her. She continued to pray even in the state of continuing spiritual dryness she was suffering. She no longer felt the joy that uplifted, comforted and strengthened her but she still knelt to pray. Moreover she never doubted that the sun still shone beyond the dark clouds that oppressed her. The novice mistress[27] liked her and thought highly of her.

Every evening the young girl from Carmagnola went to the old nun who welcomed her warmly. They had conversations that deeply impressed her, whispered wise advice, in the oil lamp lit room. The religious life, living in a community was an art to be learnt over the years and living together with others whose characters, up-bringing and ideas were very different from one's own was itself a great sacrifice. If the little continued insignificant irritations did not get you down, community life slowly revealed its riches. But gradually, and if love and understanding failed it was difficult to go on. Sometimes enthusiasm was not shared, impatience for action misunderstood, virtue mistaken for showing off. They were together to understand each other but there was misunderstanding too. All this was caused by lack of love which was the only thing that could unite them, help them to overcome difficulties that appeared insurmountable. Nevertheless a vocation was too precious a thing to be lost for such trivialities, although these did cause suffering.

Such conditions found an echo in the decision taken by Caterina after three days of spiritual exercises in which 'the preacher spoke of the charity we should have for one another, especially in our judgments':[28] I wrote more in my heart than on paper, among my other intentions, this particular one, never to judge anybody, particularly not my dear sisters and always to think well of everybody as charity requires, and when an action was inexcusable, always to excuse the intention'.[29]

She set out firmly on this way of love. Watching, learning what had to be learnt, working joyfully and patiently, according to obedience. To observe obedience without comment: 'From the moment I entered the convent I decided never to let anyone know the repugnance I might feel, and this, I confess, demanded many sacrifices and painful self-denial.'[30] The strength of her character enabled her to carry this through, although it was this very character that in some ways, at other moments, had led her to doubt whether she would succeed in following her vocation.

The days went by according to a strict timetable of work and prayer in common. At that time the novices studied much less than they do nowadays. Not a great deal was expected of a sister. It was enough if she could teach a little, write and speak correctly, inspire respect and trust in the habit she wore.

During the eight months of trial before she took the veil, Caterina was employed in a variety of jobs: 'In the kitchen, in the sick-room, in the nurseries, making soup for the poor which at that time was done in the Barolo household and distributed every day at the

Mother Foundress's expense'.[31]

Side by side with her spiritual training went a real practical apprenticeship to hard work and exhaustion. Apart from recreation times, which were always over too quickly, or a communal walk, the days flew by without a moment's break and she went to bed at night exhausted, with aching back and aching feet, and in winter her hands red with chilblains. Her difficulties were great and her health was not standing up well to the hard work. She was pale and weak, exhausted by the work she had to do, in spite of her goodwill. The Sister Superior was worried, and so was the Marchesa di Barolo who visited her daughters every day.

Obedience became harder for Caterina in this state. 'Sometimes it was beyond nature and only the thought "God wants me to do this – it's God's will" enabled me'.[32]

'Something to suffer every day'

At the end of June 1851 the novice mistress gave her the news she had been waiting for: on the next feast of St Ann she was to receive the habit. She felt all the responsibility involved. When she heard the news the first thing she did, excitedly, was to run to the chapel. Her heart was full of joy: 'Such good news consoled me, or rather filled me with wonder and gratitude to the divine goodness, which had granted my wishes at last and fulfilled my desires'.[33] The chapel was empty. She knelt at the foot of the altar as she had decided to do a few days before when she heard the reading from St Margaret Mary Alacoque: 'From now on I too will go and take refuge in the sacred and loving heart of Jesus. There I will abandon myself and there I hope to find the strength and faith I need to follow, as God wills, my vocation'.[34]

From that day on she tried to spend a lot of time preparing for such an important event which was fast approaching, and while it gladdened her heart it also made her reflect. She became thoughtful, did not talk much to her companions, and absorbed in the knowledge that very soon she would put on the habit. Usually she was chatty, joking and smiling and sharing the fun of the novices who frequently at recreation times exploded with laughter. Such a big change in her behaviour was noticed and some of the sisters thought the reason was that she was not pleased by the news the novice mistress had given her. This wasn't true: 'God was witness to my thoughts and my ardent desires and I did not take much notice of what the others thought. The thought of the change I wanted to make inside me corresponding to the change in my clothing that was about to take place so filled my thoughts that nothing else mattered. I tried to stay always in silence with my God'.[35]

The religious habit is not the vocation but the external sign of inner conviction. It is a constant reminder of a free choice made to seek perfection and the good of many others. That was why when she took the habit Caterina wanted to change her life, be truly converted, become a different person renewed by the light of grace. She did not want there to be any incompatibility between her habit and her daily life. So she wrote some resolutions in an exercise book which she afterwards quoted in her autobiography:

'I will carefully observe the silence, not only in the hours when it is imposed by the Rule, but also during the day, as far as I can, being silent with creatures in order to be more closely united to my heavenly bridegroom;

I'll try with all diligence to avoid the slightest divergence from the Rule, because it is usually these small transgressions that weaken the community;

I'll do every action, even the least important with the sole intention of pleasing God, never creatures, never for my own satisfaction;

I'll practise this by beginning every morning by making an intention that everything I say and do, every slightest thing, shall be to please God;

I'll detach my heart from everything that God leads me to understand is an obstacle to my perfection;

I'll make it my duty not to show what I like and what I don't like;

I'll never form a judgment against charity, so that I may be judged favourably myself on the day of my death, because our Lord said that those who do not judge will not be judged;

I'll try my hardest to acquire the beautiful virtues of humility and patience, and carefully take advantage of the means and the opportunities the Lord offers me to practise them;

I'll spend at least half an hour every day trying to know myself well, and in order to obtain this greatly desired and necessary grace, I'll turn often to my great protector St Franceso Saverio'.[36]

The awaited day arrived, 26 July 1851, the feast of St Ann. The Institute's chapel was crowded. The sisters were in the front seats, then the guests, then the novices, with the postulants and many children from the school and their families in the wings. Giulia Barolo, with her secretary and confident Silvio Pellico[37] beside her, sat in a place apart. All eyes were upon the lady kneeling in prayer: she was the foundress. She was a high society lady, who in spite of being noble and rich did great good and helped the poor. Beside her sat the distinguished looking gentleman with his grey hair falling on his broad forehead. He was the editor of Spielberg, the author of *My Imprisonment* the book 'which did more harm to Austria than a lost battle'.[38]

During the ceremony celebrated by the spiritual father of the community, Caterina received the religious habit from the hands of the Mother General, Sister Mary of the

Angels[39] and also the name Sister M. Enrichetta. And at the same time another girl Lucia Rovei[40] di Rivoli was received and called Sister M. Fedele.

The name Enrichetta had been suggested by the Marchesa herself and was a proof of her esteem and affection: in fact it was the name of one of her dearest nieces, Enrichetta de Vibray, who was to follow her famous aunt in the path of charity.

We may well imagine that for such an important occasion her uncle, don Andrea would have come to Turin, and possibly her mother with her sister and brother who had that year just passed brilliantly in his teachers' certificate exams at the University of Genoa.[41] At any rate a family party, although from Sister Enrichetta's writings this does not seem to have been the case: 'I spent the day I had looked forward to, when I took the veil, quietly, full of the thoughts of the reform I wanted to make in my life.' And she adds in all simplicity: 'But in practise, what I could do I don't know. I trust in my God's never failing goodness.'[42] Meanwhile her health began to worry the Sister Superior. The doctor was called in and could find no cure. She was pumped full of medicines which instead of making her better, made her worse. The cause was easily diagnosed: the hard way of life was taking its toll on a constitution already delicate. Moreover her strength of feeling and the tension of striving always to meet an ever higher ideal were adding to her weak health. In spite of these attentions paid to her by her superiors, she wanted to continue sharing in the common life in every way she could, and neither to be privileged nor excused from any duties. And what was there to be surprised at? It was the cross she had asked the Lord to send her when she entered the convent. It was the confirmation of the 'pact'[43] she had made with him: to have something to suffer every day. And just as she had asked in her 'pact', although she had permission from her superior to get up later or go to bed earlier, she never did because she wanted to live the full life of the community.

In particular the long Lenten fast did her harm and her weakness increased, with bad stomach pains and headaches. She was plainly wasting away and she did not ask to be exempted from fasting because she was afraid 'it was not really necessary'.[44]

She was dispensed from heavy labours 'such as carrying water, wood, doing the laundry'[45] but continued to perform them: 'We had agreed, my God and I, that my sickness was not to prevent me from attending to my own (sic!) duties and make me a burden to the community'.[46] This 'agreement' was to be the guideline for her whole life, even during the most difficult times.

During her first year's novitiate she was employed in the nursery school. Her first day in the classroom was memorable. She wrote: 'I was delighted to find myself among so many innocent little souls. I did in fact feel tired but I felt great satisfaction with the work. I often lost my voice because you need to shout so loud with children who will not listen to reason, and I suffered from a continual headache. But I was always able to carry on working in the school, to my great pleasure'.[47]

Some pages in the archives of the *Opera Pia Barolo di Torino*, written by the Marchese Tancredi, give us some small idea of what the first children's home in Italy was like: few or no comforts, constant hard work for the sisters: 'Four mistresses were employed, two for each group, to teach, look after and take care of the physical and moral welfare of the children for most of the day, from early morning till evening, without interruption except for taking it in turns to go and prepare their food or a very short break to have their own dinner. There were no holidays except feast days, when the school was not open and a month's summer holiday, necessary because it would be bad for the children to be shut up all together then, and because time was needed to do cleaning and necessary repairs'.

Caterina, in spite of her ill-health, adapted very well to this gruelling timetable. The only trouble was that, under obedience, she was often sent from one class to another, to discover where her talents lay and also inculcate docility of spirit into her, as was the practice then. 'When I had got used to one class and knew the boys or girls and could cope with them, then I was sent to another and had to get to know a new set of children all over again: I had four different classes in ten months. This was also God's will! I was quite content that God should arrange things in this way, but I still felt exhausted at having to keep beginning my work all over again'.[48]

Death cannot kill love

On 26 April 1852, while Sister Enrichetta was having supper in the nursery kitchen with two other nuns, a tremendous explosion rent the air. The windows were shattered, the doors crashed in with an infernal noise. This was followed by rumblings, banging and then silence. After a seemingly endless pause filled with anxiety and fear of what could have happened, people's voices were heard in the streets and the sound of galloping horses.

The powder magazine in the nearby village of Dora had exploded: there were twenty six victims and the disaster would have been worse had it not been for the courage of a soldier to whom the road from Porta Nova is dedicated today: Paolo Sacchi.

Huddled together and terrified the sisters went out into the court-yard or the threshold of the convent door and looked up at the flashing red sky and the rising columns of thick black smoke. Calm amid the confusion, the young novice quietly tried to encourage her companions with words of trust in the Lord: what was there to fear? The religious life was a joyful preparation for death when they would meet their true love for all eternity, and if the moment had come, they should only rejoice.

'Whatever happens, I told myself, it can't be more than death. I made an act of contrition and thought myself lucky that such was to be my fate, but I had to resign myself to go on living. The time for the fulfilment of my desires had not yet come'.[49] This was the courage of one to whom the thought of dying was familiar, an ever present touchstone for judging people and things.

Shortly afterwards on 19 June of the same year, death struck one of her nearest and dearest. From Carmagnola she received news that her brother Giovanni Battista was dead of 'a slow and painful lung disease.'[50] The family heard the news from Father Calandri,[51] rector of the college of Casale. It was a terrible blow which made her feel the whole weight and responsibility of the way she had chosen. If she had felt comfort in the thought that one day she would see her brother a priest, all that was over now. She no longer had the consoling hope of sharing the same road with him, as they had had when the two boys served Mass with her kneeling at the altar so carefully prepared in the Borgo San Bernardo. It was difficult to find an explanation for the death of one so dear. It was even more difficult to see the work of Providence in the cutting off of a life at the very moment it was about to be dedicated exclusively to God. However the far-off memory of those prayers said so fervently together as children with joined hands, comforted her, and led her to think of a mutual help that should last beyond life. Death could not kill love. She would have one more angel close to her.

In spite of all her efforts, the death of her brother made her feel even more lonely and she could not be with her mother as she would have wished. Her days were dark and lonely, her dryness of spirit seemed to grow worse but she did not give up and continued her devotions. Her health suffered from the struggle and her worried superiors decided to give her a change of air and send her to 'The Santena foundation, in a village not far from Turin'. The sisters of St Ann had been at San-Salvo in Santena since 1836. The Marchesa di Sambuy, a friend of their foundress, had offered them her castle and its large surrounding park. Here they opened a school for the children of the workers on the vast farm which employed hundreds of labourers. Set right in beautiful country, it was an ideal place to restore her damaged health. The community was reduced to an essential minimum who led a family life without pretensions and indeed at that date especially, life in all the houses of St Ann was unpretentious.

According to her autobiography, the community was in fact reduced to Sister Enrichetta and another nun who was her superior: 'I had as my superior and companion a good old woman, whom God used to make my novitiate humanly painful to the greater profit of my soul'.[52] In these words she hinted at the many misunderstandings between her and her superior. 'However hard I tried, for my part, to give her no cause for complaint, I never managed to satisfy her and she always had something to reproach me with. If I did her some service she reproached me; if I didn't she reproached me the same, and however hard I tried to find what she wanted I never succeeded'.[53] This was the first set-back she had met in community life, which was a far cry from the ideal picture she had had of it during the years when she had dreamed of convent life as a paradise, apart from the world, freed from human miseries.

However, the young novice was able to distinguish between the ideal and the reality which was the only way of reaching it. She was always ready to forgive, excuse, feel sorry, faithful to the promise she had made never to judge anybody. She wrote: 'I believe that this superior was faultless in the sight of God and did not even realize how greatly she made me suffer'.[54]

Her sufferings, which perhaps derived partly from her extreme sensitivity, were made worse by her state of health, which did not improve. She felt generally unwell and continually exhausted, in spite of constant care. 'I was obliged by my superior to put mustard plasters on my feet every night'.[55]

However, every morning back to teaching, with the continual struggle to keep the students in order, prepare lessons, and then correct exercises until late in the evening. And that was not all, there was doing the kitchen, making soup for the children, fetching water from the well, cleaning, stacking wood for the winter. Manual labour, sometimes very heavy, occupied part of the day and she also had to perform even humbler duties. In doing these jobs, either through inexperience or through constant tiredness, she often had accidents. 'Often during that time I broke or ruined things. My pride suffered at being thus constantly humiliated and having to ask pardon, as was the custom in our community, but I understood that this was good for me, and as my mistakes were not offences against God, I was content'.[56]

Her pride which had always been part of her character, rebelled, but as well as offended pride she felt the power to conquer it and she did conquer it, kneeling — as was the custom — to ask pardon. This action, which belongs to an age now past, may smack of external formalism. But this age was capable of forming great souls and in her act of penance Caterina found joy in the deep value of community life.

Sister Enrichetta was outwardly calm and submissive and for this she was accused of being 'melancholy and unfeeling'.[57] About this she wrote: 'God knows whether I was unfeeling, and I too know how much it cost me to control myself and keep quiet!'[58] She admits freely how hard it was for her to control her tongue: 'Although I was determined not to surrender in any way, I sometimes felt like it, and sometimes I found it immensely difficult to keep quiet when I felt the need to answer back'.[59]

These misunderstandings and difficulties with her superior made her suffer greatly during this period of her novitiate, especially as she was still saddened by the death of her brother. She suffered greatly, but in silence. She didn't tell anyone about it, there was no one she could talk to, and her days were a hard trial.

The whole day was taken up with teaching and housework, with few pauses. Her only relief was to walk in the country round the castle, stop to admire the landscape, the freshly worked fields, the vines now loaded with grapes, the flocks coming home from the pasture, and sunset-reddened sky. If she met a child they walked along together. Then she seemed like her former cheerful self and held the child's hand and chatted as they walked. If she had no other duties she would take him all the way home, leaving him at the door. She rarely accepted an invitation to come in, although she often felt a certain nostalgia at the sight of the table laid for supper, the head of the family sitting by the fire and the mother bustling about like all mothers.

Children liked her and the village girls ran up to her if she was in the square. She got on well with the young and when she was with them she forgot all her anguish. But perhaps through shyness — as she herself admitted — she detested accompanying the girls on processions,[60] which walked solemnly through the decked streets of Santena on feast days. She was disturbed by all the pomp: the bustle, the band, the people extraordinarily devout for the occasion. She would have greatly preferred to stay alone in the Institute chapel. She had a great need to pray, reflect and meditate, and her busy day seemed to give her less and less time to dedicate to the Lord. But she had to go, she could not refuse, and although she did not enjoy it she accompanied the children and school girls on these processions. 'My God was pleased to repay me abundantly for the mortification I felt on these processions. When we came back from the procession there was benediction of the Blessed Sacrament and during the time Jesus was exposed on the altar, I felt such a deep, profound sense of the |vanity| and futility of all worldly things that it would be impossible to describe. I felt not only contempt but also disgust for everything that was not God and his holy will. This feeling lasted at its most intense not longer than five minutes, but it made such a deep impression on my spirit that I thought I should never again feel unwillingness to do the things that had previously so greatly repelled me'.[61]

This seems to have been a ray of bright light in the continuing darkness of her spirit. During those moments at the foot of the altar she realized how small and unimportant were the problems she encountered in community life. She discovered their true value. It was not she who had chosen the path to follow. She had merely agreed to a plan which went beyond all her experience, to advance further and further into the supernatural: a loving plan whose intricacies she sometimes failed to understand but knew at least whose hand had made it. She would surrender herself into those hands and let the miracle happen.

Sister Enrichetta's self-abandonment into God's hands after this episode, is described in these few words:

'Only my God could fill and satisfy my poor heart, and I cared about nothing else'.[62]

Where God is, every other law gives way
'During the final carnival days of 1853'[63] she went back to Turin for a short rest. During her stay she heard from her superior that she was to be a school mistress. She would be at the 'Monastero'[64] as the house in Rue Paysanne[65] was then called by the sisters.

It had been built by the Marchese Tancredi. She was to leave Santena where she had by now settled down.

The new post was a mark of esteem, but turned out much harder than she had expected. She was to teach in the 'second or middle school'.[66] It was the first time she had faced a class of girls aged from thirteen to fifteen, a difficult age, sometimes rebellious, and requiring sensitivity and firmness.

This was Sister Enrichetta's first experience of teaching this age group, and it was a new, not always edifying world to her. It was not at all like the way of reaching inner perfection she had imagined. There is only a hint of this in her autobiography: 'Some of the girls were undisciplined and insubordinate which made it hard and painful work for me'.[67]

She spent the whole day with them from morning till night, when silence fell on the row of white beds in the dormitory. This constant attention to them was a hard sacrifice. She got up before them, saw that everything was in order, then prayers and mass together, the long hours of lessons, dinner, recreation, more lessons, even though her head ached and her eyes were dropping with tiredness. Finally the appointed daily walk, which often gave the teacher a good deal of anxiety.

She wanted to be their elder sister, their confidant and friend, but did not always succeed. She tried every means of approach and was sometimes misunderstood either because she was too strict or too kind and patient. She never succeeded in finding the happy medium of a good relationship and suffered greatly on this account. She had the support and advice of the old mistress of novices, who thought highly of her, and this was the only comfort she felt apart from what she found at the foot of the altar. Every evening before she went to bed, she stayed late in the chapel. She recalled her students' names one by one, thought about each girl and her particular needs.

Her method of teaching, if she had one, had not been learnt from books but from her living experience of the mystery of the Eucharist: the bread that becomes flesh by a miracle of love and is broken for all for the salvation of many. She also gave herself to everybody, and teaching was not her only task. She admits candidly: 'For anyone of good will who does not try to spare herself, there is always work to be done in communities'.[68]

When the wardrobe mistress fell sick, she freely took her place and in her rare free time — and even giving up her rest — she ironed, sewed, mended and collected clothes from the laundry.

'Quite frequently when I came out of school which was on the ground floor and went up to the top floor where the wardrobe was, I felt so exhausted after climbing the stairs, that I nearly fainted and had to sit down a moment to rest. After this I got on with my work and usually nobody noticed my suffering'.[69] There was some bitterness in this last remark: in communities, as often happens in families, people live together, but have so much to do and are so busy, that there is no time to say a word of comfort to anyone else, even though you eat at the same table, pray for the same intentions and have the same vocation.

In spite of all her good will and her worrying poor health, she did not always succeed in pleasing the older nuns: 'I wanted so much to help my sisters and do my duty but I did not succeed in pleasing everybody, and this hurt me. But as my conscience did not reproach me and I thought I was doing as much as I could for them, I stayed calm and I did not mind what they might say or think of me, although I tried hard not to give them any reason to be displeased'.[70]

During this period she was intimate with the sister teacher who was her 'companion and senior mistress'.[71] The class had two mistresses, the novice of Carmagnola was thus an assistant, the junior. The senior teacher was 'full of the spirit of God, and very like me in her way of thinking and doing'.[72] They worked together, they exchanged experiences and advice, and a deep understanding grew up between them, based not only on mutual sympathy and pleasure in each other's company, but above all on a common friendship in God. They had animated conversations when they were taking the pupils out for their walk. They talked about 'paradise, God, the way to serve him and love him perfectly,'[73] they were so intent on these discussions that they did not even hear the military band which played in the Piazza San Carlo and proceeded to the Piazza Castello to form a guard of honour in front of the royal palace.

If the weather was good, the Sunday outings were arranged on the spur of the moment. Fresh air, games, then home, tired but happy. Sometimes they went as far as the slopes of the Superga Hills, but only to the bottom slopes because at that time the only way of reaching the basilica was by mule, which could be hired at the famous 'Posta del Mulo'. On other occasions they went to the Monte del Cappuccini, a traditional place to go for Easter Monday excursions, or to the ruins of Cavoretto castle set among green woods. They always stopped to look up at the sky: 'If we looked up at the sky one or other of us would say: "God is there", our conversation stopped and we enjoyed savouring this sweet thought a long while, God! a great word which is enough on its own for continual meditation'.[74]

The Sunday outings were breaks in a life which might have seemed monotonous if it had not been filled with love, all work and prayer, even though Sister Enrichetta regretted that she was often so busy she could not take part as she would have liked in the common meditation in the chapel. However, although she strictly observed the Rule, she did not think it necessary to tell her confessor, because she did not consider it a fault: 'I always felt inside me that I had fulfilled this most important duty, even during my daily occupations, and I always felt calm about this matter'.[75]

This is a particularly interesting point against the idea that Sister Enrichetta was meticulously devout, full of scruples and her spirit mortified by the law. Quite the contrary. Her devotion was a true manifestation of love and not conventional; it was founded on a personal relationship and insoluble union with God. He was always present in her life and made up for her apparent failings: 'It was not that I didn't want to join my sisters in our common devotions, but when God did not allow it, I tried to make up for it in the best way I could, or rather he himself made up for it in a wondrous way'.[76] And where God is, every other law gives way.

Meanwhile the day drew near for her final religious profession. She was not troubled by the grave thought of accepting a religious vocation for the rest of her life, but she was afraid she would not be allowed to do so because of her poor state of health. But one thought consoled her: 'If it is God's will I'll certainly stay here, and if it isn't, I ask for nothing more'.[77]

Towards the middle of July 1853 the spiritual exercises to prepare for the great day began; her fears were unfounded, she would be admitted. Even during the period of most intense preparation she continued her work in school, she could not leave it. The convent needed her help. But her work did not distract her, she was absorbed in the thought of what was soon to happen in the Lord's name. She added to the resolutions she had made when she took the veil:

'I will never complain either internally or in words of any duty or command imposed on me by obedience, unless I have to explain my difficulties to my Superiors. I will fight self-love and say faithfully: God commands me to do this, or sends me this duty or to this place;

I'll do everything possible to do everything with a

humble heart and I'll seek every means of knowing my own badness;

Before I speak I'll reflect on what is my reason for speaking, and how my words may be taken by others;

I'll accept everything in a true spirit of poverty. I'll never complain about food or clothes, but receive everything from the community, my dear mother, like a poor person who deserves nothing and receives everything from charity.

I'll often meditate on the agony in the garden and Mount Calvary, from which we learn the most important useful lessons which give us the truest knowledge.

I'll accept with joy, in so far as I can, my weakness, all the pains and difficulties that may come my way, regarding them as instruments of divine Providence to make me enter into myself and detach my heart from the frivolities of this world'.[78]

They are unpretentious words which show that she had managed to come through her period of settling down in the community she called 'my dear mother': every difficulty could be overcome by thinking of the agony in the garden and the foot of the cross would be her refuge. The problems she met with the people she lived with were 'instruments of the divine Providence.' The changing circumstances of her life from now on would be her way to attaining love.

On 26 July in the chapel of the Sisters of St Ann in Turin, Sister Enrichetta pronounced the vows that were to bind her for the rest of her life to an ideal which became reality.

Notes

1.   A.V. *Turin, portrait of an unknown city*, p.531.
2.   Silvio Pellico: *Reminiscences of the Marchesa Giulia Falletti di Barolo*, (Turin, 1914).
3.   The precise details are as follows: By letters of 25 March to the Secretary of State of the Interior, also, it seems, by personal request to King Carlo Felice, the Marchesa Giulia di

Barolo argued that an alms house was needed. She suggested that rules should be drawn up and that the house with a garden, in the Valdocco region, would be a suitable site. On 7 March 1823 the royal licence was issued, approving the foundation of the house in question and adding that the king wished to support the zealous effort made by the important persons concerned, who were inspired by the sentiments of a noteworthy piety. The king gave his approval to the regulations. By a document dated 4 April the king took possession in his own name of the house and the Marchesa was appointed sole administrator of the new Institute.

4.   The first article of the regulations of the almshouse said that 'there should be admitted only poor married women and spinsters who had broken the law and suffered a financial penalty, but had acknowledged their fault and shown willingness to do regular work, and had given proof of their repentance'.

5.   'On a visit to Naples the Marchesa went to see the tomb of the virgin martyr St Philomena. She was very anxious to see a hospital for young girls built and asked the saint to beg for divine help in establishing it. On her return she bought a house at Moncalieri to serve as a hospital, and next door built a chapel which was dedicated to the saint of Mugnano. As the plan developed it was realized that it would be better for the hospital to be built at Turin where it would be easier to get doctors. Accordingly she built it on a site which she had acquired next to the Homes of the Magdalenes and put to another use the house she had bought at Moncalieri. It admitted girls between the ages of three and twelve who suffered from illness at an age when they would not be received in other hospitals. It was put in the charge of five sisters of St Joseph'. (Silvio Pellico, *Op. cit.*, pp. 83-84.)

6.   Silvio Pellico, *Op. cit.*, p.51.

7.   The Marchesa, working with poor families, saw babies who were suffering from the neglect of their parents. She recalled having seen such homes in France. Inspired by a philanthropy which was not only worldly, but founded on religious faith, she realized the valuable purpose such a home could serve. She was the first to found such a home in Piedmont and put it on her own property. There were two buildings, one for boys, the other for girls, and altogether 260 children were received. At first the direction was carried out by seculars, but later by sisters of a congregation which Rosmini had established at Locarno. These were later replaced by the Sisters of St Ann. (Silvio Pellico, *Op. cit.*, p.57).

8.   G. Fenoglio, *The Palace of Marchese and Marchesa di Barolo*, pp. 65-67.

9.   'She caused to be built an extension of the property by the

side of the Convent of St Ann, which was a home for thirty orphans who were given an education there. They were called the 'Juliets' and were taught and managed by the Sisters of St Ann, and when their education was complete and they left, each 'Juliet' was given a dowry of five hundred lire.' (Silvio Pellico, *Op. cit.*, p.87).

A manuscript of Pellico contained in the archives of the Madonna at Turin gives a summary of all the charitable foundations of the Marchesa up to 1845, which states that 'in the teaching establishment of St Ann, over and above the children instructed there, there were girls who had become orphans in the cholera epidemic and were received and cared for by the Marchesa'. From this we may conclude that the 'Juliets' took their name from this group.

In the same document, after mentioning the children's home in the convent already described, it added that the Marchesa had built a house where she received and maintained at her own expense thirty orphans. This was opened in 1846.

10. *Monssu Druent* was for Turin a type of wildly extravagant man, whose counterpart in Rome was the Marchese Grillo. His name was Ottavio Provana di Layni-Druent-Altesano.

Ottavio's daughter married Gerolama Falletti, but the father's extravagance soon wrecked the marriage and the unhappy young man committed suicide, throwing himself out of a window at the corner of the palace. In 1735 the palace was inherited by the Marchese Ottavio, great-grandfather of Tancredi Falletti, who married the refugee from the Vendée, Giulia Colbert; he was best man at Napoleon's wedding.

11. G. Fenoglio, *The Palace of the Marchese di Barolo*, pp. 27 and 33.

12. Giovanni Lariza made a complete catalogue of the works of art and portraits of writers then kept in the palace. These works are now mostly in the Royal Picture Gallery in Turin. A Madonna by Sassoferrato was, at the wish of the Marchese presented to the chapel in the Palazzo Comunale.

13. *Ibid.*

14. 'They left me at liberty only eight days in which I was to make all the preparations for entering the novitiate. I was asked to stay in the country until the festival of the Immaculate Conception was over. But I knew what those days of delay would mean for me, and what strength it would require to hide from the gaze of other people in the proud struggle between nature and grace. So I refused the request'. (Autobiography, p.125).

15. *Op. cit.*, p.125.

16. *Op. cit.*, p.126.

17. *Ibid.*

18. *Ibid.*

19. *Ibid.*
20. *Ibid.*
21. *Op. cit.,* p.127.
22. *Op. cit.,* pp. 127-128.
23. *Op. cit.,* pp. 128-129.
24. *Op. cit.,* p.130.
25. *Op. cit.,* p.132.
26. *Ibid.*
27. At that time the mistress of novices was Sister Maria Bracotti, a secular born at Giaveno (Turin) on 29 October 1836, died 19 April, 1857.
28. *Op. cit.,* p.130.
29. *Ibid.*
30. *Op. cit.,* p.136.
31. *Ibid.*
32. *Ibid.*
33. *Ibid.*
34. *Op. cit.,* p. 135.
35. *Op. cit.,* p.137.
36. *Op. cit.,* pp. 138-139.
37. Silvio Pellico lived at the Palazzo Barolo between the years 1838 and 1854. First as librarian and financial secretary, then as the friend and indispensable confidant of the Marchesa Giulia. 'Among persons of the highest character' — so Pellico wrote to Cesare Balbo on 19 November — 'the first to commend me was the Marchesa Barolo, who honoured me with a letter dictated from her heart just after reading *My Imprisonment*'.

On 31 January 1854 when Pellico died in the Palazzo Barolo, Giulia paid his funeral expenses and put up a handsome tombstone in Turin with the inscription composed by herself 'beneath the weight of the cross he learnt and taught the way to heaven. Christians, pray for him and follow him'.

The Vicomte de Melun, who was among the most representative personages of the Catholic revival in the last century, was to write of the meeting of Pellico and the Marchesa: 'God brought together two persons of completely opposite sides, different in rank, character and opinions, and united the writer with the woman of action, the liberal conspirator with the realist from the Vendée; the hidden prisoner living on bread and water to the *grande dame* who lived in a luxurious palace and had one of the largest fortunes in Italy. They spent their last days under the same roof in the most complete harmony, a contrast which is vividly described in the gospels and lives of the saints and other great personalities, between the active life and contemplation, between the callings of Martha and Mary.' (Vicomte de Melun, *The Marchesa di Barolo, her life and works,* Paris, 1869).

38. The famous saying, attributed by some to Cesare Balbo, by

others — with greater authority — to Metternich (Cf., *La Confutazione autriaca delle Mie Prigioni*. Acts of the Royal Venetian Institute, 1913-1914, Vol. LXXIII, Part 2, pp. 1163-1192).

In a letter to his brother Luigi dated 22 August, 1838, Pellico alludes to the intrigues of the Austrians to get his book put on the Index. This emphasized Silvio Pellico's own words: 'the stratagems Austria used to have my book put on the Index of Prohibited Books were in vain. They were prolonged and repeated, but as no one could point to any passage which was liable to censure, the censors declared that they could not give way to the Austrian demand. (*Lettere familiari inediti di Silvio Pellico,* Sales, 1883. Vol. 1, p.60).

39. Sister Mary of the Angels, in secular life Anna Maria Metilde Fraheia, born on 15 November 1806 at Pisa. Became a religious on 24 February, 1835. Superior of the new Congregation in 1839 and 1845; first Mother General in 1847. Left the Congregation on 21 May, 1865.

40. Sister Maria Fedele, in secular life Lucia Rovei, born at Tivoli on 15 September 1840. Associate in the novitiate of Mother Enrichetta; in 1864 was appointed Bursar and worked to acquire a house in Rome, and founded one in the Via Massena. Died 11 July, 1893.

41. Research in the Historical Archives of the Somaschi Fathers shows that Giovanni Battista Dominici was assistant teacher in the elementary schools in December 1830, and was due to take the public examinations prescribed under the new regulations relating to public instruction. He took the examinations at the University of Genoa in May 1851, 'which he passed with distinction, and gave the promise of a brilliant future' (Letter from Fr Giulani, Professor of Rhetoric at the University of Calandri, 22 May 1851). Later by unanimous vote he was appointed Professor of Grammar.

42. Autobiography, p.139.

43. *Op. cit.*, p. 126.

44. *Op. cit.*, p.141.

45. *Ibid.*

46. *Op. cit.*, p.142.

47. *Ibid.*

48. *Ibid.*

49. Autobiography, p.143.

50. From the records of the Archives of the College at Casale.

51. Fr Francesco Calandri wrote on 19 June 1852 to the Father General, 'today our beloved brother Giambattista Dominici left us in the peace of the Lord, leaving this religious family memories of a model priest and a man of the most upright character. He was born at Carmagnola in December 1826. In his early studies

he showed such diligence and perseverance that he grew in the esteem of others and received many tributes. He became a model to others in his conduct and in his austere dignity of speech and manners. When he reached the right age he asked for and was granted the habit of the Minor Observants. But his delicate health prevented him from continuing such a rigorous vocation. So he reconsidered his position and was allowed to become a member of our Institute. He finished his novitiate in Genoa and was assigned to our College where he was able to study under the distinguished scholar Domenico Berti, who was full of his praises and entertained the highest hopes for his future. But unhappily these were not to be fulfilled. Fr Dominici was successful as an instructor to the younger students, and gave proof of uncommon ability and excellent judgment. Nor did he ever omit the usual exercise of piety and study, though he was of such frail health. This admirable character gave glory to God more and more, and devoted himself to the service of this Congregation and of his fellow-men. Last year he decided to take the examination of Professor of Grammar, and was successful in passing with honours. His strength continued to fail, but he was resigned to divine Providence and bore with religious constancy months of suffering from a painful illness. He turned more and more to the thought of heaven. Very often he was comforted by the sacraments and commended his soul to the God of mercy, and prayed that his misery should have an end, and that he should be made worthy of entering into eternal light. To this end he entreated the prayers of our congregation. Knowing your charity I am sure you hastened to offer the prayer he asked for'.

52.   Autobiography, p. 143.
53.   *Op. cit.*, p. 144.
54.   *Ibid.*
55.   *Ibid.*
56.   *Op. cit.*, p. 154.
57.   *Op. cit.*, p. 144.
58.   *Ibid.*
59.   *Op. cit.*, p. 145.
60.   'One thing that displeased me much at this establishment was to have to accompany the girls on the Processions' (Autobiography, p. 146).
61.   *Ibid.*
62.   *Ibid.*
63.   *Ibid.*
64.   *Ibid.*
65.   Then the way of the Consolata, where the house of St Ann still stands today, was called 'rue Paysanne'.
66.   *Op. cit.*, p. 147.
67.   *Ibid.*
68.   *Op. cit.*, p. 149.

69.   *Op. cit.*, p. 147.
70.   *Op. cit.*, p. 149.
71.   *Ibid.*
72.   *Ibid.*
73.   *Op. cit.*, p. 150.
74.   *Ibid.*
75.   *Ibid.*
76.   *Op. cit.*, pp. 150-151.
77.   *Op. cit.*, p. 147.
78.   *Op. cit.*, pp. 148-149.

IV The thousand wishes of Sister Enrichetta

The stars are always in the sky
On 17 September 1854[1] the Mother General called Sister Enrichetta to her room.

While going up the stairs, the young teacher considered all the reasons why she might have been called. All the reasons she could think of were both plausible and promising, but the matter had to be serious for the Mother General to wish to see her in the small study next to her room on the first floor. During the day she frequently encountered Sister Mary of the Angels who valued her highly and was like a mother to her, wanting the best for her, and ready to do anything for her without being asked.

She hesitated before the half opened door, adjusted her starched head-dress which tended to slip somewhat, and the cross which hung round her neck, and then she knocked.

She talked with the Superior for a long time, and before returning to her pupils she went to the nearby chapel. On her knees, in silent, meditative prayer, she reflected on what she had heard from the Mother General; grave words, laden with responsibility and obedience, about life in the community. But no matter how sublime or lofty the words, it was still difficult to actually fulfil them obediently. It was on precisely this point that so much rhetoric had been spun about the religious life: here today, there tomorrow, totally detached and without preferences; nor had the modern notion of the necessity of virtue come into being.

She joined her hands in prayer and gazed towards the altar, towards the sacred Host, whose presence was indicated by the lamp burning to one side. And slowly she came to understand that nothing is serious as long as there is love.

Two days later she would have to leave Turin, and even Piedmont, and go to a distant place she had never heard of: Castelfidardo. Yes, she meant to talk to the sisters sometime about certain rumours she had heard about the community there. As was usual with rumours, they had grown out of all proportion because of the distance: rumours, suppositions and suspicions about the convent so far away from Turin, due not so much to the lack of a railway connexion, as to the different attitude to organization adopted there by the sisters of St Ann who referred to the community at Castelfidardo as 'the nuns of Vetto' or the nuns of King Vittorio.

The Mother General would accompany her on the journey, which comforted her. She would then remain in that community to carry out the task of observing, reporting and tactfully helping to bring everything there back to normal.

At that time the convent at Castelfidardo was the Institute's most important one after the mother-house in Turin. At the end of 1835, the municipal council of the town, which was then in the Papal States, had solved the problem of elementary education for the masses by entrusting the sisters of San Benedetto, already in existence, with the total responsibility for the education of children from well-off families.

In 1847 Mgr Luigi Zampetti, then Bishop of Rimini,

met the Marchesa di Barolo, accompanied by Silvio Pellico, in Loreto to discuss the plans for opening a school and kindergarten near the shrine. This was how she came to accept the offer of the prior of Castelfidardo, Attilio Sciava, to have the Sisters of St Ann in the district. The local council declared its willingness to provide land and buildings.

The project had already reached an advanced stage by 1849 when it had to be suspended until matters improved, following the declaration of the Roman Republic. The first five sisters, accompanied by the foundress and Silvio Pellico, all in civilian dress because of the political situation, arrived at the small town in the Marches on 17 April 1850 and opened the school, which was subsequently followed by the boarding school and the novitiate.

On 20 September 1854, having packed the few things she would take with her, Sister Enrichetta left Turin together with Sister Mary of the Angels. It was a long and tiring journey, despite the frequent stops to rest and change the coach horses. One can only speculate as to which precise route they took. It is conceivable they went by train, using the line between Turin and Genoa finished in 1853, then through Aurelia to Pisa. From there they would have gone via Florence to Perugia, through Flaminia and the Furlo pass to Ancona. However, it seems far more likely they went the whole way by coach through Piacenza and Modena, along the endless, dusty Via Emilia until they reached the blue expanse of the Adriatic.

One can easily imagine the young teacher's astonishment at the sight of so much blue. For this girl from the lowlands in an age when travel was by no means easy, the sea had only existed in her imagination before that moment. From then on, it became a reality; the pull of the waves, the infinite shades of blue and green merging with the sky, the white sails on the horizon. Seated side by side, the two sisters gazed in wonderment from the windows of the carriage, at the same time slowly reciting the rosary. They would shortly see the outline of the shrine of Loreto, high on the hill. Their prayers, almost inaudible so as not to disturb the other passengers, were all the more intense, following the rhythm of the galloping horses' hoofs. 'In those days the roads were not surfaced properly, so our journey took two weeks because we had to stop so many times (sic!). We arrived at Castelfidardo on 4 October 1854 more dead than alive from the discomfort of being jolted around on the wooden seat'.[2]

Having come from the north, their first impressions of Ancona were not exactly encouraging. The countryside was beautiful, the views were wonderful, soft, misty hills dotted with villages. But the living conditions of the people were very different from what they were used to in the more humble surroundings of Piedmont. The accordion industry which was to make Castelfidardo famous had not yet been established.[3] The people were virtually enclosed within the little town by the old medieval walls extending along the whole ridge on which it was perched. Houses huddled together, built of light-coloured stone, with terra cotta tile roofs, dominated by the bell towers of San Francesco, the collegiate church and the crenellated towers of the prior's house. The houses were all built along one single street with a surface of trodden earth worn smooth by the hoofs of the mules which the inhabitants used as beasts of burden to carry heavy loads and bundles of logs from Porta Marina to Porta del Sole, then the centre of the village.

The people lived on very little. They were simple artisans, scarcely able to meet their daily needs, with a small piece of ground down in the valley where they would work from dawn until dusk. Those who were better off would go down on their mules, while the less fortunate carried their tools slung over their shoulders.

The ideals and promises of the republicans and supporters of Mazzini seemed to have taken root more strongly in the Marches than elsewhere; nevertheless, whether in the Papal States or in the liberal Kingdom of Sardinia, misery and drudgery, the fruits of poverty, were always the same.

The house of the Sisters of St Ann was just beyond the Porta Marina in a street that sloped gently up the hill. The facade was of red brick, vaguely reminiscent of the house at Loreto. It was a modest, single-storeyed building.

Sister Enrichetta's first task at Castelfidardo was to take the place of one of the sisters who was 'a mistress in the municipal school'.[4] She was also to act as deputy to the Superior. In this first job she found herself very occupied by the lack of discipline among the pupils who had been fond of their previous mistress and were suspicious of the new arrival. She was also confused by their almost incomprehensible dialect. But with time the differences eventually vanished, and they were able to establish a dialogue based on affection and mutual esteem. Her other task was far more delicate since all the sisters knew the real reason for her stay with them. On her departure, the Mother General had made it explicitly clear: 'Remember, Sister Enrichetta, that if anyone has caused trouble, they will have it on their conscience'.[5] This warning dismayed her, for though she felt a certain dependence on the local superior she was still more convinced that her duty was to obey the Mother General. A conflict she found very tiring and which could come to a head at the slightest provocation. The task was out of the ordinary, and most unusual for a nun barely twenty-six years old.

Life at Castelfidardo was difficult from the very beginning. Given the situation, it was hardly surprising that the teacher from Carmagnola was treated so cooly by the community: 'I was regarded somewhat suspiciously in the house and I almost had the feeling that one of the sisters was watching me in order to be able to report everything to the superior in charge'.[6] The hostility was silent and indirect, but none the less strong. Conversations held almost in a whisper came to an abrupt halt when she appeared. Smiles of intrigue, frequent unkind comments behind her back, but no courage to speak openly. A tense atmosphere, laden with suspicion and fear, which for all her good will she could not succeed in dispelling.

There was no lack of work to be done and the most unpleasant tasks were assigned to her, such as cleaning out the hen-house, which she did not hesitate to call a 'revolting task'.[7] Nevertheless, she did not rebel but did it 'diligently'[8] and confessed to having experienced a certain 'pleasure' in it and to have been glad to do it 'for its meanness and baseness'.[9]

Tasks from morning to evening. At school, which already took all her strength, she was given all the heaviest work to do. Despite all this she nevertheless endeavoured to make herself useful in every way, as we can read in her autobiography: 'The community did not know how to handle me so I could not help feeling uneasy all the time. It was a most unpleasant situation to be in'.[10]

Prayer was her only relief, for her many tasks gave her very little time free. Walks were a rare event. At the most she went as far as Fornaci or Crocette, hamlets at that time surrounded by fields. Then, on Sundays, a quick break for vespers in the collegiate church of St Stephen. Only late at night, before going to bed, did she have time to stop in the garden and admire the view of the valley below. In the distance she could see the dim lights of Osimo and Recanati. The stars reminded her of the stars at home, not so much in Turin, as in Borgo San Bernardo and Carmagnola.

In these peaceful moments so many thoughts passed

through her mind, even sad ones. But on looking at this landscape they all disappeared, suddenly seeming totally insignificant. The sky dominated both the landscape with its undulating hills, and the anguish in her heart.

She believed that 'a nun is an angel in the world'.[11] She had no doubts that every nun had the potential to be an angel, that in fact many were, but that others sometimes forgot their real vocation, and allowed the petty distractions of life to lead them away from the one, true love. She was overcome by sorrow. She had no regrets as to the path she had chosen; on the contrary, these difficulties strengthened her conviction. Nothing of consequence could be accomplished without sacrifice, and whatever she did in her daily life she did not for her own sake, but in response to an invitation that was not of this world. A vocation was something immense, infinite, extending way beyond the four walls of the convent. Whatever form the community took, it was only a means to an end, not the end itself. The end was something quite different. One had to persevere along the chosen path, for the stars were always in the sky.

A statue of the Madonna for the angels of the hospital
At the beginning it seemed impossible, absurd. Then came the first victim. They tried as far as possible to conceal the news, to avoid groundless fear among the population. One had to be certain. The local doctor and pharmacist were awaiting the results of some tests being carried out by the health authorities in Ancona.

It was July 1855. It was the height of summer, and there had been no rain for more than a month. The fields were arid, the Aspio and Musone rivers were dried up, exposing the caked mud of the river-beds to the sun.

The crowd that gathered in the first few days beneath

the shade of the prior's house in the square to hear any further news about the epidemic, which had not at the time been declared as such, grew smaller and smaller. Although the authorities made no specific statement, fear spread. A latent fear which made each person suspect the other of being a carrier of the unknown disease.

Further deaths were declared near Figuretta and Quercia, all with the same symptoms. The number of deaths increased, the population was alarmed, frightened; they stayed in their houses. There were less and less people to be seen on the streets.

The school of St Ann was deserted. The majority of the pupils were absent and the number of empty seats increased from day to day.

Finally, a proclamation from the authorities was read out in the three main areas of the town.[12] The town-crier had to read it out; there would have been little point in posting it on the walls, since very few of the people could read. To the accompaniment of drums the piercing voice of the town-crier rang out, mournful and sinister, along the alleys, squares and paths leading into the surrounding countryside. The people were asked to boil all drinking water, to wash fruit and vegetables carefully, and to report any suspected case immediately.

The town had been stricken by cholera. Castelfidardo was in isolation. The few inhabitants who could, shut up their houses and left before it was too late. They departed secretly, at night, offering sums of money to the guards from the sanitary corps sent to the district. Some of the guards allowed themselves to be bribed, ignoring the explicit orders of the prior. Within a month, the cholera had reached Recanati.

In the face of such despair, the petty controversies within the community faded, even disappeared. At the sight of the suffering and the immense enigma of death which struck so many families, the entire community of St Ann rediscovered the true significance of their vocations. Not one held back, not one was afraid. Together, they would find the true justification of their existence in endless works of mercy.

'We spontaneously offered to go and help the cholera victims in the hospital for infectious disease, and the proposal was readily accepted by the town council. For my part I went with the greatest of pleasure, offering myself up to God, and prepared to die from the disease if it so pleased Him. . . . But I came to an agreement with my loving God that he would not call me to Him until the plague was over, so that I might be of service to the last, helping the poor victims of the evil disease and helping the other dear sisters carry out their works of mercy'.[13] Sister Enrichetta was up night after night sitting beside the sick in the provisional isolation hospital set up in the fields outside the town. Nothing was too much for her; she performed the most humble tasks. I was greatly distressed by the constant vomitting of the victims, and in my weakness I found the painful tasks I had to carry out utterly repugnant'.[14] At the end of her period of duty she could go back to the convent for a rest, but she preferred to stand in for one of the nurses, or for one of the sisters who was absent or more tired than she. Her mercy was boundless. She continually pushed herself further because, in the last analysis, her only aim was the life hereafter. Ever further, surpassing human logic, and in her generous urge to do everything possible to help she was fully aware that it might cost her her life. But her deep sensitivity and her profound sense of the meaning of the religious life raised the following doubt in her mind: at what point could she dispose of her own life which she had after all given to the order?

'I was overcome with scruples at the thought that I was disposing of something which no longer belonged to me, namely my life. I therefore wrote to my Mother General, asking her permission to renew my sacrifice.

She replied that she could not grant this wish, that I should concentrate on living and working, and I would have to be satisfied to comply with her wishes'.[15]

She was tireless; fatigue never seemed to touch her She was so busy dispensing aid and consolation that she no longer felt her former uneasiness as she grew more exhausted. She moved anxiously from one bed to the next, ready to go wherever she was called, and everywhere she found pain, despair and death.

Beneath the awnings of the provisional hospital, illuminated at night by torches which contrasted starkly with the pallor of the suffering countenances, she found herself face to face with death. It was probably the first time she had encountered it in such an uncompromising form; foreheads bathed with cold sweat, wide open eyes staring into space, hands clutching hers in desperation. They tried to hold onto life by grasping her delicate, white, slender hand. Hand in hand, they would recite prayers together while waiting for that terrible moment which can only be overcome by love; that moment unlike any other, the most important moment of all. And its significance was to be found in the crucifix round the neck of the sister of St Ann, an ordinary, unknown woman who had chosen love instead of life.

The doctor came past, making a sign to indicate that it was all over, that medicine could do nothing more to help. Patient and understanding as a mother, Sister Enrichetta waited and prayed. Between one mystery of the rosary and the next, a tremor, a shudder, and the victim's heart stopped beating. Then the sister tried to compose the defeated limbs and drew the sheet over the face of the deceased.

She had often thought about death, she had made it the theme of her meditations, she had even wished to die for the sake of others. But to look death in the face was quite a different matter. It is easier to die than to watch someone dying. Here, she was seeing both the young and the old die, even infants.

'At midnight I often found myself alone with one other sister whom I left near the poor invalids while I went to light the way for the grave-digger who used to come at that hour to remove the corpses of the wretched victims'.[16] These few words conjure up the drama of the time spent in the hospital. One can almost visualize Sister Enrichetta, a lamp in her hand, lighting the way for the messenger of the dead.

These were painful days, with no respite, and yet full of inspiration. On 16 December 1855 she wrote to her uncle, don Andrea: 'No paid help could be found to look after these poor victims of the plague. That is why our Mother Superior offered to carry out the work of mercy for nothing with the complete agreement of all the sisters who took it in turns working day and night at the hospital, at the bedside of the poor wretches, many of whom died a mere couple of hours after being struck by the disease'. At this point she remembered her sister at home. Different though they might be in personality and outlook, they had something in common. for she then added: 'Tell dear Teresa that I should have liked to have her here so that she could have helped care for these poor wretches in case we were so surrounded by the dead and dying that we no longer had time for meditation'.

Half way through October, the cholera disappeared. But the village was no longer the same; many families had been decimated, countless people had died. A solemn 'Te Deum' was celebrated in the collegiate church on 13 October 1855, and the same day the prior of Castelfidardo wrote to the Marchesa di Barolo: 'I cannot sufficiently commend the remarkable conduct and religious courage shown by the Reverend Mother Superior of the Institute of St Ann and of Providence, followed promptly by all the sisters subordinate to her, when this place was stricken by cholera. They spontaneously offered their help to the sick who were cared for in hospital at the cost of the town council. The tireless care of these true daughters of mercy brought great comfort to those afflicted by the disease. Those who recovered were full of their praises, and even the dying, as the end drew near, did not forget to show their appreciation of the care and help they had received, and of the religious comfort bestowed on them in their final hour. With these humble words I should like to thank Your Excellency, as foundress of the Institute, on behalf of the whole town. The people here would like to express their eternal gratitude and will pray constantly for your prosperity and for that of your Institute'.[17]

The bells of the collegiate church pealed loudly in unison with those of San Francesco, of Our Lady of Mercy and of San Pietro at Sant'Agostino. Life returned to the town, the shops opened once more, the streets were filled with noise as before, people stopped outside the Porta Marina to admire the view. In dry weather, when the sky was clear and the air bracing, one could see as far as Mount Conero, Sirolo and out over the blue Adriatic towards the faint silhouette of the Dalmatian hills in the distance. Once the plague had passed and they had overcome their fear, the survivors realized that life would go on as before, that they were still the inhabitants of the same town.

The children returned to school, playing happily in the garden which was redolent with the scent of geraniums and citronella. And with them, the sisters.

At the meeting of the town council held on 13 November 1855 they discussed various ways in which the inhabitants of the town might express their gratitude to the sisters from Piedmont for the work they had done. They were no longer referred to as 'the sisters of Vittorio' but as the sisters of St Ann, of Castelfidardo.

They voted unanimously to donate to the community,

in the name of the whole town, a statue of the Immaculate Conception to be placed in the convent chapel. The choice of statue was determined by the fact that the dogma of the Immaculate Conception had been solemnly proclaimed the previous year, 1854.

The report of the meeting contains the following specification: 'The cost of the said statue may amount to about twelve scudi. It would be the only way of obliging them to accept a gift because it would be dedicated to the worship of the Virgin. Anything else they might not accept, and even perhaps consider an insult'.[18]

The 'escalation' of love

Sister Enrichetta distanced herself somewhat from the joy that greeted the passing of the epidemic. She did not participate in the general rejoicing, for her spirit was still more oppressed than ever. It was very hard for her to act as though she was filled with joy.

'In addition to the many difficulties I encountered constantly in the course of fulfilling the duties imposed on me by obedience, I was also beset by such intense spiritual suffering that I could not possibly express my anguish in words; at that moment I did not know what to do with myself, and even began to wonder whether I was not in hell, rather than in this world. Heaven seemed to be of bronze, my heart harder than marble; I was so emotionally disturbed that I would have been capable of any excess if God had not sustained me by the power of his mercy'.[19]

While in this state she received no comfort either from the Superior or from her confessor, with whom she talked very little and who was 'everything in that little community'.[20] These words from her autobiography refer to the situation which had arisen in the relationship between the sisters and their confessor whose excessive interference, if well-meaning, caused considerable trouble. Nothing serious was meant by the gossip circulating in that very restricted, provincial setting, but it could easily lead to disagreement and once the clouds were there they would not disperse as easily as they had come.

Sister Enrichetta watched and said nothing, drawing her own conclusions. She faithfully carried out the task that had been entrusted to her, reporting everything — with utmost discretion — to the Mother General who came to visit Castelfidardo. It made no difference to her that the other sisters regarded her with suspicion. That belonged to the past; now, she was ready for anything. To speak openly and frankly was far better than to disregard altogether. If she did that, she would have fulfilled her mission.

The Mother General held her in high regard, not just for what she was able to report, but for her own sake, and listened attentively to what she had to say.

She was not interested in influencing the young teacher. Her concern was of a much higher order, and she had the ability to clarify problems and advise others how to cope in any given situation. Her judgment was serene, she never said an unkind word about anyone, and always remained eloquent, even detached, when informed of matters that did not concern her.

The following measure was proposed to take effect immediately: 'The bishop of the diocese[21] was then asked to appoint a priest as Superior of the community, according to the stipulations of our Constitution. The bishop agreed, and God desired that an excellent canon be appointed. In addition to many other benefits, he also arranged that from time to time one of the fathers of the Society of Jesus at Loreto would come to the convent to hear confessions or to preach on spiritual exercises.'[22]

In the Chronicle of the Institute we read: 'In 1850, after our sisters had settled at Castelfidardo, some local girls wanted to enter our order. So the Mother General conferred with the bishop of the diocese and our foundress, the Marchesa di Barolo, and it was agreed to set up a novitiate there'.[23] This duly happened, but the novitiate left a lot to be desired because it lacked a proper mistress of novices. Sister Enrichetta was of the following opinion: 'In my view there was no one in our little community who had the necessary qualities to carry out such a delicate task'.[24] She was therefore greatly surprised at the unexpected news that she had been selected by Sister Mary of the Angels to be mistress of novices.

Sister Enrichetta confessed: 'I almost regretted having mentioned it, but I could not have done otherwise, for my conscience and my duty explicitly bound me to do'.[25]

Despite her perplexity, she accepted. It was the least she could do; indeed she had to obey. Her only fear stemmed from the persistent spiritual anguish she had been struggling with for years. She was assailed by doubts as to whether she could inspire enough confidence in the novices, whether she would be able to bring certainty and enlightenment to those in her charge. These noble aims seemed remote and unattainable to her. She loved God, but she no longer felt the reassuring echoes of this love to guide and comfort her.

The following passage from a note written at the time is significant: 'Gone the human consolation, gone the pleasures of the spirit. From that moment on I had to renounce them all. Others may derive satisfaction from them, but for my part I sought to fulfil to perfection the supreme and divine will of my heavenly Spouse!'[26] Yet again she had the generosity of soul to help her overcome such a difficult period. And to those novices who were affectionate towards her and were moulded by her, she would bring the light she herself could not see.

She was full of love and sympathy for all. One of her pupils confirmed this: 'What made her leadership so successful and ensured the most perfect relationship among us novices was the fact that she was totally impartial and had no favourites. Whether we were educated or not, rich or poor, ignorant or cultured, she showed the same attention to us all, the same loving interest and affection in the education of every one of us'.[27]

When teaching or giving instruction she always managed to be tactful, to respect the other person. Her words were never empty rhetoric, even if it were justified. She always led the way by putting her words into practice immediately. Example was of primary importance. She was the first to tackle any task or sacrifice.

At that time misdeeds were punished by acts of mortification such as eating one's meal kneeling in the middle of the refectory, a type of penance no longer permitted. One day, to the amazement of the community, Sister Enrichetta knelt down in the refectory and silently consumed her meal in that position. She had not committed any misdemeanour, but simply hoped to show an example to the novices by her act of humility. Her pupils grasped her meaning and one by one did the same. Obviously, there was no virtue in performing a similar act, but to do it with the approval of the teacher from Carmagnola surpassed even virtue itself.

Red in the face, almost mortified to be the focus of the attention of all the sisters, she thought about how often, too often, food was wasted in the community; food which was the gift of God. They would sit at table without giving a thought to the fact that they had plenty of food to eat while so many others went hungry. On her knees, dipping the spoon into her bowl, she thought about the multitudes of poor. She had come into contact with them at Borgo San Bernardo, at Turin, at Santena as well as at Castelfidardo; the poor wretches who knocked at the convent door, for whom a bowl of hot soup did more good than all the words in the world. Words lost all meaning or powers of persuasion in such circumstances; there could be no meaningful communication between those who had enough to eat and those who did not.

Sensitive to every need of the novices, she became inflexible with regard to the Institute as a whole. She was able to see beyond the surface right into the soul of the individual, hence she knew exactly if a girl who desired to sacrifice her life for the love of God was suited to the religious life or not.

Once she had made up her mind not to admit a certain girl as a novice she stuck to her decision in defiance even of the Superior and the confessor: 'I examined the girl and was convinced she should not join the community. I could not say she was bad or that she could not fulfil her obligations, but I did not feel her piety was sufficiently convincing, or her faith strong enough, which aroused great feelings of compassion in me'.[28]

Her decision was greeted by much comment in the chapter. It was considered to be very extravagant, many of the sisters being of the opinion that time would mature and form the novice and that she would make a good sister. Even the Bishop of Loreto was consulted, since he was making a pastoral visit to the region at the time. The prelate interrogated the mistress of novices for a long time, the latter was polite but firm in defending her decision. She regretted it very much, but she had to abide by her idea, which was not just an idea, but a mature conviction reached through prayer and deliberation. This was countered by the objection that there was so much work to be done in the community, the houses were in the course of expansion, the Institute needed vocations, and that to turn a young girl away from entering the convent was a grave responsibility. The girl in question offered no serious grounds for complaint; she was devout, intelligent, and carried out her duties carefully. But Sister Enrichetta insisted again and again that this was not enough for a sister of St Ann. She was quite convinced of this, even though it caused her pain to say so. Human qualities, a certain devoutness and the ability to accustom oneself to the ways of convent life were not enough. Much more was demanded, for in times of crisis and great suffering, when everything seemed in vain, love had to triumph, sustain and overcome inertia. The fame of religious orders is not based on the number of their members, but on the spirit which inspires them. It was probably for this reason that she refused to give in to all the arguments advanced.

'Neither this long interrogation nor the many others I had already had with the Superior made any difference. A special confessor, the most reverend Father Pellicani, was sent to us at about that time. He conducted further investigations and was very prejudiced against me, almost as though I had invented the whole thing out of caprice or antipathy. I told both Monsignor the Bishop and my Superior many times that if they would take responsibility for the case, I wished, with their permission to reverse my decision: but neither of them would agree to such a procedure'.[29]

This debate demonstrated Sister Enrichetta's strength of character. But her strength did not come from obstinacy or partiality; rather, it originated from a deep-rooted conviction which permitted no compromise, and strove courageously for the realization of the ultimate good. In the end, the young novice in question was in fact asked to leave, and she later became a wife and mother.

'A few months after this event my superior was ordered by the Mother General to accompany one of my novices to Turin. So I was left in charge of our small house for about eight months'.[30] It was the end of February 1857.

Although it was against her nature to give orders and she was unwilling to take command, she managed to overcome her reluctance and proved herself to be in every way able to cope with the responsibility. She approached all matters with directness and intent, even though she was often torn between two decisions and longed to be relieved of the burden: 'I found the burden of supremacy over the others harder than ever, and for a long time I reflected on how I could free myself of it'.[31] This thought constantly recurred, and she discussed it with her confessor who assured her that whatever happened was the will of God, and so she could not back out.

The sisters at Castelfidardo grew to appreciate and respect her, no longer regarding her as an intruder come from Turin to report on the running of the house to the Mother General. In these eight months love worked wonders. The whole community was transformed and instilled with new life. There were no further petty disagreements and obedience was respected, not out of fear or convenience, but out of love. Each sister carried out her duties and all came together in prayer.

The victory had been achieved by Sister Enrichetta's example, by her loving, sympathetic approach while deputizing for the Superior. An open, frank and constructive dialogue was established between the sister who bore the responsibility for the house and those who lived according to her ideals. Her ideas were no longer abstract but had become a living witness, day after day illuminating and motivating every action carried out for the good of others.

In her autobiography Sister Enrichetta summarized the union of minds with the following words: 'The novices were already greatly attached to me and even the other sisters showed me great affection; thus I could organize all my beloved sisters without encountering any resistance'.[32]

The Church is neither Rome nor Italy
On 17 May 1857 Pius IX visited the Marches, an extra-ordinary event which gathered a great crowd. That day, the Holy Father was at Loreto and granted an audience to all religious in the diocese. The meeting took place in the hall of honour of the Apostolic Palace almost filled to overflowing by the large numbers of sisters who had gathered there from all parts of the diocese. There were many kinds of habits, and the starched head-dresses of various different orders all in a flutter of excitement as they awaited the arrival of their sovereign and pontiff. Among the crowd was Sister Enrichetta, and the chronicle records that even Sofia Barat was there, the foundress of the Sisters of the Sacred Heart who had a house not far from the shrine.

The sister from Carmagnola along with some of the other sisters mingled with the crowd, trying to get further forward in order to get a better view. It was the first time she had seen the Pope. While waiting, a myriad of thoughts swept through her mind: a confused tangle of sensations. Emotion, faith, and love for the man who carried the same cross as the Lord.

Absolute silence preceded the arrival of the papal procession. First of all the altar boys carrying the cross, then the attendant monsignors, the bishops, the cardinal Secretary of State, the noble guards and finally the Pope. Pius IX was still young, but was an imposing figure. His expressive face indicated the presence of a sharp wit softened by a kindly, paternal disposition, so that he seemed almost to detach himself from all the splendour surrounding him and establish a sense of familiarity with each individual present.

'When the Supreme Pontiff entered the hall, he

glanced round him with pleasure and exclaimed: "Chorus Angelorum!" The various orders were then presented to him one by one. When Sister Enrichetta's turn came, the Bishop of Loreto added: "Holiness! The sister now kissing your foot comes from Piedmont." Stooping down the Pontiff looked at her. "If you are from Piedmont," he said smiling, "I want to give you a good penance. But will you do it?" "Holiness," replied Sister Enrichetta, "Yes, I shall do it, and with all my heart." "Well then," replied the Pope, "the penance I give you is to say three Hail Marys for me." The gentle father of all the faithful said these words with such an ingenuous smile, that they filled the heart of the good sister with joy and she counted that lucky day among the most beautiful and happy of her life'.[33]

At the end of the audience, emerging into the square in front of the gleaming white marble facade of the shrine, Sister Enrichetta entered the basilica. She knelt down among the crowds of pilgrims in the church and prayed. Faithful to her promise, she slowly pronounced the Hail Mary, enunciating each word in a low voice, speaking from the depths of her heart. Old words, yet somehow new each time the mystery was re-invoked: and the Word became flesh and dwelt amongst us.

Throughout the short journey from Loreto to Castelfidardo, she thought about her encounter with the Pope. She could not forget the expression in the eyes of that sovereign, white-robed figure, his hands raised in blessing, and his fatherly manner. Every word and gesture of Pius IX was engraved in her heart.

Sitting in the gig carrying the sisters back to the convent she noticed the sea away in the distance, and it reminded her of an idea she had been nurturing for ages: the idea of going to work as a missionary in India. She had first thought about it in 1856, when reading the life of the martyr Giovanni de Britto, and had entrusted the possibility of being able to carry it out to her patron saint, Francis Xavier. Her hopes of being able to realize the idea had not diminished; on the contrary, she wanted it more strongly than ever. She even mentioned it to her Superior, who pointed out that missionary work was not one of the tasks of the order.

Her meeting with the Pope filled her with an even more powerful desire to achieve something far greater for the Church. And the Church was not Rome or Italy, or the country where one was born, but the whole world, or better still, the hearts of all men called to the same holiness.

It was not enough simply to possess faith. She wanted to help others share in it too; hence to go out to the missions overseas was her greatest desire. She spoke about it to Father Pellicani, her confessor from the Society of Jesus.

'When talking once to the Reverend Father I involuntarily let him know about my desire to go and work in India and, if it be God's will, to shed my blood for the faith. After that he questioned me many times before granting me permission to make the vow'.[34] This vow is amply explained in her autobiography, which gives in full the formula approved and granted by Father Pellicani on 2 February 1858. With this vow she consecrated herself to the missions 'for the love of God and souls,' 'with the firm intention of doing everything possible that others may know, love and serve you, even if it means suffering or, with your divine help, sacrificing my life.'[35]

Although her plan to go and work as a missionary could not really be executed, it gave her renewed enthusiasm and inspired her to take her vocation more seriously. Magazines and books about the missions became her favourite form of relaxation, but she did not have as much time for reading as she would have liked. So her daily work and sacrifices became her missionary tasks, because she carried them out with a perspective for exceeding the given situation. The future was in the hands of Providence, of that she was convinced; it was impossible that such a noble aspiration based on love could be frustrated for long. Some day she would perhaps go to India. She did not know when, but she was certain that she would go. And in her prayers she imagined that she would not be alone; she would take other sisters with her over the seas.

She made her plans with meticulous precision and on a scale worthy of the aim in view: 'First of all, I denied myself everything but the bare essentials and any commodities I would not be able to obtain in those distant lands. So I often slept under just one blanket and in the refectory I was careful to give myself the least nourishing food'.[36] Then, with charming naivety she added: 'This was, so to speak, my training for India'.[37]

In November 1857 the Superior returned from Turin, and things went back to normal. All the sisters were preoccupied with the beginning of the new school year which was about to begin. Although it happened year after year, it was an event that never lost its fascination; it always seemed as if it were the first time. Both the sisters and the children had their preparations to make for the big day. All sensed the same feeling of trepidation, though for different reasons, the same hope of doing well and the same anxiousness to meet again in class. Even if the children seemed to prefer the holidays, they were nevertheless fond of school. And the same applied to the teachers preparing avidly for the great day. In fact they did not know what to do with themselves without the children rushing about, shouting, at times reducing them to despair. This was confirmed by the fact that in the summer months the convent seemed to be shrouded in lethargy. They still worked, and prayed and did some good, but they missed the happy, lively voices, for example when the children were waiting outside the convent walls before school began.

Sister Enrichetta was back with her novices again. She no longer bore the responsibility of running the house. She had the opportunity to have some peace and quiet. But she could not relax, she was disturbed by a vague presentiment which made her feel very uneasy: 'Without anyone saying anything to me, I felt that I was not meant to stay there much longer'.[38] She had a feeling that before long she would be leaving Castelfidardo.

The following spring, the Mother General came on a visit. She did not give the slightest hint of her plans, but one of them was to take Sister Enrichetta back with her to Turin. This notwithstanding, Sister Enrichetta wrote: 'I got everything ready and took all the necessary steps as though I were certain to be leaving. I was so sure I was not deluding myself into thinking it might turn out differently'.[39]

It was not long before her presentiment became reality. In the course of Sister Mary of the Angels' stay, the mistress of novices was informed that she too would be leaving for Piedmont. When she finally received this not wholly unexpected news, there were only two hours left before they were due to depart. Rapidly, she prepared her few things; she had nothing of her own and was ready to obey 'with the greatest calm in the world'.[40] However, it was only a superficial calm: 'My poor heart, although I was not aware of it, was torn apart with grief, and if my novices were making a sacrifice, mine was every bit as great'.[41] When the time came to say farewell, she could hardly restrain her tears: 'I refuse to describe the final act of separation. All I can say is that we were all struck dumb with grief'.[42]

'There was no end to our farewells, grasping each other by the hand and embracing impulsively; but the coach was waiting outside Porta Marina. Before leaving, a quick visit to the chapel; a prayer in front of the statue of the Immaculate Conception donated by the townspeople in commemoration of those terrible days glowing with loving mercy'.

The two sisters set off on their journey: 'We went as far as Ancona by coach, and since the railway had not yet been completed, we then went by boat via Trieste to Venice; from there we took the train to Turin, where we arrived on 23 June 1858'.[43]

Notes

1.   The date of 17 September 1854 may be concluded from several passages in her autobiography: 'I was informed by my dearest Mother General that I had to go to Castelfidardo and that there were only two days to go' (p. 151); '. . . for the journey lasted two weeks . . . and I arrived at Castelfidardo on 4 October 1854' *(ibid.)*.
2.   *Ibid.*
3.   The manufacture of accordions for which Castelfidardo is so famous, in fact began in 1860. Its origin is wrapped in legend. Paolo Bugiolacchi described it as follows: 'In about 1860 an Austrian pilgrim on his way to the nearby shrine of Loreto, stopped for the night at a local farm house, owned by the Soprani family. The story is that young Paolo Soprani was very curious about the instrument (a concertina) the pilgrim had with him. He studied it at length and when presented with it as a gift by the foreign guest, he set about dismantling it and putting it together again, introducing remarkable improvements in tone and aesthetic effect. And so it is said he constructed the first accordion. To start with, the instruments were made in a small way by artisans, but before long the industry had grown enormously and after a short time it became the economic pivot of the little town in the Marches' (P. Bugiolacchi, *Quattro frescacce in dialettu,* Ed. Mari, 1965, p. 12)
4.   Autobiography, p. 151.
5.   *Op. cit.,* p. 152.
6.   *Op. cit.,* p. 153.
7.   *Op. cit.,* p. 154.
8.   *Ibid.*
9.   *Ibid.*

10. *Ibid.*
11. *Op. cit.*, p. 122.
12. The three stylized towers appear in the coat of arms of Castelfidardo, representing the three different areas of the town: Cassero, Verugliano, and Montebello.
13. *Op. cit.*, p. 155,
14. *Ibid.*
15. *Ibid.*
16. *Op. cit.*, p. 156.
17. On the same day, 13 October 1855, Romano Sciava, the prior of Castelfidardo, wrote as follows to the Superior of the Sisters of St Ann, Sister Maria Gabriella Gionetto (born in Paris on 26 April 1824, died in Turin on 12 October 1861): 'Thanks to God, and to the prayers of many devout persons, the disease that has ravaged this wretched place is over. In my capacity as priest in charge of this town I should like to express our gratitude to you for the Christian piety shown by you and your sisters in coming to the aid of the cholera victims admitted to the hospital. I shall not dwell on eulogies because I am more than aware of your religious humility. I shall only say that the least I can do is to write to your Foundress in Turin expressing as best I can the people's gratitude to your sisters, a gratitude which is extended towards every member of the community entrused to you. Please accept my humble tribute of thanks. You will always be remembered in my prayers'. On 19 September 1855 Father Sciava wrote to thank Canon Giuseppe Cattarelli for his work on behalf of the cholera victims. At the same time he asked him to act as spokesman in thanking the Sisters of St Ann in the name of the entire population: 'The gratitude of everyone in this place towards all the Sisters of St Ann, even for repairing the bed linen when necessary, which was often, it being so old. But more still, for their Christian love and mercy which was a constant source of comfort to the sick'.
    The letters are to be found in the town archives at Castelfidardo; tit. VIII, rub. 2,I.
18. The following statement is all that remains of the minutes of that council meeting: 'Above all we owe praise and gratitude to the Sisters of St Ann for their exemplary Christian charity in spontaneously offering to nurse the sick brought into the hospital. The great deeds of this holy Institute will be recorded for posterity in these pages, but the council would nevertheless like to make a public gesture of the people's gratitude, and so we thought of presenting them with a statue of the Immaculate Conception to be placed in the chapel of the Institute. Our idea is to present it to them clothed, if time permits, although we may have to commission the clothes elsewhere. The cost of the statue may amount to about twelve scudi. It would be the only way of obliging them to accept a gift because it would be dedicated to

the worship of the Virgin. Anything else they might not accept, and even perhaps consider an insult. It was due to them that the sick were well looked after, and things ran smoothly. With the help of only two attendants and one boy they were able to fulfil so many of the needs of the sick, even the most repulsive. And this was not the limit of their philanthropy. For in their spare moments they sewed new bed linen and repaired and patched up the old sheets, without wanting to be recompensed in any way. If the Assembly is prepared to show its gratitude to those who came to our help in this distressing situation we shall find that they will help us again, should it ever be necessary (May God preserve us from it for a long time) . . .' In the margin, the person who wrote the minutes noted: 'Proposal unanimously accepted'.

19. *Op. cit.*, p. 157.
20. *Ibid.*
21. At that time it was Mgr Gianfrancesco Magnani, Bishop of Loreto, whose official residence was in that town. Castelfidardo was included in the diocese of Loreto.
22. *Op. cit.*, p. 158.
23.   The Chronicle does not state when the novitiate was closed; but it is to be assumed that it happened after Sister Enrichetta's departure for Turin in 1858, because after that date no further mistress of novices was appointed at Castelfidardo.
24. *Op. cit.*, p. 168.
25. *Ibid.*
26. *Op. cit.*, p. 165.
27. Pietro Paolo Gastaldi, *Umiltà e grandezza*, (Turin, 1926), pp. 170-171.
28. *Op. cit.*, p. 169.
29. *Op. cit.*, p. 170.
30. *Ibid.*
31. *Op. cit.*, p. 173.
32. *Op. cit.*, p. 170.
33. Pietro Paolo Gastaldi, *Op. cit.*, pp. 189-190.
34. *Op. cit.*, p. 174.
35. *Op. cit.*, p. 175.
36. *Op. cit.*, p. 178.
37. *Ibid.*
38. *Op. cit.*, p. 182.
39. *Ibid.*
40. *Op. cit.*, p. 183.
41. *Ibid.*
42. *Ibid.*
43. *Ibid.*

V Wooden promises will not heat the house

Happiness is to serve others
The thought of seeing Turin again filled her heart with joy. As the coach moved rapidly along the banks of the Po, she already felt at home. The Po plain does not have the pleasant, colourful landscape of the Marches, but for anyone born in the region it stirs up an indescribable emotion.

The rows of poplars, tall, agile, ready to rustle at the slightest breath of air. The fleeting movement of light and shade in all mutations of green, and then a larger clearing through which one caught a glimpse of the river flowing majestically towards the sea. The farmhouses, the villages clustered round the bell-tower of the parish church, fields stretching as far as the eye can see, until they merged with the horizon. As the journey progressed the countryside became more and more familiar. After crossing the Ticino river, she found herself in Piedmont.

At sunset the two sisters arrived at Turin. But before going to the convent of St Ann, regardless of the luggage, they stopped for a prayer of thanksgiving at the nearby sanctuary of the Consolata. At the feet of this image so dear to the people of Turin, Sister Enrichetta prepared to confront a new phase of her life.

116

It was late, the church was deserted and the sacristan was shuffling from altar to altar extinguishing the candles. Only the image of the Madonna was illuminated, a painted altarpiece which, according to tradition, had been miraculously discovered in about the eleventh century by a blind man called Giovanni di Brianzone.

So she returned to the house where she had lived as a postulant, but now strengthened in her vocation, matured by the experience of charity, and above all having acquired the ability to judge people and situations. On her return she requested to be delegated to the most humble tasks. For one month she worked in the kitchen, preparing the soup, peeling potatoes and washing dishes. All great achievements seem insignificant to start with; but in reality they are only trivial and irrelevant in the eyes of the world.

She did not remain in the kitchen for long, not because she despised such work, which did, after all, offer her scope for reflection, prayer and meditation between one job and the next, but because Sister Mary of the Angels appointed her as novice mistress.

She accepted the post *pro tempore* until the next elections due to take place in a year's time.[1] Every new post entailed a certain amount of suffering. So here too, some of the novices treated her at first with a coolness bordering on diffidence because of their attachment to the previous novice mistress.

'Most of the sisters then in the novitiate welcomed me with genuine affection, but some of them caused me a great deal of suffering and trouble before I could gain enough authority over them at least to make them accomplish their given tasks. However, with the help of God and much self-sacrifice I finally surmounted the difficulties'.[2]

Self-sacrifice above all else. Disregarding the irrelevancies, keeping one's thoughts constantly on higher things. Accepting people as they are and with optimism, confident that love, good example and understanding can achieve everything. Love is a flame which spreads, though it demands complete renunciation. Love means not thinking about oneself. It encourages one to give without expecting anything in return. And it is the best school for novices.

Prayer is the food of this ideal flame. Not formal prayers of devotion, but a living witness rendered day by day. For Sister Enrichetta prayer was not confined to the steps of the altar or to the silence of the chapel. For her, prayer and action were one and the same thing. The hours she often spent praying in the middle of the night when everything was quiet gave a supernatural glow to everything she did. The novices were gradually affected by this spiritual light, so wonderfully fused with extraordinary human warmth.

When one of the novices was taken ill, Sister Enrichetta was the first to come to her assistance. She gave her encouragement and help and was closer to her than a mother. She would spend entire afternoons at her bedside reading books about the saints and stories and articles from the popular weekly journal 'La Famiglia'. She always devoted herself personally to the sick, making sure that they lacked nothing, that the diet prescribed by the doctor was kept to, and that they were given light, nourishing meals.

Being so modest she would not hear of any attention being paid to herself. Rather, she insisted on every possible care being given to the novices, whom she saw as the future of the congregation.

At this time the young members of the convent spent their time in prayer and study alternating with periods of manual labour. This involved keeping the convent buildings clean, doing the weekly laundry and working in the kitchen preparing food both for the community and for the children who attended the school.

The morning call came at half past four.[3] In winter it

was still dark at that hour. Sister Enrichetta was always the first to rise, always ready and energetic, tirelessly giving strength and courage to those who possibly lacked them. She did not like to see long, sad, reserved faces. One smile from her was enough to smooth away the deepest frown. To her, happiness was to serve the Lord, to be able to devote herself lovingly to her vocation. Such true, genuine happiness which does not diminish even when confronted with the greatest possible difficulties, can only exist in that way in the Christian faith.

Once the initial difficulties had been overcome, she inspired the novices with total confidence. Convinced that every problem could be solved by mutual understanding, she was always prepared to listen. All she demanded was sincerity. Whether talking to older or younger members of the community, she did not focus on what they were saying but studied the speaker's facial expression so as to interpret her state of mind.

She tried to understand the particular problems of each individual and by identifying with them was always able to find a solution.

She was still only thirty years old, having taken her vows just five years before, yet many of the sisters, even the older ones, already regarded her as their irreplaceable guide. Her guidance was undemanding; it was neither conceited nor presumptuous but inspired exclusively by the charity and love she felt for the Institute. That this was possible and in such a spontaneous manner, was a sign of the growing esteem for the sister from Carmagnola.

She was not in the slightest affected by all this esteem. Nothing could be further from her thoughts than to think she might be better than the others. On the contrary, troubled by the mysterious spirit which tormented her, she nevertheless forced herself to continue giving light, comfort and hope to others. This was the secret cross she had to bear. 'The prayer I directed most frequently to the loving God was that I should always have a secret martyrdom to suffer and that I should achieve perfection in a way totally concealed from the eyes of the world. In his infinite goodness the Lord answered my prayer, for it pleased him to lead me through the darkness of the spirit. Yet even in the midst of this darkness he always gave me immense strength to overcome my weakness, so that even in the deepest gloom I could say: My Lord, let me not offend against you, this is my only fear. If it please you to increase my sufferings, I shall not only resign myself to them, but I shall be happy to be able to suffer anything for your love'.[4]

In the meantime, she continued to think that some day she would go to India. She felt intuitively that she would go there as a missionary, and at times tried to imagine what that distant country might be like. Her idea of India was a vague one based on travel books and her reading of the life of her guardian saint, Francis Xavier. This idea was constantly alive in her and she could face up to any sacrifice when it came to helping those working in the missions. This missionary ideal which she nourished during her years in Turin was the synthesis and crowning of her vocation.

While praying in the chapel she dreamed of dying a martyr's death. She had no fear. She was prepared for anything, but she felt that to lay down her life for the one who loved her would be almost too great a favour. She brushed the idea from her mind, disturbed that she had even thought of it. But she was never able to free herself from the idea of going overseas as a missionary to bring others the love which sustained her.

One day she discussed with her confessor the vow she had made at Castelfidardo, only to be still more discouraged, as the Sisters of St Ann had no overseas missions at the time. So she abandoned this vow 'made in a moment of stress'[5] and which, most important of all, was 'contrary to the spirit of the Institute'.[6]

Her hope became transmuted into a utopian ideal. But she did not lose heart and persisted in her resolution. 'I told them that I did not remember having been unhappy at the situation and that my desire to go to India did not override my being a sister of St Ann; that in fact my first stipulation was that I desired to be sent overseas by my legitimate superiors, in the same way that a sister is sent from one house to another'.[7] This explanatory statement from her autobiography proves that for her the only true vocation was the missionary one.

To make progress in life means solitude
During this period the entire congregation experienced a grave constitutional crisis, as is inevitable in a relatively new, still growing organization. Pontifical approval was not granted until 1846.

Over a space of time a variety of factors combined to aggravate an already delicate situation, itself a reflection of the anxieties and disturbances of a difficult period in the history of Catholic organizations. These factors have not always been examined objectively. On the one hand, there was a certain disagreement between the foundress, the Marchesa di Barolo, and Sister Mary of the Angels as to how the order should be run. On the other hand, this conflict seemed irreconcilable, owing to the lengthy rule and character of the Mother General, who often acted in an autocratic manner causing bad feeling among those who thought differently.

Sister Enrichetta recalled: 'How many times in the last two years of my duties as mistress of novices was I sent to pray until midnight before the blessed sacrament, in the hope that the dear, good Marchesa might come to see things differently. What I in fact did was to pray for Sister Mary of the Angels instead!'[8]

For the exhortation to such prayers came from Sister Mary of the Angels, and made extremely apparent the degree of tension existing in the higher ranks of the order.

The criticism levelled against Giulia Barolo was generally instigated by persons who did not understand the fervour of her charity. She was and remained a figure of undisputed moral rectitude, and is regarded as one of the most important personalities of the Catholic revival in Piedmont in the nineteenth century.

In addition to the differences arising from the clash between two strong, authoritarian personalities, other aspects of life in the community must have been less than perfect; for in 1858 an authoritative appeal was lodged with the Holy See for disciplinary measures to be taken. No one has ever been able to establish who was responsible for this action, which could have led to the dismissal of the Mother General. Maybe some visiting cleric made himself spokesman for the discontent growing within the order. This view is supported by a passage in the letter dated 14 January 1859 from the Vicar General of Turin to Cardinal Della Genga, Prefect of the Congregation of Bishops and Regulars, which reads as follows: 'Charity leads me to believe that the person who drew up this complaint is not well acquainted with either the Mother Superior or with the management of the convent'. (This in fact referred to the complaint which led to the intervention of the Holy See on behalf of Sister Mary of the Angels who had been incriminated). The possibility that the Marchesa di Barolo herself was involved must be ruled out, for on 22 November 1858 she wrote: 'I repeat in all honesty that this Mother Superior possesses great qualities and abilities'. However, later on in the same letter we read: 'I do not share her confidence, indeed I lost this many years ago. I do not wish to blame her, poor dear. Having numerous faults myself I can forgive her. Seeking only the general good, and not my own satisfaction, I must not complain, for that little Institute has achieved some good'.[9] And again on 3 November 1858 she wrote: 'Without any doubt this Mother Superior has faults; I have had experience of

122

some of them. But she has so many beautiful qualities that I have forgiven her with all my heart, recognizing in her a clear mind, an intense spirit, true ability and a head for organization which render her extremely useful to the community'.[10] Her words confirm the existence of many differing, at times irreconcilable, opinions. But they also throw light on the efforts made by the foundress to avoid or minimize any disciplinary measures. Nor could there be any question of Sister Enrichetta being involved, it being contrary to her nature to take any action which would make her stand out from the crowd. Her whole life supports this.

The Chapter, which was to be held in April 1859, drew closer. The situation was still tense, and deteriorated still further, according to a letter dated 24 October 1858 from Cardinal Guisto Recanati, patron of the order, to its foundress, Guilia Barolo. This document is phrased in unequivocal terms, stating explicitly that it was the will of the Holy See to exclude the present Mother General, Sister Mary of the Angels, from a possible re-election or any other appointment.

This news caused a sensation, creating much dissention within the community. Sister Enrichetta remained unperturbed. During this period she began to read the writings of St John of the Cross. This choice, dictated by the spirit, made a profound impression on her mind. She confessed: 'At the time I knew nothing whatever about his works. I expressed my wish to read these books to the Superior, who asked me why I wanted to read such books dealing with nothing but mysticism'.[11] From the Mother Superior's answer she realized that she had asked too much. 'I prayed to God that if it be his will, I should be permitted to read these books; for I had no other desire but him, and in him alone I wished to live. After this I felt even more strongly compelled to request the said works. This time I was assured they would be granted to me without difficulty, as was in fact the case'.[12]

She found comfort in St John's wonderful descriptions of the difficult path to perfection achieved through the experience of years of tormented 'dark nights'. They opened up new horizons to her progress. All through this very difficult period in the order, in the midst of controversy and frequent arguments, Sister Enrichetta preferred the silence of meditation and prayer, and did not allow herself to be distracted from her duties as mistress of novices.

Following the harsh decision of the Holy See, an inquiry was set up by the diocesan authorities to investigate the case. Thanks to the intervention of the Marchesa di Barolo, the truth was established, and by a decree dated 18 April 1859, Sister Mary of the Angels was reinstated as head of the Institute for a further two year period. At the end of this time the Chapter was to reconvene to elect a new Mother General. Sister Mary of the Angels would no longer be eligible for re-election.

'During this period', we read in the autobiography, 'things grew more and more gloomy. Many sisters were bitterly disappointed on behalf of the Mother Superior, and they came to me for comfort, confiding in me their troubles and sorrows. All I could do to help was to cheer them with kind words so that they would find the strength to cope peacefully with any trial sent by God and to cling to him only who never fails when one is in need'.[13]

The sisters frequently stayed talking to her until late in the evening. Some were worried about the consequences of the next Chapter; others supported the unjustly accused Mother General; and yet another group was convinced that after twenty-two years of rule, sweeping changes were necessary. She received them all warmly and listened patiently to all points of view, but she refused to be drawn into futile discussions, and was especially averse to unconstructive complaints. Whenever the conversation drifted unintentionally into pettiness, she was able to lead it back to more positive topics.

She herself remained neutral, rarely expressing her opinions about others. Nor did she subscribe to any criticism of or hypothesis on the future organization of the Institute. She was convinced that the Lord takes care of all things; that events, however difficult, are subject to Providence; and that in the end the best possible solution would present itself.

She always spoke calmly, without any trace of personal involvement. Her meditated words were almost imbued with light by the sublimity of her thoughts. They were simple thoughts; old, yet eternally new and true, and always clearly expressed and deeply intuitive. When listening to her, even the greatest problems dissolved as if by magic.

In times of difficulty she never ceased to advocate union with God. To those who sought her advice she frequently read passages from the works of St John of the Cross: 'This divine union consists in having a soul which translates the will into the will of God; whatever stirs it will be the will of God'.[14] The transition from reading to meditation is brief, for, once appeased, the soul turns heavenward. These intimate discussions often ended up in chapel, with those involved praying together at the foot of the altar.

The winter of 1859, the year of the second war of independence and of Villafranca, brought worrying news from Carmagnola, concerning the health of her uncle Andrea. The gravity of his condition was confirmed by the letters she received and by some relations who visited her. The same old troubles were recurring in a more alarming manner, and due to old age his condition was not improving.

Her uncle died on 11 February 1860 and on hearing the news from her Superior that evening, Sister Enrichetta could not restrain her tears. She would have liked to have seen him one last time, to have given him her loving assistance. But her duties with the novices, the distance and above all, the rules, had prevented her from doing so. As the years go by it is inevitable that one becomes more lonely. People dear to one pass away, often leaving a permanent void. Kneeling in chapel, Sister Enrichetta prayed from the depths of her disturbed soul, that through faith she might overcome the void which oppressed her at the loss of her uncle.

In the warm light of the lamp burning beside the altar, she saw the tired face of her uncle, as she had seen him the previous summer, so frail that he could only just move from the armchair to the bed. It had been a brief visit home, only giving her just enought time to greet those she loved. She remembered his blessing when she took leave of him, the expression in his eyes still attempting to be authoritative; the way he had given her advice as though she were still a child, telling her to be good, to persevere along her chosen path, and not to fear the difficulties which are the salt of life. She would never forget how he placed his bony old hands on her head as she bowed to receive his blessing: hands to which she owed so much, the hands of a father.

These distressing emotions reminded her of her mother. Now she was alone she would go to live with Teresa, who was married to Guiseppe Oscella. They would look after her, and she would be with her loving grandchildren.

There are moments when a religious feels the full weight of the decision she has taken. That evening, Sister Enrichetta was overwhelmed by the gravity and enormity of her choice. Whenever anxiety overtook her and she longed to go home, she understood the real meaning of detachment. In pursuing her vocation she had bidden a definitive farewell to the world. She needed great strength of mind not to give way to her emotions. But the thought of the sacrifice she had made for a great cause lead her to discover the love which comforted her, that boundless love which is the love of God.

Two asterisks by her name

The two years granted to Sister Mary of the Angels by the Holy See to continue her duties as Mother General drew to a close. 'The two years passed with great speed and there was much talk about the election of a new Mother General, something which had never happened in the Institute since its foundation. For my part, I listened to them all and said nothing, content to unburden my heart to the loving God, especially late at night. Kneeling at the sacred feet of Jesus, I placed everything into his hands and implored him to provide the Institute with someone capable of running it according to his holy will'.[15]

As the days passed and the convocation of the Chapter approached the voices of those who considered the teacher from Carmagnola the most suitable successor became more and more insistent. They felt that such a delicate and controversial situation required the energy and enthusiasm of a young person. This opinion was further strengthened by the approval of the foundress.

Sister Mary of the Angels also valued her highly and, at a meeting, indirectly suggested that she might indeed be elected. And this was not all. In a letter to Cardinal Gabriele della Genga on 10 January 1861 she enclosed a list of the nominees, placing an asterisk beside the name of the most suitable candidates. A double asterisk indicated 'those who could be proposed as Mother General'.[16] Beside the name Dominici there was a double asterisk.

Many voted for her, seeing her already as future Mother General. Sister Enrichetta did not seem to see herself in this light and looked towards the future with apprehension. She sincerely believed herself incapable of such a task and for as long as possible did everything she could to deny the suggestions. She simply could not conceive the possibility that she might be elected.

It was against her nature to accept a post of such importance, She wanted to work behind the scenes, to pray without distractions, to live the love which was the guiding force of her existence. Nevertheless, at the bottom of her heart she knew it would be futile to fight against the inevitable. She remembered the intuition she had had before entering the convent in 1849, when reading the life of a female saint who had suffered greatly in order to instil the fundamental spirit of charitable love within her order, that she too would have to undergo similar suffering were she to undertake this post in the Institute. These were only premonitions, but so deeply ingrained as to cause her considerable distress. 'I hardly slept and was scarcely able to eat. During meal-times I was subject to the most painful and disturbing thoughts'. In another passage of her auto-biography she states: 'I spent days of acute misery, not knowing what was happening to me. Constanly in torment, I was obliged to control myself forceably so that the novices with whom I was still working would not notice anything. I feared I should go mad, so immense was the suffering I endured in that miserable and turbulent state of mind. I felt I had lost all sense of faith, hope and charity. I seemed to have lost that trust in God which had always been so alive in me. Nothing whatever could console me or even give me a little relief'.[17]

She turned to her father confessor, hoping to receive some comfort, but in vain. The kindly priest's advice did not bring her the desired calm. Frightened of the future, she fought with all her strength, becoming ever more firmly convinced that she would be elected Mother General. This conviction was not based on any presumption, in fact she did everything she could to dissociate herself from it. She tried to convince herself it could not happen. Others had qualities she did not possess; intelligence, higher qualifications, a more intense spiritual life.

Despite all these arguments her presentiment gathered force and became a dominant certainty. A certainty she feared greatly. At this point she even distanced herself from the sacred heart of Jesus.

'Every time I went into the church, no matter for how short a time, I used to entrust my novices to the sacred heart of Jesus. I felt they were all embraced by the fervour of his love. At this difficult time I tried to do the same thing for myself. But because of my unutterable sorrows I felt I was being rejected, and with me all my beloved daughters. "My Jesus", I said, deeply wounded, "My Jesus, if you do not wish to receive me, I accept willingly. I deserve it for having been rebellious and ungrateful towards your love and your will; but I implore you at least receive my daughters who have had no part in my infidelity" '.[18]

To be Mother General seemed inconceivable. She felt she was too young and knew from experience just how hard a task it would be, as she wrote: 'Were I to become Mother Superior I should certainly not permit things to continue as they were'.[19] She knew the situation in the Institute at the time and was aware of the complaints that had led to the intervention of the Holy See. However, her belief in the religious life was so profound that she never ceased to hope that things would change for the better. At times she was overcome by a thought which she immediately dismissed from her mind: the thought that the Lord might use her and her limited energies as an instrument to lead the congregation along new paths towards other, wider aims. In other moments she returned to her original idea of missionary work which she had put aside, but never abandoned. She thought it might be possible, attainable, even in the not too distant future. These more consoling thoughts alternated with periods of great unease. The more sublime the thought, the greater was the depression that followed.

It was at this time that she felt she was being inexorably

overpowered by a miraculous plot; that, despite her human frailty, the will of God was to be accomplished through her suffering. She was bewildered. Nevertheless, her great fear and mental distress was in complete contrast to the universal esteem she enjoyed on the part of the community.

She described her distress in the following passage of a letter written but never sent to her confessor: 'Words cannot express how I feel. All I can say is that it seems absolutely impossible to ask for help, nor can I hope to receive help from anyone'.[20]

On the evening of 13 January 1861 she was in the refectory with the novices. During the meal they usually took it in turns to read aloud from a spiritual work. The novice delegated that evening read in a clear voice several passages from the life of Maria Maddalena dell' Incarnazione. Sister Enrichetta ate with reluctance, absorbed in the thoughts which preoccupied her. 'My heart was filled with the greatest sadness. All during the day I had had to constrain myself forcibly to conceal it from my sweet daughters. Only at meal-times did I finally have a few moments more or less to myself in which to reflect on the distressed state of my soul'.[21]

Her 'sad reflections',[22] her anxieties about the future, her fear of being elected to a post she thought beyond her capabilities all suddenly faded, and she felt an immense confidence surging through her. It was like when the sun returns in splendour after a foggy day. This change was brought about by the words she listened to during her scant meal. The reader's voice, not really distinguished in any way, careless even in its diction, echoed insistently in her mind. 'To God nothing is impossible, nor to his servants if they allow themselves to be guided by him like blind instruments . . . *Nemo accipiat coronam tuam*, are God's words to all. The crown prepared for you will never be given to anyone else'.[23] In her autobiography we read: 'Having been at the brink of hell, thinking that mercy would never be granted to me, the sound of those words struck me like lightening. In a flash it was as though I were consumed with flames. But at the same moment the Lord also made me understand his previous indignation towards me, and I realized that I had been excluded from his sacred heart because I had not given myself completely, without reserve. For God had commanded me many times to abandon myself entirely to his loving embrace. Unhappy creature that I am, I was always more ready with words than deeds. Though prepared to make him many offers, even the most painful sacrifices, I did not and could not make myself give him that one thing he so strongly desired of me; namely, to place myself completely at his disposal'.[24]

From that evening on, though still profoundly distressed, she was able to approach the situation with a different frame of mind. She accepted her troubles as the most precious gift of the God who loved her and whom she loved with all her heart. 'From that time onward a sweet calm pervaded my heart, and I was no longer assailed by great fear. Which is not to say that the possibility of being elected Mother Superior did not weigh heavily on me. But I trusted utterly in God and placed the running of the Institute in his hands alone'.[25]

On 18 April 1861 the extension granted by Rome to Sister Mary of the Angels and her assistants expired. It formed the only topic of conversation in the convent, and the *Veni Creator* was recited every day in chapel for the souls of those responsible for making the serious decisions involved. Everything was ready for the meeting of the General Chapter to commence.

The Rules of the congregation at that time established precise conditions for a valid election.[26] Once the correct information had been supplied, it was up to the Cardinal Patron to approve the list of sisters eligible.[27] So it was that in his letter of 29 March 1861 the Vicar General of the Archdiocese of Turin enclosed the list of ten names, including that of Enrichetta Dominici.

The bishop being ill at the time,[28] the 'sealed envelope' containing the votes cast was to be sent to the Congregation of Bishops and Regulars.

From correspondence exchanged between the Holy See and the Curia we know that instructions were given for the Chapter to convene on 29 April. By 7 June it was over, and the final results were sent to Rome, though the 'ballot-papers of the congregation in Bagnorea',[29] where the sisters had had a house since 1851, were still outstanding.

Although no official announcement had been made, everyone in the community knew who had been elected to succeed Sister Mary of the Angels. All that was needed was the decree of her nomination and the necessary approval. The only one who refused to believe it was Sister Enrichetta herself. She continued to work with her novices just as before. During her hours of prayer and meditation she felt sure she would not have the strength to carry out such a responsible task. Despite her apparent calm she was suffering immense inner turmoil. 'I was so convinced of my inability that I felt obliged to decline the post for the well-being of the community'.[30] She seriously considered turning it down, although the Rule 'forbade anyone to reject any post or office to which they had been elected'.[31] Furthermore, to renounce it would be to reject God's plan, to doubt that Providence guides all things, and to distance herself from her promise to devote herself completely to the heart of Jesus. This was at the heart of her perplexity: on the one hand her conviction that she must remain faithful to her resolution, and on the other her obsessive fear of not being able to fulfil the demands of the office.

Sometimes, in moments of depression, she was filled with nostalgia for her original vocation to life in the cloisters. She dreamed of being able to live withdrawn from the world; not in order to escape from it, but in order to understand its true significance more fully, and to devote herself to expiating some of the many sins committed against love, which is the most important thing in the world. The silence of prayer, the concentrated peace of meditation, the joy of feeling united to that sublime love. All these thoughts filled her with sorrowful regret. Perhaps she was not meant for the active life. Nevertheless, she had a passionate desire to work as a missionary, and while nursing the sick at Castelfidardo she had discovered the overwhelming fascination of charity, which is what people expect of a sister. She was afraid of the decisions and struggle she would encounter, and she would have to struggle if she wanted to give a new structure to the Institute. There were many things she could not do, and any changes eventually effected would not be for the sake of novelty, but because her vocation, and that of other sisters, would bear witness to their validity. She would have to be full of strength, to become accustomed to authority, something that could not be learned from one day to the next. She was disturbed by a thousand such thoughts detracting from the courageous spirit she would need to cope confidently with the task ahead of her.

In order to overcome the confusion of these doubts and especially in order to have a frank, comforting discussion, she used to go to Canon Luigi Anglesio, Cottolengo's successor as superior of the neighbouring Little House of Providence (Piccola Casa della Provvidenza), a well-known and much loved figure in the town and a worthy man to continue Cottolengo's work, so aptly described as 'not philanthropy, but evangelical charity'.[32] He was a priest with immense experience as a spiritual adviser. For years he had been coming into contact with every kind of suffering and was gifted with tremendous sensitivity in the spiritual advice he gave to others. The hospice founded by Cottolengo was at that time the centre of charity in Turin. But it had not yet benefited from the recent architectural expansion, so all the work had to be squeezed into one modest single-storeyed building near the market garden and looking out over green fields dotted with houses which stretched away towards the Meana canal. It was where the country-side gave way to human habitation, the narrow alleys of the Fiando district and the colourful market at Balon with all the second-hand dealers, their wares spread out on the ground in the streets and little squares of this typical 'storehouse of infinite poverty'.[33]

She was accompanied by a sister,[34] and before being received by the Canon she visited the inmates of this house ruled by Providence: faces ravaged by pain, limbs stiffened or disfigured, expressionless eyes staring into space. The least she could do was to stop and bend lovingly over such suffering and with difficulty she succeeded in chatting to a man whose voice was reduced to a hoarse, incomprehensible rattle. She grasped hold of trembling hands, tried in vain to follow deadened gazes and a great feeling of compassion overwhelmed her. It was not just compassion, but also love, the desire to help them. The sight of such wretched poverty and suffering made her still more intensely aware of the responsibility of her vocation.

She would be Mother General. By that time everything seemed to confirm it. She would have liked to turn it down, to draw back, but at the sight of these wretches another thought took shape in her mind. She had done nothing to be elected, indeed she had tried every expedient to avoid it. That it should have happened was solely due to the will of the Lord; it was part of a scheme of love which surpassed all feelings. She could not go against the will of the Lord. She would therefore accept it in good faith, just as those poor wretches had accepted their cross of suffering with resignation. She had to accept the post, not because she wanted to, but for the good of the Institute, for the good she could do for so many suffering people. And the most difficult suffering to cure was that of the spirit.

Such were her thoughts while going up the stairs to the Canon's office. She then met him. He was an old priest in a shabby, worn-out cassock, yet impeccably neat. At first sight, his expression seemed very strong; but on examination, it had a gentleness that inspired all who talked to him with confidence.

'I explained my reasons to that holy servant of the Lord and he assured me I could not refuse this post without opposing the will of God manifested in the community's vote for me. And when I wanted to stress my inability to run the convent well enough he added: "Put all your confidence in God and then if you are not able to manage you will at least have the humility to step down" '.[35]

On hearing these words, she fell silent. Greatly moved, she bowed her head and knelt down with her companion to receive the good priest's blessing. In her heart she had accepted, she resigned herself to what the future might bring. Submissively, she would let love guide her where it chose. And love had no limits, it was always pushing forward, inexorably.

Before taking leave of her, the priest accompanied her into the reliquary chapel, a room containing a display of numerous famous relics which can still be seen by visitors to the Little House of Providence. Sister Enrichetta stayed there for a long time, her hands joined, praying fervently. Comforted by the discussion with the Canon, but confused by the outcome which she had perhaps wished otherwise, she consented with all her heart to do the will of God. 'That blessing', she wrote, 'comforted me wonderfully, and I returned home resolved to do the will of the Lord'.[36]

Sister Enrichetta as Napoleon III

Though still awaiting the decree of approval from the Holy See, the sisters were happy that the election was over. They already talked about it as though it were a *fait accompli*. There were, however, a few who thought they could profit from the new situation and they tried to avoid her, but Sister Enrichetta was still the centre of attention.

The more solicitous sisters congratulated her and expressed their willingness to collaborate, though not all these compliments were sincere. The previous Superior had ruled for too many years, and her methods of subjection had differed greatly from the more genuine spirit of the Rule. The convent would have to go through a period of adjustment and the disadvantages inevitably manifested themselves. The political climate and the historical moment always play a crucial part in such changes. One need only think of much older and more established religious orders where the same thing has happened.

From 17 March 1861 Turin became the capital of the Kingdom of Italy. The ideal dreamed of for generations became a reality, a reality that emphasized the acuteness of many grave problems to which a solution had been hoped for years. These included, in addition to the much debated Roman question, the problem of relations between state and Church which had not been improved by the Siccardi Act of 1850 and the compulsory confiscation of Church property in 1855. And there were still vivid memories of the sentence imposed on Archbishop Franzoni, arrested for circulating a pamphlet among the Turin clergy protesting at the suppression of the ecclesiastical courts of justice.[37]

It was not surprising that, despite some wonderful examples of holiness, religious life was affected by this corrupt atmosphere of anticlerical sectarianism. The result was that many weaker souls drifted away from religion, the number of vocations inevitably dropped, and there was a growing indifference towards religion, openly professed by many. As in any period of transition, the Institute of St Ann suffered likewise from this general disorientation.

The decree from the Congregation of Bishops and Regulars approving and confirming the election of Enrichetta Dominici bears the date 1 July 1861.[38] In this document we read that the votes cast amounted to twenty-nine, far exceeding the necessary majority, given that the total electoral role was only thirty-one. Sister Enrichetta duly became Mother General, with Sister Maria Gabriella and Sister Maria Angelica as her first and second assistants respectively. The gilded pages of the Chronicles of the Institute contain the following comment on the event: 'From that time a new era blossomed in the Institute and we could not thank God enough for having looked so bountifully upon us, giving us reason to have still greater faith in the benificient effects of his infinite mercy. Following the election our venerated Mother Foundress returned to live in the midst of her daughters. She loved the Mother General and all of us sisters with a tenderness which words cannot express. Completely satisfied to see peace and order reigning in the congregation she had founded, she could happily intone the *Nunc Dimittis*'.[39]

Leaving aside the ponderous style of the period which now strikes us as rather amusing, this passage testifies to the conflict within the order — especially evident in the reference to the Marchesa di Barolo — which was probably largely responsible for provoking the Holy See's decision of 1859. It also proves that the election marked a crucial turning point in the history of the order.

There were numerous difficulties to overcome before these auspicious changes could be effected. Most important of all was the task of dealing with the older sisters who from force of habit favoured Sister Mary of the

Angels and felt she had been victimized. The younger sisters, on the other hand, were sympathetic towards Sister Enrichetta. Many of them had been novices under her tutelage and so knew her well. Appreciating her good qualities, they were prepared to respond warmly towards her in her new post.

One cannot overlook the fact that some welcomed her appointment because they wanted to have a young superior whom they could easily influence, even possibly persuading her to introduce ideas of their own. This factor is supported by the following comment from her autobiography: 'For a long time before my election as Mother Superior I constantly remembered that a newly appointed Mother Superior is entirely dependent on the advice of her predecessor'.[40] Further on this is stated even more explicitly: 'I must emphasize that my predecessor as Superior loved me very much. She loved me like a mother and gave me to understand that she had the greatest confidence in me. As she told me many times, in particular on those occasions when she wanted to make me aware of the ungrateful way I had responded to her love and kindness, it had been at her instigation that the sisters had chosen me to be their Superior. She wanted me to be totally dependent on her advice. I should have been only too happy to do this, but I soon realized that I could not reconcile this arrangement with my own conscience'.[41] Sister Enrichetta immediately rejected deception of this kind and wisely decided to follow the path dictated by her own conscience.

28 July 1861 was a day of celebration in the convent of St Ann in the via della Consolata. In order to lend a more authentic flavour to the new Italian capital the street had forsaken its former French name, rue Paysanne, for the more native-sounding title of the nearby pilgrimage church. It was the day of the solemn proclamation of the recently elected Mother General. Feverish preparations had gone on for more than a week. All except

Mother Enrichetta were in a flurry of expectation. Though almost none of the sisters knew it, she spent the evening before deep in prayer, even preferring to take her meal alone so as not to interrupt her meditations.

That hot summer morning, Mass was said in the chapel, attended by the sisters from the neighbouring convents. They came from Santena, Altessano, Sansalva and Bra. As well as the novices and pupils there were also some small children, but despite the crowd everything ran very smoothly. The chief absentee was the foundress, the Marchesa di Barolo, who was away on a visit to Lyons. The chapel was full to overflowing and the smell of incense wafted through the open door and down the adjacent corridor. From the threshold one could see the altar, and near it the diminutive figure of the Mother General. Seen from a distance, she seemed fragile, absolutely immobile, sunk in prayer.

At the close of the liturgical ceremony and before going to the Chapter Room for the general assembly of the community and her official installation, the Mother General wished to visit the infirmary to see some of the sisters incapacitated by old age. This gesture truly demonstrated her loving care for others. It was touching to see the young sister appointed to the highest office in the Institute remember its oldest members in this way. They had spent the best years of their lives in the convent, yet their tired eyes still reflected a childish innocence, like the children who had been in their charge. Now, when they fell asleep in the sun which streamed in through the window they imagined they were back running, playing and spelling out loud; a sweet, imaginary, sleep-inducing dirge which merged with the voices of the children playing down in the courtyard or in the classrooms on the ground floor. It was a unique dirge allowing them to drift miles away as it filled the silence which would otherwise have overwhelmed them with fear.

This visit to the infirmary was a simple gesture, but a significant one. One can never move forward along one's chosen path without first looking back with love and respect over the past. For however fascinating the future may be, it is only a continuation of what has been, and one must have an understanding of the past if one is to find the strength to make genuine progress towards the future.

The proclamation was greeted by warm applause, after which all the sisters present made a vow to obey their new Superior. Mother Enrichetta embraced each one in turn, with a kind word for each. She then rose to address the whole assembly. Standing before the assembly she looked paler than usual. Her voice sounded calm and convincing, without emphasis, yet firm and clear. She thanked Providence for guiding all men and all things and quietly exhorted them to beware of reason and to persevere in the faith which would sustain and mould them. She thanked all those who had placed their trust in her to bear a burden which she felt was beyond her strength. But if they all shared this burden together, keeping their gaze constantly directed heavenwards, it would become far lighter. In undertaking her new responsibility she asked for the prayers and goodwill of all the sisters who, united by their vocation, would from that time on form one large family.

That afternoon, in the main reception room reserved for special occasions, pupils from the school gave a recital of piano-playing, singing and poetry. Sister Enrichetta chatted in a friendly manner with the participants making lively, apposite comments. Many of those present were full of admiration for her youthful versatility; her distinguished, reserved manner; and her simple, dignified bearing. She was just thirty-two years old and had been a member of the Institute of St Ann for ten years.

It was late in the evening before she could be alone.

She would be sleeping for the first time in the small apartment set aside for the Mother General. It consisted of a fairly small room in which the bed occupied most of the available space and next to it another room which served as a study. A soft breeze entered through the open window, gently ruffling the curtains and relieving the sultry summer heat. The chirping of the crickets reminded her that the countryside was not far away. In May one could even see glow-worms in the convent garden, the same glow-worms that flew in swarms along the edges of the freshly ploughed hemp fields at Salsasio or at Borgo San Bernardo.

When the bells of the church of the Consolata struck eleven she was still not in bed. The following day she had to rise as usual at four in the morning. This was stipulated in the regulations applying to the summer months, and she could not grant herself any privileges. Before, she had had to obey the Rule. Now she herself had to be the Rule.

Seated at the table, her head bent as her pen slid over the page that was illuminated by the oil lamp. She wished to lose no time in informing the foundress of all that had happened. The Marchesa was on a pilgrimage to the French shrine of Fourvière. On hearing that Enrichetta had been elected, the latter decided to celebrate the event in a manner worthy of the occasion. She turned to the priest in charge of the shrine and asked him how an event of such importance was usually celebrated there. The rector regarded the noble lady with curiosity. He knew her name with its aristocratic sound, and thinking she might be a very generous person, began to describe the various traditional ways of commemorating an event of exceptional importance. Having enumerated countless possible solutions he then recalled that when Napoleon III had visited the shrine, the entire church had been brilliantly illuminated. Great was his astonishment, almost verging on disbelief, when he realized that this decisive, energetic, forceful lady intended to do the same thing because, as she confided to him, a favour long desired had been granted by the gracious intercession of the Madonna.

On the appointed evening, thousands of flares shot up into the night sky, highlighting the delicate silhouette of the shrine of Fourvière. The illuminations could be seen down in the valley, and unless they asked, no-one would have guessed that such a magnificent display was in honour of a nun from Turin, an ordinary sister as well as a Mother General, and not for the visit of any illustrious personage. The flares lit up the hot summer night sky until the break of dawn when they were extinguished one by one by the wind descending from the Alps.

Notes
1.   Autobiography, p. 183.
2.   *Op. cit.*, p. 183-4.
3.   It would seem relevant to quote this regulation in full from the *Constituzioni e Regole dell'Istituto delle Suore di Sant'Anna e della Provvidenza* (Turin, 1846) p. 32.
'However, from the first day of April until the end of September the sisters will rise at half past four, except during the months of June and July when they will rise at four, because of the long hours of daylight. From the first of October to the end of March they will rise at five o'clock.

Given a quarter of an hour to dress, at the sound of the bell they will go to the church to meditate and to recite the office as prescribed in the Rules, after which will ensue precisely half an hour of meditation. Then they will attend Holy Mass. It shall be in the hands of the Superior to decide whether the Holy Mass precedes this period of meditation or not, depending on the particular circumstances and needs of the community. From then until eleven o'clock they will perform the tasks and manual labour required by their vow of obedience.

At eleven o'clock they will examine their consciences for a period of about ten minutes before going in to lunch, during which they will listen to spiritual readings. After lunch they will have a recreation period for about one hour, during which the sisters may undertake some simple manual tasks, depending on the judicious and merciful will of the Superior.

At midday they will say the *Angelus Domini*, to be followed by an hour of silence as prescribed by the Rules. At two o'clock there will be a spiritual reading for a quarter of an hour, after which there will be a discussion on the theme of the reading, lasting until three o'clock. But before that they will recite the *Veni Creator*. Then the catechism for half an hour. At three o'clock the bell will ring to remind them of the hour of the death of Our Lord and they will say an act of contrition. At four o'clock they will say a third of the holy rosary except on Sundays when they will say the *Corona del Signore* and on Fridays the Sorrowful Mysteries. At a quarter past five they will assemble to say the evening office. At half past five, meditation followed by the *Pater, Ave* and *Gloria*.

Dinner will take place at six and during it, as at lunch time, there will be a spiritual reading. Thereafter, recreation for one hour after which they will occupy themselves with various tasks until half past eight, when the theme for meditation the following day will be announced. After this they will proceed immediately to the church to venerate the Holy Sacrament and the five sacred wounds of the divine Saviour. They will then recite the five so-called psalms of the Virgin contained in their prayer books. They will finish up with a brief examination of conscience, an act of contrition, the hymn from compline, *Te Lucis*, and the canticle *Nunc dimittis*.

At nine o'clock exactly they will go to bed in silence, which they will observe until after Holy Mass the next morning. This timetable must be strictly adhered to by the novices; those sisters involved in teaching or in other works of charity will fulfil these same spiritual duties, but at times to be specified by their own Superior.'

4.   *Op. cit.*, p. 185.
5.   *Op. cit.*, p. 184.
6.   *Ibid.*
7.   *Ibid.*
8.   *Op. cit.*, p. 199.
9.   Letter from the Marchesa di Barolo to the Cardinal Patron of the Institute, Giusto Recanati, 22 November 1858.
10.   Letter from the Marchesa di Barolo to the Cardinal Patron, 3 November 1858.
11.   *Op. cit.*, p. 186.
12.   *Ibid.*
13.   *Op. cit.*, p. 187.
14.   Salita, I, II, 2.
15.   *Op. cit.*, p. 187.
16.   From the letter of 10 January 1861.
17.   *Op. cit.*, p. 189.
18.   *Ibid.*
19.   *Op. cit.*, p. 188.
20.   *Op. cit.*, p. 190.

21. *Op. cit.*, p. 191.
22. *Ibid.*
23. *Op. cit.*, p. 192.
24. *Op. cit.*, p. 192-193.
25. *Op. cit.*, p. 195.
26. *Costituzioni e Regole*, (Turin 1846) p. 9-12.
27. The names of the sisters were as follows: Maria Luigia, Maria Angelica, Maria Silvia, *Maria Enrichetta*, Maria Fortunata, Maria Maddalena, Maria Zita, Maria Giuliana, and, belonging to the house at Castelfidardo: Maria Gabriella, Maria Alessandrina.
28. We know this from a letter in Latin from the Congregation of Bishops and Regulars, dated 20 April 1861: *SS.mus omnes facultates tribuit supplendum defectum E.mi Protectoris . . .*
29. Herewith in full the text of the letter from the Vicar General of Turin, Canon Celestino Fissore, dated 7 June, 1861, to the Prefect of the Congregation of Bishops and Regulars:
'Most Reverend Eminence,
On 29 April last, as soon as I received the letter from Your Most Reverend Eminence dated 20 April, I lost no time in organizing the election of the Superior General of the Institute of St Ann in accordance with your instructions. But only yesterday did I receive the packet containing the relevant ballot cards which I feel it my duty to return to you immediately. The Superior General points out that there are two votes missing, namely those of two sisters from the house at Bagnorea, which are delayed by mistake. Since it would take several days for them to arrive, in order to minimize the inconvenience and to save time, she has asked the sisters in question to send their votes directly to the Congregation. I herewith enclose her letter together with the ballot cards. Bowing reverently I kiss the Holy Purple, and have the honour of remaining your most venerable servant. . . .'
30. *Op. cit.*, p. 195.
31. *Ibid.*
32. A. Gorrino, *S. Giuseppe Benedetto Cottolengo*, no. 118, Ch. III.
33. C. Merlini, *Palazzi e curiosità storiche torinesi*, p. 223.
34. 'Taking advantage of the authority of my new position, and not daring to speak to anyone about this, I left the house with a sister to visit him. I explained my reasons to this holy servant of the Lord and he assured me that I could not refuse the post without contradicting the will of God' (Autobiography, p. 195-196).
35. *Ibid.*
36. *Ibid.*
37. Archbishop Franzoni was arrested in 1850. With reference to this pamphlet Jemolo wrote in *Chiesa e Stato in Italia negli ultimi cento anni.* (1949), p. 213: 'The pamphlet contained

nothing irreverent about the state. Its sole aim was to ensure the implementation of the law without impinging upon matters of principle. An action was brought against the Archbishop on the grounds of abuse and he was duly sentenced ... The Archbishop of Sassari received the same treatment.'

38.   As reported in the Decree of the Congregation of Bishops and Regulars dated 1 July 1861: *Reservatis schedis a sororibus Instituti a S. Anna nuncupati ad hanc S. Congregationem Episcoporum et Regularium transmissis, pro eligenda Moderatrice Generalu eiusque generalibus Assistentibus, die 25 Junii 1861 coram me Cardinali Prefecto, et infra scripto Secretario eiusdem S. Congregationis, reperta sunt suffragia vigintinovem favore Mariae Enricae pro munere Moderatricis Generalis, suffragia vigintise favore Mariae Gabrielis ad officium primae Assistentis, et suffragia vigintiquator favore Mariae Angelicae ad officium secundae Assistentis. Idcirco S. Congregatio respectivas electiones approbat atque confirmat, cum dispensatione quoad Mariam Angelicam ab interstitiis ob exercitum officium primae Assistentis. Datum Romae ex Secretaria memoratae S. Congregationis die 1 Julii 1861. N. Card. is Parraociani Praefectus.*

39.   From the *Cronache dell'Istituto*, 1861, p. 51.

40.   Autobiography, p. 197.

41.   *Op. cit.*, p. 198.

VI Fruits of an overwhelming faith

Washing dishes is worth an audience with the Pope
The kitchen in the Convent of St Ann in Turin was spacious and filled with light, with a wide chimney blackened with smoke and a wood stove which warmed the whole room in the winter months. A grey stone sink worn with use stood near a tub always filled with water. All betokened belief in having the necessities of life in good order.

The room was on the ground floor and had two glass doors opening on to a courtyard. As midday approached, the inviting smell of soup spread through the neighbouring rooms, rose to the upper floors and disappeared into the air round about.

The room served both as kitchen and refectory. The children of the hospice took their meals there amidst a clatter of crockery and the confused babble of voices only quietened during the saying of Grace; the Grace was short and hurried, but said with conviction; appetite does not wait at that age. Later, when their duties allowed, now one and now another of the sisters ate a hurried lunch, whereas in the evenings they could eat quietly together in community.

Every day there were piles of plates to be washed and

all the pans with their clinging grease as well. A holy monk[1] once said that the spirit of charity in a convent could be measured in the kitchen. If any food is wasted it means that they don't know who is hungry; if on the contrary there are just piles of plates to be washed, it means that all the soup is given away to those who would otherwise go hungry. The sisters of St Ann were well placed in this respect. There was the daily hot meal that the Mother Foundress wished given out punctually every day in the porch of the Barolo Palace to the poor of Valdocco.

Mother Enrichetta, although she was Mother General, did not feel exempt from her duties in the kitchen, especially on feast days, when she would go downstairs in silence, appearing in the kitchen with a smile on her face to roll up her sleeves without saying anything and happily lend a hand wherever necessary. 'I remember that once the Mother came up beside me when I was washing the dishes' — witnessed someone who was very close to her — 'and since she chose the heaviest ones for herself, I, being younger, allowed myself to tell her that the more difficult bits should be for me, to which she replied, "Hush, hush, my bones are harder . . . and you are already doing too much". She used to behave in the same way with the sisters who were dealing with laundry and ironing the linen, working beside them like a simple maid'.[2]

And another testimony: once in the kitchen she said to Sister Pierina: 'If we do things to comply with the will of God and give him this pleasure, washing dishes is just as meritorious as going to an audience with the Holy Father!'[3]

Everything she did with this simplicity was not mere humility; it was done out of love for the sisters who tried to relieve her of these everyday tasks.

Moreover, working side by side with them, elbow to elbow, she came to understand them better. She could study their characters, watch their development, encourage them to better things in the kitchen. Confidences easily became more spontaneous; they made plans, talked about the school, just like in a family. There were a few occasions when to alleviate the fatigue, Mother Enrichetta intoned a song to raise morale and the others all joined in.

She ruled in a new way, based on charity and mutual respect, totally different from the authoritarian, somewhat detached manner of her predecessor. 'Too much flexibility, too little sense of the dignity of her position', criticized the older ones, still mentally bound to the deposed Mother General. She paid no attention to such comments, although they hurt her. As far as possible she kept a more than respectful relationship with Sister Mary of the Angels, who gradually saw her plans to enslave the former novice mistress evaporating.

Although gentle in her dealings she nevertheless showed strength of will and a consciousness of the importance of her position. The attitude she took, against her will, in arguments with those who tried to sway her is proof of this. Her will was not mere caprice or an impatient desire to change; before taking decisions she took advice from those around her and regularly summoned the council of the Institute; but she always found her final decision at the foot of the altar in the silence of prayer.

Faced with the obstinate hostility of the most conservative sector in the convent, she tried to find a way of meeting them and to clarify a worrying situation once and for all.

On the subject of Sister Mary of the Angels she wrote, 'I tried to consult her in everything to see if I could win peace and win her over through my fulfilment of my duties and the obligations placed on me by my office, but I soon realized my mind was getting muddled by this and took the decision just to wait calmly for any sign of reciprocal respect from her'.[4]

It was a hard choice and caused her much grief, because in the final analysis she was bound by gratitude and affection towards someone who only brought her sorrow.

'I do not know how to put into words', she wrote in the pages of her autobiography,[5] 'how painful it was and how much it hurt my heart to behave like this and set myself against a person whom I have always loved and still love and from whom I have received all manner of benefits. If the good God had not helped me with a more than ordinary grace I feel certain that I would have given way to natural tenderness and through affection would have done less of my duty since I felt the contrast between his grace and my nature so strongly'. Thus in a few lines of touching sincerity she sums up the drama of a sensitive but not a weak soul.

The election that happened then re-established normal relations between the community and the foundress who regained her due place in the life and heart of the convent of St Ann. There was now perfect understanding between the young Mother Superior and the aged noble lady. This had always been the case even at the most difficult moments, and this fact constituted a further motive of criticism on the part of the most stubborn element in the convent who gathered round Sister Mary of the Angels and her one-time faithful follower Sister Maddalena. These two nuns could not bring themselves to bend their ways to the new route taken by the Institute, and preferred to live apart from the others; they spent the whole day in their rooms, rarely coming out and when they did come out, doing so only to spread rumours and suspicions on everything that was being undertaken for the general good.[6]

Mother Enrichetta's response to such a worrying situation was one of love. While her preferred way was one of gentleness, this was not a weak but a strong form of gentleness, patient and true to the essential principles she could not give up. It would have been too easy to use her authority and force the two rebels out of the congregation. She preferred to wait and pray.

Sometimes when, in the evenings, she retired to her room to write or to read reports from the distant houses, a thought assailed her, a doubt she could not put from her. She thought, and was even convinced, that another in her place would have known how to handle the situation, would have made a decision and resolved the whole matter. Another would have been right not to hold back when faced with such a task. 'Strong fears of having been perhaps myself the cause of the unhappiness of that poor soul do not cease to assail me. I think and believe that another Superior, better than I, would have known how to win her back to God and to the practice of virtue'.[7] The reference to the former Mother General is clear but what is still more significant is the way in which it is expressed. Besides the delicacy of not mentioning her name, what stands out is the pre-occupation of one used to seeing in people not the natural defects of their character, but the supernatural aspect. She was not worried about her personal prestige or about the calumnies that often came back to her, but about the person's soul, about 'that poor soul'. Hers was a manner of seeing and judging that summed up a whole style of life.

Despite appearances, she did not give up. She could not even imagine it possible that a nun should possess such pride as to overcome all her good intentions. Yet her pride and rancour, perhaps stemming from her deposition, disturbed relationships that should have been composed of mutual esteem and common sense. The two sisters, who increasingly refused any dialogue with the community, remained uncompromisingly opposed to all gestures of generosity and understanding. This, during the four years until their departure from the Institute, was the secret thorn in the flesh of Mother Enrichetta, who was even inclined to give up her generalate for the sake of renewed peace.

'My God' she often said in her prayers, 'if you think it would be good for that soul to return to the position she had before, so that she could look after herself and the affairs of the Institute according to your holy will, here am I, ready to be deposed from my office, even ignominiously, and reduced to the last and lowest place in the house. If this should redound to your glory, you cannot lack the means of bringing it about. Do it then as soon as possible and I will be happy!'[8] Whatever sacrifice, whether of herself or of her reputation, would not matter: what matters is that the congregation should continue its work and that there should not be dissentions amongst them. She often asked the Lord to make her suffer: now she was on the Cross and was neither surprised nor distressed. The final end of any vocation is the tremendous solitude of Golgotha.

The strongest blow

Even if disillusionment, reverses and bitterness were not lacking in her life, there were still some shafts of light. The Mother General's essential goodness, good example and gentleness of mind were not without fruit. They bore fruit above all in the young nuns, many of whom had had Mother Enrichetta as novice-mistress during their novitiate. When virtue is an example it is just as catching as evil, and perhaps even more so.

In this way she created a nucleus of sisters who lived more deeply in the spirit of their religious calling, bringing new and sometimes surprising experiences to their old vocation. More emphasis was given to the spiritual life. Prayer and meditation came to occupy pride of place; obedience was placed at the service of love. At the heart of this group was Sister Candida, whom the diaries speak of as possessing a special intuition in the understanding of souls. Another was Sister Maria Teofila, all ardour and enthusiasm, who did not hesitate to use her own outgoing nature to comfort and advise her own Superior. The autobiography recounts two episodes about these two sisters which emphasize the confidence and identity of view that came to be formed in this group of chosen souls.

One evening, in the summer of 1863, Mother Enrichetta was tired and with her fatigue her usual afflictions became heavier than ever. Sister Candida went to find her in her room, excused herself for disturbing her, and lent her a book, *The Directory* of Scaramelli, a work of spirituality then much in vogue. 'Mother, read this chapter which might have been written especially for you. You will find your own problem precisely in it as the book explains'.[9] The Mother General took the book, thanked her, read it and indeed found consolation in those pages. 'I found there exactly what I wanted in my present need and realized that God had shown her the state of my mind, even though I had spoken little with her about myself and had not done so in any way in those circumstances'.[10] This was the time at which possible suppression of all religious congregations by the Government was beginning to be spoken of. Anti-clericalism was the general rule and the Mother General expressed her fears to the sisters in an address to them: 'I did this so as not to appear presumptuous in front of the others, although in my heart I felt very differently'.[11] It was Sister Teofila who pointed out to her that her words did not correspond to her inner convictions: 'She told me that, in speaking of those things, I was not saying what I felt in my heart and that it would have been to the greater glory of God if I had in fact demonstrated my own trust in him and his paternal goodness'.[12] These are little things but they prove the existence of a living dialogue, a mutual exchange of experiences and intuitions, that formed the heart of the new community. The whole community benefited from this and flourished once more even while there remained the unsolved problem of the behaviour of the deposed Mother General and her companion.

In the summer of 1862, the Marchesa of Barolo, despite a serious illness that gave grounds for fears about her health, thought of opening a school on one of her estates in the Vercellese at Villarboit. On 12th October, two sisters from St Ann's went out there and the work began.

On 1st November of the same year, Canon Alberto Ariccio, who had known Mother Enrichetta's teacher, wanted to open an orphanage in Carmagnola.

Mother Enrichetta accepted the invitation joyfully. This was her native town and sending the sisters there was like sending them home. The new foundation was called 'The Retreat of the Immaculate Conception'. The first stages were very tiring, with only two sisters but more came later and a workshop for embroidery and needlecraft was added to the school for boarders and day-girls.

Meanwhile plans were going ahead for another house at Orio in the diocese of Ivrea. The new school was opened at the end of 1863 on the property of the Count della Torre, a friend of the foundress. In all this rush of work the Marchesa Giulia was close by her side, not concealing her hopes for the future of the Institute. These hopes, however, were veiled in sadness at the thought of life passing from her: she still saw so many things to be done for her foundations. She spent whole days without leaving the palace, her carriage was seen ever more seldom on the streets of Turin, and she finally had to give up her habit of going every Sunday on foot to visit prisoners. She felt tired and old and was tormented by a repetition of disturbances of the liver, that no doctor could succeed in curing. And yet she did not give up; she was carrying out a project that had been taking shape for some time: the building of a church for the popular quarter of Vanchiglia. This was a suburb of the city in which the worst kind of poverty was found, in which the chief problem for every family was finding enough to live on from day to day. The number of houses grew daily without any overall plan, due to the inexorable growth of the city. It would be the ideal place to set up a medical centre, with an oratory and a cheap kitchen, in the shadow of the parish church that was to be built. It was a bold scheme that seemed to give her back a spark of youth.

The nearly octogenarian Marchesa often spoke of these and her many other hopes to Mother Enrichetta. Her fervour for works of charity was not wasting away but rather increasing and becoming more impatient because her only fear was not to be able to have time to bring her plans to completion. From the depths of her room she followed the dealings with the planning authorities, asked for the necessary permissions and, despite being prepared to subsidize the building works from her own funds, fought against snags and opposition that lasted a long time.

On her feast day, 22 May 1863, the ceremony of laying the foundation stone finally took place. The noblewoman who had struggled beyond her strength to bring this about preferred not to be present at an event that would call for authority and citizenship.

She did not want applause, thanks or useless rejoicing, even though the building was to be named after her and called St Giulia. It was to be an institution in the van of social reform, particularly in those parts of Turin where there was then no parish church but only the Oratory of Don Bosco.

Yet her health inexorably declined and the chances of a recovery grew gradually less and less, the old liver troubles being augmented by a persistent heart murmur which caused new worries for Mother Enrichetta, who felt more than a daughter's fondness for the old lady. When she had to go to Castelfidardo in the summer of 1863 the foundress' state of health was desperate. Despite this she went — she could not do otherwise — and during the entire journey her heart was with the sick lady so dear to her: she was afraid she would never see her again.

She went on a pilgrimage with some of the sisters, to the sanctuary of St Joseph of Copertino at Osino, to pray for the Marchesa's recovery and had a Mass celebrated there; kneeling in front of the holy Franciscan's tomb she prayed fervently and — as she recounts in her autobiography — she felt these words welling up from her soul: 'Do not pray for the Marchesa to get better but rather for the strength to make a great sacrifice'.[13]

This inspiration or premonition left her very much alarmed.

Yet she did not speak to anyone or brood on this intuition that had come to her in the silence of prayer. A few days later she went to Loreto to ask for the same grace, and the result was identical. Recalling the episode some years later she said: 'When I went to Loreto I warmly begged the most Holy Virgin for the same favour; I did not tell her that I had already asked her son Jesus and that he had denied it to me, but they must have spoken to each other and not kept any secrets from each other because the Madonna also made me feel in my heart that she was giving the same negative reply'.[14]

Her fears were confirmed during the winter of 1863. The Marchesa's state of health became desperate; by December she was prostrate with exhaustion: her insomnia had become unbearable and the pains were increasing. The Sisters of St Ann took turns beside her bed even though the Marchesa had asked for her housekeepers so as not to disturb the nuns, who nevertheless kept close to her.

On the Feast of Epiphany 1864 she received Extreme Unction. The chaplain don Ponte, a friend of the family, brought her the sacrament which she received fully conscious. Then the gradual decline and final agony went on with no further hope.

In the evening of 19 January all the sisters and children, together with the whole community, prayed together. The walls of the twilit chapel echoed the invocations of the litany of Loreto repeated slowly and rhythmically. The thoughts of all were turned to what was happening in the nearby Barolo Palace, where a life was drawing to its close.

The latest news was desperate. 'It is a question of hours,' the doctors said. She would perhaps live through to the dawn, her heart could perhaps stand another night. Despite the imminent reality of the situation they still hoped for a special favour, even though don Bosco had replied in a letter when asked to pray: 'The time is close when the merits of the Marchesa will receive their reward, and her dearest daughters be put to the test'.[15]

Towards ten o'clock the convent was in deepest silence. From the snow-covered courtyard a light could be seen burning on the upper floor. The Mother General could not sleep; she was reading when someone came to tell her that the foundress was in her last agony.

In the great four-poster bed in gilt wood the Marchesa lay dying, her heavy breathing the only note of life filling the room.

She was deathly pale, her eyes half closed, all expression gone from them. Mother Enrichetta lent over her and quickly whispered a few words in her ear. She seemed to recognize her and slightly moved her hand, which immediately fell back. Her last words — as her confessor don Ponte recalls — were : 'May God's will be done in me and through me, in time and in eternity!'[16]

Then the silence of death. It was 11.30 on the night

of 19 January 1864.

It had originally been the Marchesa's intention to make the Holy See the sole beneficiary of her possessions: an act of attachment to the Holy Father which she had not discussed with him. However she had eventually been convinced of the difficulty that would have arisen from such a decision, particularly in the political climate of the time, and had taken the advice of experts and left her goods in trust to a 'Pious Administration' legally approved by the government.

That was the origin of the Barolo Foundation which is still in existence, which was established on 10th June, 1864 and finally legally ratified on 22nd September, 1867.

The Sisters of St Ann had lost a mother. More than a mother for their Superior General, who wrote: 'For several days I was unable to hold back the tears that abundantly and spontaneously fell from my eyes, and if on the one hand I was certain of having acquired a protectress in heaven, on the other I could see all the consequences that would follow for the Institute from her death. However, God alone could be my support and my hope and trust in him was the only thing that could lighten my deep sorrow to some extent'.[17]

Greetings from God

In May of 1865 Mother Enrichetta went to Rome. This was an unforgettable journey, a revelation for her soul, devoted to beauty and truth. It was the first time that she had a chance of kneeling in the Basilica of St Peter and of praying by his tomb. She saw the Holy Father perhaps during a public audience. It was probably a rapid visit to carry out official business with the Congregation of Bishops and Regulars, but she had time to mount the Scala Santa on her knees and to pray in the various basilicas, remembering the whole Congregation, particularly the difficult question of Sister Mary of the

Angels, praying for her before the tomb of Leonardo da Porto Maurizio in the lonely Franciscan convent on the Palatine hill.

These times, which should have been full of sunlight, were times of suffering. She was oppressed by her habitual spiritual aridity. It was a burden she bore within her and which no one could alleviate, pray as she might more fervently than ever. In the rare moments of light in the midst of so much darkness she had the feeling that her main worry would be resolved and in fact she did not have to wait very long.[18] Almost as if in answer to such a definite presentiment, she received a letter from Piedmont telling her of the decision of the two sisters to leave the Institute finally. There was no way she could stop this. She had done everything possible, but all her most charitable approaches had been repulsed. Her good will had not been understood and presumption and selfishness had triumphed.

When she came back to Turin at the end of May, all that had to happen had already taken place. The event caused a certain amount of fuss even though it was the logical outcome of behaviour over the years. Mother Enrichetta accepted the challenge and confronted it with firm serenity. There is always some merit in choosing freely the line one should follow; it is much better to leave the community if one no longer possesses the spirit to live in it. In any case, a serious obstacle to the smooth running of the life of the Institute had been removed.

For her part, Mother Enrichetta felt no resentment toward the deposed Mother General. For as long as she lived, she continued to treat her with deference, though always saddened not to have been able to do more to hold her and to bring her back to that path that they could have travelled together. Faced with the inevitable, she did not abandon her charity. She did not let slip any remark except of compassion and of bitter resignation.

She also took care to see that the two sisters had enough to live on and somewhere to live. She acquired an adequate amount of household goods for them, hired a lodging for them at her own expense and generally saw that they could live decently.[19]

These events, however, left her in a state of deep depression: 'I found myself one day oppressed by the virtual certainty that God had gone from me forever and that I could no longer hope to win him back to me'.[20] Trying to rouse her out of this condition, the lovable Sister Teofila, with the simplicity of the saints, sent her a letter. It consisted only of a few lines in laboured handwriting: 'Greetings from the good God who had charged her with telling me that I was very dear to him and that he loved me very much'.[21]

Greetings from the good God, a sign of the familiarity with the supernatural to be found in a religious community! 'He told it all to me in a letter whose reading made such an impression on me that I shook from head to foot and two huge tears fell unbidden from my eyes. Something unusual for me, not being used to relieve my innermost sufferings in this way'.[22] Her reaction to the spontaneous friendship of the gesture to such a real evidence of love was one of shock: 'In the state I was in it seemed to me impossible that the good God could remember me, let alone love me with his infinite charity'.[23]

It was Sister Candida who made her decide on the choice of a spiritual father who would be a secure and understanding guide to her for many years. The choice fell on don Pellegrino Tofoni, secretary to Cardenal de Angelis, Archbishop of Fermo at that time in exile in Turin. Mother Enrichetta had known him at the Barolo household and had been struck by his manner, his inspired mode of speech and the piety shown by his comportment. In her diary from December 1865 to

November 1866 she wrote: 'When I met Your Honour for the first time and had finished speaking to you in the company of our beloved Mother Foundress, the Marchesa of Barolo, you impressed me as a voice that told me, my dearest Father, that it could benefit my soul and that I had found in you the support and comfort that I was so much in need of'.[24]

Her first feeling was the certainty of having found someone who could strengthen her soul; then there came a certain fear 'of finding a satisfaction for myself in this and, however slightly, of diminishing the faithfulness with which I wanted to stay abandoned to divine leadership'.[25] Up till then she had not had a stable spiritual guide. She had resorted to various chaplains, confessors to the community, and in the same way she had received little understanding. When she was more advanced in spiritual experience, she saw the need for a spiritual director and prayed that the choice of a suitable person would be inspired. She invoked the aid of the Holy Trinity, to which she had been very devoted since the last years of her childhood, spent at San Bernardo. She did not have to wait long for an answer to her prayers. One evening Sister Candida confided in her that she had heard an inner voice murmuring to her after Mass: 'Tell your mother to talk to don Tofoni, who is a faithful servant of mine, who loves me a great deal and is beloved of me. Tell her to listen to him'.[26] This was in the month of November, 1865, and from then on her soul had a guide.

This providential decision contributed greatly to lifting the fog of the spiritual night in which she was wandering. After the first few conversations the light came back. This was a new sensation that invaded her whole being and the fervour that she thenceforth never ceased to give to the things of God came to be a joy to her.

Her main route to this joy was the thought of the

goodness of God. The good Father — as she called him — truly loved her and offered his heart, full of love, to her. She had to spread this love, united to her own imperfect love, over everything she met without any distinction. This became the meaning of her vocation for her.

In her diary on 23 December 1865 there is evidence of her re-born sensitivity and of the effect that the regular meetings with don Tofoni were having on her: 'When you come to the convent we move a little deeper in discourse on matters of the soul, and you leave me with an indescribable consolation. The good God keeps me awake almost all night in continual admiration of his divine goodness, making me aware how much I should be grateful to him, showing me the extent of his love and the benefits he is always bestowing on me. He makes me feel in particular how grateful I should be for having given me you as father and guide to my soul. For the last fortnight I have spent four or five hours each night without closing my eyes in continuous admiration and thanks to the divine goodness and in the short sleep I have had I often woke up and my thought was always fixed on the goodness of God. From that time on I have always been certain that it is God's will for me to place my will in his heart, having given me such clear proof of his approbation'.

Faith can move mountains
At this time talk of suppressing the religious orders and houses was growing. Mother Enrichetta nevertheless had the courage to agree to the requests from the citizens of Bra, who wanted the Sisters of St Ann to teach in the infant school of Saint Andrea. Five sisters were sent there in addition to the other five previously sent by the Foundress to the infant school of Sant' Antonino.

This was a true act of courage, in view of the fact that the Italian parliament was proposing to ban the so-called interference of Catholic teaching in the schools. A wave of anti-clericalism was rising throughout the whole kingdom, the Church was called an outdated institution, destined to perish in the course of a few years.

Mother Enrichetta had no fears. In order to invoke the protection of heaven against the possibility of any suppression she caused a tabernacle to be built in the courtyard of the convent on the Via Della Consolata; she had it decorated with a painting depicting the images of St John, St Ann, St Stanislas Kostka and St John Berchmans; in the central niche there were statues of the Virgin and St Joseph.

The political situation nevertheless worried the community. To whose who showed their fears by telling her of this or that suppression that had taken place elsewhere, Mother Enrichetta replied: 'I am not afraid of the law, but of infidelity to our Rule, as it is this and not the law which will tear us away from our convent, if we admit it in our hearts'.[27]

But the Rule was respected by all, and the quarrels of the past, and the tepid approach to religious life once found in some of the sisters, were things of the past. The convent lived like a single soul.

There is one episode from this period that stands out. The convent steward had been suffering for some days from a worrying infection of the eye. The Mother General went to see her, took an interest and on an extraordinary impulse felt in herself the certitude that she could cure her, if she only touched her bad eye.

She tells of this in the letter dated 2 November 1866, to her spiritual director: 'For the last two or three days a dear daughter of mine has had a bad eye and I felt in myself that if I touched it with my hand it would be cured. I fought this thought for a day and a half fearing some deceit on the part of the enemy, as indeed I still fear it although I do not, thanks to God, have any anxiety left. Finally on Saturday 17, meeting this sister in the corridor of the church I could no longer restrain my impulse or put off the reproach that tormented me, whenever I saw her suffering through my fault and my obstinancy, through not daring to give way to the thought of doing as I have written above. Finally I brought myself to do it and while I was pretending to look at her eye, I touched the infected part saying to God with all my heart: "My God if it be your will and not an illusion of the devil let this eye be cured at the touch of my hands, and cure it then through your omnipotence in the way that most pleases you, for I am but a most vile worm". About an hour later I saw an improvement that continued towards the evening of the same day.

At that time I was very much afraid of my presumption and of a deceit, fearing to have given way not to an impulse from God as at first I believed, but rather to have fallen for the deceit and the cunning of the devil. These fears lasted from about five o'clock in the evening till ten o'clock the following morning, and I went on without resisting them and during this time this poor sister's eye went back to a state almost worse than before. It was with great sorrow that I saw that the infection was growing and I turned back to God asking for the cure since her health was very close to my heart, particularly in view of all that she had to do as steward. I then felt an inner reproach, telling me it was because of me and my diffidence that that poor creature was suffering, so I felt inspired to turn back to God with the following words: "My great Father in heaven, I know that you are all-powerful and that you can consequently make use of even the vilest of instruments, amongst whom I count myself. Through your grace you use them for the good of our neighbour, so that even I your creature, however unworthy, can become through your goodness alone an instrument for the benefit of others and I also believe that by my touch I will be able to cure all the ills that you wish with your most holy will to be cured in this way". After this prayer the infection improved and on the following day, Monday 19, it had entirely disappeared. In all things may the bountiful and omnipotent Father, the only author and protector of all true good be praised'.

From the same letter it appears that a few days later, when she asked the steward how her eye was she received this reply: 'There is no longer any trouble; the eye doesn't hurt me any more. Mother has cured me!' In confusion, Mother Enrichetta tried to change the subject, but her whole life was shot through with episodes like this: events that surprise and fascinate us, make us reflect on things that we can only find lovable because they stem from the depths of a faith equal to any challenge – a simple, spontaneous, genuine faith like that of the first apostles, the faith that in the end has the power to move mountains.

The secret of the strength that springs from such a faith is soon said, and she herself said it in her own words: 'I do not know how to conceive that the infinite might of my God could sink so low as to virtually unite itself to my vileness and lowness, because it seems to me that I see these two so opposed beings involved in the same thing. This flash of knowledge brought about a mixture of sorrow and joy in me and I do not know how to describe how much it made me both suffer and rejoice at once'.[28]

Union with God, the consciousness of the human condition inserted and transformed in the supernatural can accomplish wonders.

Once, on 5 December 1866, she heard from the recently opened house in Bra that a sister was needed to take the place of the sick Superior: 'I should have been able to fill the gap, but what was I to do if even in my own convent I was short of people? But the good God to whom I have recourse in secret did not fail to come to my aid'.[29]

164

She thought of a plan whereby she could make use of a 'sister who was herself in poor health,'[30] and was in the infirmary. She went to see how she was and on seeing that she was still feeble and could hardly get out of bed she still did not lose heart.

'I asked Sister Olimpia (the name of the sister in question), how she was and she told me that she did not feel able to get up. It is better like that, I replied and I would soon have dismissed my first idea and looked elsewhere but somehow I was unable to. I went from there to the church to take the matter a bit further with my dear eternal Father. When I had done this I was even more convinced that I should put my first decision into effect. I went back to the infirmary to make her get out of bed ... Doing this seemed a little hard to me and therefore I told my good God how important it would be for me if, when I got into the infirmary I could already find her out of bed, and so it happened'.[31]

This inspiration in decision-making, this recourse to prayer, and the immediate effect of turning to her 'good daddy', as she affectionately called the Lord, were all fruits of an intense faith in a life that overcame and conquered all difficulties.

It is interesting to read how simply she told don Tofoni what had happened. From the immediacy with which Sister Olimpia agreed to the plan one can perceive the high degree of esteem in which obedience, the basis of living the same vocation together, was held.

'My God, you see how much I need to be able to send this sister to that school. Give her sufficient strength and virtue so that she can do well, and with benefit to others, the task I am now putting upon her. Saying this, I left the church more decided than ever in my first plan. I went to the infirmary and I found the sister already getting dressed, I asked how she was and she told me that the worst of the pains had gone, but that the headaches and a number of other aches and pains were still with her, as I believe they will continue to be to some extent . . . "My dear sister", I said to her, "I need you, are you ready to go and work in the vineyard of the Lord?" She replied most generously, "Yes, Mother, I am ready to do whatever you tell me to". I told her, "My dear little daughter, I need you to pack up and go to Bra, not some time this week, or even tomorrow, but today, in an hour and a half. Meanwhile let us now recite together three Paters, Aves and Glorias to our dear St Ann, so that through her intercession we will obtain from God the graces we need so much". When we had done this I made the sign of the Cross with the relics of St Ann over her head, where her pains were worst, and gave her the relics to kiss'.[32]

From then onwards Sister Olimpia suffered no more from headaches.

When you have to put an end to it . . .
While Mother Enrichetta's way of ruling was loving, prudent, understanding and respectful of other people's personality, at the same time it was firm and unyielding on the principles handed down to her and through which the vocation was handed down. In speaking of the duties of the religious life, she did not use half measures. She was extremely honest and came straight to the point, to the extent that she sometimes appeared hard and unyielding – so much so that she sometimes regretted.it.

'On the last day of last year I was very naughty and spoke straight out and said things I would not have believed myself capable of wanting to say. At dinner I spotted some signs that the sisters at the end of the table wanted to give me their New Year wishes and I prayed with all my heart to the Holy Trinity and to my guardian angel for inspiration in the words that I should address to the community. I then felt their help very palpably and said what they inspired me to say. Amongst other things I said that it was now time to make an end of our self-love, our scruples and our own comfort, to ensure that this coming year would be one of triumph of God in our hearts and minds, I said that we could not go on with the laziness of past years, that God was knocking at the doors of our hearts and had been for a long time, but that we had too long been resisting his grace, had not been allowing ourselves to be conquered even by God, but that he well knew the way to win over his creatures, and that in one word we had to put an end to it, one way or another, because if we didn't finish with our faults then God would have finished with us!'[33]

One must read what she then wrote almost in secret to her spiritual director:

'You see, my dear Father, how naughty I was, so before I finished I softened my words and asked them to excuse me if I had said too much, but that I had felt constrained to do it by my sense of duty, that I loved them all and God alone knew what I would not be capable of doing for the good and advantage of each one of them!'[34]

On 14 March 1867 she went to Castelfidardo to visit that community and she went to the sanctuary of Loreto to pray for the Church and Pius IX. These were decisive times for the Holy See. The Roman question was a burning one in everyone's mind, and the law presented by Ricasoli and approved by Rattacci on the confiscation of ecclesiastical goods, risked aggravating an already tense situation. There were demands from many parts for Rome to be made the capital of Italy, the threat of a coup by the most impatient elements in society was in the air and the unforseeable could happen from one moment to the next.

'I find myself in a continual act of sacrifice', she wrote on 15 April 1867, 'always on behalf of the Church and I continue always to pray the good God for the desired triumph of the same'. She was ready to give her life for the victory of the Apostolic See and was even more inspired on receiving a letter from Sister Teofila who gave her to understand, on behalf of 'good Daddy', that truth would triumph 'but the victims would be few'.

In May of the same year she went to Bagnorea where the Sisters of St Ann had had a house since 1851 and besides teaching in the school had for some years helped in the running of the civil hospital there. Here too she was assailed by the consistent thought of doing something more for the Church and the Pope:

'I feel almost all the time', she wrote on 15 May 1867, 'at one and the same time both the immense goodness of God and my own extreme unworthiness. I have moments of Paradise and I still have moments of hell, but in general I am usually calm and very happy with the state in which the good God holds me, without any other desire than that of sacrificing myself continuously for the good of the Church, and this seems to be the will of my good God. "My God", I ask him, "how long will the sacrifice go on? Till when, my God? . . . The Church! The victim! Look at her!" '

Meanwhile, time was marching on, the six-year term of her generalate granted by the Holy See was coming to an end. There was talk of a forthcoming Chapter, to be held on the Feast of Pentecost, 1867. Mother Enrichetta was worried, afraid of being re-elected. The pages of her diary show her worry: 'I continued to make the offering, several times a day, as my habit had become, but every time I renewed it, I always felt an inner reproach telling me: it is not complete, you are still keeping a part back. I then did a bit of examining my conscience, and found this to be true. I was offering myself for any sacrifice that God might ask of me, except that of being re-elected Superior, and this was the missing part that made my offering displeasing to God'.[35] On another page, telling of the extraordinary dialogue with

God she undertook every day in prayer, she wrote: 'I told my good God all the difficulties I had found and still found in my office and insisted above all on my total incapacity to govern the Institute well. And he replied kindly: What are you doing now? Was it not I who supported you, and the community with you, in the past? What have you got to fear for the future? These words left me somewhat confused, and from then on I became more convinced than ever that it was God who had done everything through me and in my place. So I said, as much from the heart as I could: I give in! But I could not feel any gratitude on God's part. I repeated, I give in! for a second and a third time. But nothing new. The offering was not accepted, and I felt myself being told clearly, though I cannot say how: From you, giving in is not enough; I want to you be pleased and even re-joice at your election. Perhaps you will not be, but you should make your offering as though you were. I seemed to see these words as if they were printed, with my mind, but my senses could neither see nor hear any-thing. All I felt, in myself, was the certainty that these words came from God. But my anxiety about and aver-sion to the office of Superior were so strong that I could not make the offering in the way that God asked me to. It seemed impossible that God should want such a thing of me, and I said to myself: It is not possible to rejoice at something so unwelcome to me. In this way I persisted in my view, contrary to the good God's'.[36]

On the day fixed — Whit Sunday — the Chapter met, and the votes cast were sent unread to Rome. Mother Enrichetta had no illusions: she knew very well she would be re-elected: 'From then on I could no longer persuade myself of the fact that weight of the superior-ship would be taken off my weak back, and I was sure it would fall back on it even more heavily'.[37]

It was June; the Feast of Sts Peter and Paul was approaching, when she was expecting the fulfilment of great things. It was the day arranged with her 'good Daddy' for the offering of herself, so that the Pope would be safe and the Church triumph over the hostility of its enemies. The kind of offering involved can be gleaned from a fraction of a letter: 'Oh! how happy I should be if I could break myself in pieces to lessen, even if only a little, the terrible trials to which the Roman Pontiff, the holy Pius IX, is being subjected!'[38]

The time for the longed-for offering came, but it was not her life that the Lord wanted. This was something quite different: the sacrifice of the person dearest to her and her acceptance of re-election.

Since her brother's death, Anna Dominici had not been well. She had seldom been able to embrace her daughter, whom she did not see for years at a time. Just one hasty visit, once, for the foundation of the house at Carmagnola. Don Tofoni went to see her. 'I am enormously grateful to you,' she wrote, 'for everything you have done for my poor mother and my sister, and thank you with all my heart. Today a Canon came from Carmagnola, and he told me that since the operation performed to drain off the water that was swelling her body, my dear Mama has been a little more comfortable, but he could not give me any hope. He did not want to talk about my sister, but I can imagine the state she is in. In any case, if this is the will of the good God, it is my will also and I am ready for the painful sacrifice. The thought of rejoining her one day in the bosom of 'good Daddy' is even a consoling one for me!'[39]

On 12 June 1867, Anna Dominici died. Her daughter received the news in Turin two days later: 'I was about to end this, when I received a letter from my cousin the Canon with the sad news of the death of my poor and beloved mother, on Wednesday at one in the morning. I had already offered this sacrifice to the Most Holy Trinity for their coming feast day but they wanted to accept it earlier. I have renewed the offering to them, not without the deepest sorrow, heightened by the hardly good news of my dearest sister, who is in bed and has had two bloodlettings . . . And the good God who has dealt this blow does all things well, so nothing remains for me but to bless him and thank him always and on every occasion'.[40]

In the first days of July, Mother Enrichetta received from Rome the confirmation of her re-election. 'The news of my appointment as Superior General did not come unexpectedly, and I had therefore been able to dispose myself in advance to receive the news of this cross, with the feelings you suggested to me. I think I can say that I embrace this great burden with joy and gratitude, and my good God knows how many times I have told him that I am content with his will, and want nothing that is not the perfect fulfilment of his most holy will in me. I finally made so bold as to tell my dear Daddy that I would be generous with him, and did not at all like to think that he would be less so with me. My Daddy, I have told him and still tell him a hundred times, I have done as you wished, but I want to be rewarded with nothing except the full carrying-out of the promises you often made me in your great goodness'.[41]

Her way of talking of her 'good Daddy' is amazing. Those who do not believe will perhaps be sceptical, or at least puzzled, but it is impossible to be indifferent to such spontaneity of faith, and authentic faith. A sense of dismay, almost of nostalgia for something lost, something that gave life a meaning, comes over us on reading her writings, with their talk of her 'Daddy' and her 'Mama', Mary, on every page. What she writes is neither rhetorical nor poetic, but a certainty that becomes a loving dialogue, a sacrifice of herself, a *raison d'être*. It is hardly possible to understand Mother Enrichetta from outside this perspective, which gave light and new vigour to the whole community. It is enough to think of Sister Candida and Sister Teofila to see this: two simple souls, but so immersed in the supernatural that they formed one soul with the Mother General, their guide, support and encouragement.

Notes
1.   St Salvatore da Horta, O.F.M. Cf. P. Foguet, *El Taumaturgo catalán*, (Vichy, 1927), p. 266.
2.   *VI Testis Rev. Sor. Maria Severina Pravettoni, Proc.*, p. 602.
3.   *XI Testis Rev. Sor. Maria Julia Spano, Proc.*, p. 1547.
4.   Autobiography, p. 198.
5.   *Ibid.*, p. 199.
6.   'They lived always shut up in one room, where they ordered their meals to be served; when they occasionally came to recreation it was only to set a bad example and spoil the serene happiness of the community with their grim faces and severe looks'. *Attestatio sor. Mariae Dariae Bonavero*, Summn. Ad., p. 49.
7.   Autobiography, p. 200.
8.   *Ibid.*,
9.   *Op. cit.*, p. 204.
10. *Ibid.*
11. *Op. cit.*, p. 205.
12. *Op. cit.*, p. 206.
13. *Op. cit.*, p. 204.
14. Pietro Paolo Gastaldi, *Umiltà e Grandezza* (Turin, 1926), p. 263.
15. Giovanni de Montis, *Nobiltà Vera*, p. 158.
16. *Ibid.*, p. 159
17. Autobiography, p. 205.
18. 'In those days I suffered an inner martyrdom that I cannot explain, and at that moment an unfamiliar feeling of inner peace took hold of my whole being and at the same time I was sure that our prayers would be heard favourably by God, and that grace would not be far away from us. The same thing happened to me on the Scala Santa, and in other places I can no longer remember, and I could no longer doubt that God had not delayed in pouring out his abundant mercies on our poor Institute'. Autobiography, p. 202.
19. 'I know that the ex-Superior and her follower, lacking the humility to serve under Mother Enrichetta, left the Institute and the charitable Mother provided them with household goods, money and, furthermore, arranged lodging for them and gave them a pension for as long as they should live, so that they could live decently'. *Attestatio sor. Mariae Columbinae Brizio*, Sum. Ad., p. 49.
20. Autobiography, p. 207.

21. *Ibid.*
22. *Op. cit.*, pp. 207-8
23. *Op. cit.*, p. 208.
24. From the *Diary* (Dec. 1865 — Nov. 1866) published in *Vigilia Eroica,* with notes by S. P. Morazetti, p. 213.
25. *Ibid.*
26. *Diary,* p. 214.
27. P. P. Gastaldi, *op. cit.*, p. 269.
28. Letter to D. Tofoni, 15 Dec. 1866.
29. *Ibid.*
30. *Ibid.*
31. *Ibid.*
32. *Ibid.*
33. To D. Tofoni, 16 Jan. 1867.
34. *Ibid.*
35. *Diary*, p. 215.
36. *Op. cit.*, pp. 217-8
37. To D. Tofoni, 14 June 1867.
38. To D. Tofoni, 15 Dec. 1867.
39. To D. Tofoni, 3 June 1867.
40. To D. Tonfoni, 14 June 1867.
41. To D. Tofoni, 19 June 1867.

VII Actions speak louder than words

To take thought for the morrow is contrary to God's plan

The Roman question kept everyone in suspense. On 3 November 1867 at Mentana Garibaldi's volunteers, in their desperate attempt to reach Rome, fell back with heavy losses under the accurate fire of the French rifles. Imprecise reports of the battle excited apprehension and indignation in the minds of the Catholics of Turin. Communications were interrupted, fragmentary accounts and some newspaper reports went as far as to announce that the papal city had fallen to the insurgents.

Mother Enrichetta was dismayed and could not believe what people were saying. This is reflected in a letter to don Tofoni of 12 November 1867, in which once again her great trust in her 'good Daddy' was made manifest: 'I was anxious to find someone to assure me of the real truth about the situation in Rome, but to whom could I have recourse when everybody was complaining of the lack of news, due, they said, to the cutting of the telegraph wires and of the railway? Amid such uncertainties I contented myself with pressing my poor but urgent prayers in the sight of the dear heavenly Father. In those days we recited together the whole rosary and the

174

Miserere, which we continue to do now also, for the present needs of holy Mother Church and for the conversion of sinners. Meanwhile there came the hour of evening meditation, and without willing it I found myself spiritually in the eternal city. I understood nothing, I saw nothing, but I experienced such quietness, such rest in God, such assurance that he must have kept his promises—namely that Rome would not be touched and that what was said to have occurred was not true. I cannot explain the experience, but it caused me such happiness that I could not keep it all to myself. Coming out of church dear good Sister Eufrasia questioned me in the way she sometimes did: "Mother, what of your 'good Daddy'?" And as usual I answered: "My Daddy is well and kind". And then I added: "Listen, dear Sister Eufrasia, to a piece of good news. The telegraph wires with the 'good Daddy' have not been cut, not at all; he lets us know that the news from Rome is good and that the city is quiet." Oh do thank dear "good Daddy" so much for the speed with which he gave us such good news; he had promised he would and I remained thenceforward with ever greater certainty that God's promises are fulfilled'.[1]

The community had events in Rome much at heart. That very evening Sister Teofila delivered a letter to the Mother General.

'My dearest Mother,' the letter ran, 'the most dear Daddy today is pressing me to come to you with the message that I now give in writing. I did not want to come for fear of further disturbing you. Mother, "good Daddy" bids me inform his daughter about what is happening in Rome; that is, he with his suite, in particular "Mama", otherwise our dear foundress, are presiding as ministers, and Daddy says that they will not set foot in Rome; moreover he wants me to give you this good news because it is the word of "good Daddy" who cannot err'. This way of expressing herself may appear simple-minded and naive, but it reflects an attitude and is evidence of a high degree of spiritual communion that can be a lesson to us even today.

Early in 1868 reports of a possible imminent suppression of the Institute were again bruited about. But the person at its head was not alarmed: 'Amid the rumours which threaten our foundations', she wrote to her spiritual father, 'I cannot explain to you how great is the peace and quiet that I enjoy and feel in my heart'.[2] The cause of her unchanging serenity was not superficiality but won by suffering and due to 'the circulation of messages from God that some of my dear daughters transmit to me from time to time'.[3] In the midst of the trials that were rising so threateningly, she believed firmly in the inspirations of those close to her. Above all she believed in 'good Daddy' and she explains it in an enlightening way: 'Now I understand better than ever why "good Daddy" insisted to me throughout last October that he was the Superior of my Institute and that it was up to him to take the necessary thought. So much so that now I make the most of his claim to the title, and of my heartfelt handing-over to him of all my rights, so as to commit him to make known, support and promote the interests of *his* Institute! "My dear Daddy," I say to him, "you have told me so many times that you are its Superior, well then, play the part, because now is the time!"'[4]

The thought that most oppressed her was that, with the threatened suppression, so many girls and an infinity of children would be abandoned: no more schools, no more nurseries. Yet her courage did not fail; indeed, she continued to press forward with further foundations and to take in more girls.

In a letter of 14 February 1868 she writes: 'The most painful idea of all is that of being closed down and throwing onto the streets the young girls whom I receive into the Institute, who will all, because of me, be forced to face endless hardships. Nevertheless I have a strong sense of my duty to continue to receive them if they present themselves; indeed I pray God to send me many of them, because I have much need of them'.

There were many proposals to open new houses. The reputation of the Sisters of St Ann was spreading: they were sought out, valued, loved by the people. In 1868 the Duchess of Aosta, Maria Vittoria, offered the Turin Congregation the management of the school for poor girls at Reano. The offer was accepted and, given the situation, it was an act of courage. It was to be abundantly rewarded once the work was put in hand.

Less than a year had passed before the Duchess, an old friend of the Barolos, again asked for some sisters to set up an elementary school on the estates owned by the family at Vettigné. The proposal was accepted and three nuns left for that countryside which at one time was mostly used for the cultivation of rice. On 15 October 1869 the school opened its doors. There was a shortage of everything and it was to pioneering work that the sisters were called.

However they were not daunted and they faced the difficulties without complaint. They were well aware that in following their vocation they had not chosen the smoothest path, and their charity won the hearts of the inhabitants.

In this great burgeoining of tasks, one project remained—the aspiration to go to the missionary lands, to set sail for India. Mother Enrichetta spoke of it again to the convent's confessor, but received vague replies which betrayed a certain lack of confidence. Missionary work was not in the spirit of the Institute; India seemed a hazardous enterprize when in Piedmont, and in Italy at large, the scope for their apostolate was so vast. These were all valid objections, but the splendid project would not be quenched. In 1858 she had registered a vow and would not go back on it now. It was for 'good Daddy' to show her the most suitable way.

In October 1870 she was at Castelfidardo. One evening in that month someone knocked at the convent door in Via della Consolata in Turin. It was late and visitors were not expected. The community, as we read in the Annals of the order, was gathered in the chapel. At the first ring of the bell they pretended not to hear. But the bell at the door was insistent. The portress, a certain Sister Anna Graglia, went to open the door and found herself face to face with a priest in a cloak, accompanied by Canon Odenino. The priest introduced himself as Domenico Barbero, Bishop of Doliche, Apostolic Vicar of Hyderabad, India. Despite this introduction there was difficulty about entering the house at that unusual hour. When the reluctance and astonishment of the portress had been overcome, the Bishop asked for the Superior, but Mother Enrichetta was in the Marches, so he was received by her substitute. The purpose of the visit was soon declared: he had come to explore a plan to engage some of the Sisters of St Ann in his Indian province.

The prospect at once enthralled the whole community and Sister Eufrasia, the local Superior in Turin, wrote on the following day to the Mother General to inform her of the event. Her letter was welcomed as a sign from the Lord, but the problems connected with an eventual acceptance were many. Before reaching a definite decision she asked the Cardinal Protector and the Archbishop for authority to proceed, which they granted. Not yet satisfied, she prayed and asked others for their prayers.

In her letter to Tofoni of 13 December 1870 she wrote: 'Once back in Turin I was able to get further clarification of the Indian issue. In conclusion it seems to me that I cannot by any means have further doubts about the will of God, although, to tell the truth, I had never had any and, in fact, always feared that the project would be realized. In the few days' time that I took before giving a final answer to the Bishop's request for my nuns, during which we of the community made a triduum to St Ann with benediction of the Most Blessed Sacrament, I was aware of a sort of fear of setting myself against the divine will by a refusal and of thus bringing divine retribution on myself. When the triduum was over I gave my favourable response to Mgr Barbero in agreement with my good assistants who awaited it with much anxiety, but greater confidence, and busied myself with the choice of who to send to India. In this too I saw the hand of the good God, and I think I can from every point of view feel at peace on their account'.

The eagerness of those sisters to set out for the mission field was overwhelming and infectious. Even if they knew so little about India, to cross the sea and carry into distant lands the seed of their Institute, there to flourish and bear rich fruit, was the dream of them all. Charity, as is said with good reason, has no need of speech to make itself understood. The most sublime and unselfish love, a love that asks for nothing in return, possesses an eloquence and a power to convince that goes beyond words. Charity itself becomes words, and a universal embrace.

A few days after Mgr Barbero's unexpected visit, Sister Maria Bonosa, who had never given any sign of a missionary vocation, wrote to Mother General, still at Castelfidardo, that she was ready to go—because 'she wished with all her heart to be a daughter to her'.[5]

Not all, however, were in favour of the plan. The convent's confessor was doubtful, and there were some who observed that such a decision was contrary to the purpose of the foundation. Others made a point of the enormous expense to be faced and the resulting dissipation of forces that could be used elsewhere. Mother Enrichetta, in agreement with the Vicar Apostolic, remained firm in her determination. To take thought for the morrow was contrary to God's plan.

In those days of waiting a cheque for 1000 lire arrived

179

from Mgr Marietti of the seminary of St Calocero in Milan: a contribution to the first expenses of the journey, and a sign from Providence. Six nuns were to leave for India: Sisters Maria Rosalia, Seconda, Margherita, Felicita, Dionisia. Sister Maria Bonosa would be Superior to the missionary community.

'The fact of the imminent opening of a house in India has produced a great effect on the community, and in general all draw renewed enthusiasm and strength from it. They are edified by the quietness, abnegation and cheerfulness that shine on the faces of each of the six chosen for the Hyderabad mission. They are widely spoken of with admiration and respect. One or two have taken it a little ill not to have been chosen for that expedition, but, Father, you must see that if it had been a matter of considering other people's pleasure and my own convenience, I certainly would not have deprived myself of those who are such a help to me here, but would have sent others instead, whose absence would have been a relief rather than a loss to me. But it was a matter of seeking the greater glory of God, the greatest advantage for the Institute, and the peace of mind of the sisters marked out to be, as it were, the foundations of that nascent house. From such a point of view I could not have taken a different line from what I have'.[6]

The days passed and, as departure drew near, many people came to the convent to congratulate the Mother General, pay their respects to the missionaries, and express approval of the decision taken by the Institute. At that period to depart for India was an exciting event. It seemed quite an adventure that a handful of women should show such daring for the faith.

The eve of departure, 23 January 1871, was spent in farewells and the final preparations. There was no lack of moving scenes. Among the gifts which they received, the most precious was Mother Enrichetta's: a silver reliquary that had belonged to the foundress.

180

Early in the morning of the 24th they heard Mass in chapel; there followed a quick meeting in the assembly hall. The Annals record that no one succeeded in saying a word on behalf of the community. After a stop at the sanctuary of the Consolata, and accompanied by the Mother General and the Superior, Sister Eufrasia, they left for Genoa where they arrived in the afternoon.

In the harbour the steamship *Arabia* was berthed, a vessel fitted out for long voyages. She had fine clean lines, enormous smoking funnels, a high broadside of steel. Mgr Barbero; Luigi Marinoni, Superior of the seminary of St Calocero in Milan; and Fr Rossi of the same seminary, awaited them on board. They were to make the voyage with the nuns and would arrange, by agreement, for their first installation.

They expected to weigh anchor at once, an hour or two later. Instead departure was postponed for three days owing to unforeseeable damage to the engines. Meanwhile the party was given hospitality in the town, in a convent of Dominican nuns, the 'Providence'.

On 27 January, at four, they were all aboard, and late in the evening the anchors were lifted. The ship drew away; darkness enveloped the harbour; there was fog and the ship's lights, ever more distant, could hardly be perceived. Mother Enrichetta was with Sister Eufrasia on the quay, tirelessly gazing out to sea, even when nothing could any longer be discerned on the horizon. She did not say a word; deeply moved, she put her hands together in prayer.

In her account of the hours of separation which she wrote on 6 February 1871 to her spiritual father, she said: 'In our grief, acute though it was, what quiet peace and serenity! I must tell you, both I and my dear Sister Eufrasia who was with me were edified by the courage of our good daughters. I promised them that I would think of them as my special favourites, my Benjamins. Poor sisters! They have made such a tremendous sacrifice and well deserve so dear a name! I see that I have enlarged somewhat on this theme, but, Father, what else can you expect? I needed to open my heart to one who knows how much in God I love all these dear Benjamins of mine, from whom I have had to separate myself, perhaps never to see them again on this earth. God, always God! In everything, God! His glory, his will!' From then onwards the Sisters of St Ann, on mission in India, were to be called the 'Benjamins'.

One of the sisters had the task of keeping the diary of the voyage, and from its pages, yellowed by time, we learn some interesting particulars.

One night, on the voyage from the Strait of Messina in the direction of Crete, the *Arabia* was battered by a storm. There was great alarm, and no respite from sea-sickness. Then, as they approached Aden, they ran the risk of being held up for quarantine. Sister Maria Felicita had a temperature; it was smallpox, a disease more feared than the fury of the waves. Detained for the necessary medical checks, under growing fear that the voyage would be interrupted and that all might be interned in some quarantine station, they very fervently commended themselves to St Ann. After two days' stop in the sultry heat of those areas of the Red Sea, the health authorities finally issued the licence to continue the voyage; the case as such did not arouse anxiety.

The voyage continued and on 19 February they were in sight of the Indian coast. They were welcomed by Mgr Meurin, Bishop of Bombay. In this city they found their first lodgings in the convent of the Sisters of Jesus and Mary. On 22 February, rested from their fatigues, they set off for Secunderabad.

Mother Enrichetta followed in spirit her 'Benjamins', and they, distant though they were, did not forget Turin and their convent there. In a letter to Tofoni of 20 March 1871 there is a mention of them: 'I venture to pass on to you a beautiful poem, composed by our good

Sister Felicita (Sister Eufrasia's sister), which my dear missionary Benjamins sent me from Suez. For several days I hadn't the heart to read it, but finally, under obligation to say a word or two of thanks to Felicita, I read it this morning, not without shedding tears. How deeply I still feel the painful separation! I imagined that I had no heart, but in this case it made itself felt and still does. How mysterious the human heart is!' The poem, alas, has not survived, but perhaps that is just as well. We would have criticised it for the naiveté of its expression and for its old-fashioned form, or we would have found something rhetorical in it.

Beyond all expectations

In 1871 the members of the Association of Charity at Cheri delivered a request for sisters of St Ann to run the nursery school, the free elementary schools (the so-called 'people's schools'), and the fee-paying elementary schools. Mother Enrichetta accepted, and despatched ten nuns. Yet another task began, and with an indifference to the human means which was a measure of her trust in God, in her 'good Daddy'.

'So good', she wrote to don Tofoni, after the chaplain had preached a sermon which envisaged the sufferings of souls in purgatory for even quite small failings: 'So for me too it will be necessary to make a long stay in purgatory, if every little failing is to be punished so severely. I kept saying to myself: My dear Daddy will then face me with a long bill to pay ... He might let me have sight of it now so that I could try to make reparation while still in time, since I would regret it too bitterly if my soul, delivered from this wretched food for worms, could not at once run into the arms of God. But the goodness of my God is ever more incomprehensible! Father, would you believe it? I had scarcely entertained these thoughts when my more than dearest Daddy enabled me to see him with a sheet of paper in his hand. I looked and looked again, but seeing no writing on it I ventured to ask my dear Daddy how in the world that sheet should be blank when every day I commit so many faults and shortcomings. A fear indeed crossed my mind that perhaps the devil was preventing me from seeing straight in order to lead me astray. Then my dear Daddy condescended to let me know that he, being the essence of justice, saw that my failings were committed through mere frailty and weakness and so did not have to be written down as they were not deserving of punishment. At an insight such as this I remained confounded, but I was not astonished, knowing as I did from such long experience the infinite kindness of my dear Daddy towards this unworthy, though so loving, daughter of his. All this happened in a few minutes, and in a way that I cannot really explain. I knew all that I have so far described without feeling or seeing anything with my bodily senses. But there remained with me such a sense of unction and assurance that I was never again visited by any doubt but that the occurrence was an exquisite touch of divine goodness towards me. This touch made itself deeply felt in me for about a week, a week I spent in an almost continuous act of wonder at such condescension and goodness on God's part'.[7]

With this great simplicity Mother Enrichetta touches on a moving theme. In words of such sincerity we catch a glimpse of the profounder meaning in the infinite goodness that is justice. The 'good Daddy' in whom she believed was not threatening or angry, ready to punish every fault however petty, but love, limitless generosity, much readier to understand than men are.

The Lord's goodness inspired her with confidence to face new and more onerous undertakings, and filled her with unexpected boldness. Already she had been working for some time on the project of founding another house in Turin. On the few occasions when she emerged into the city, with her inseparable companion Sister Eufrasia, she stopped to look at this or that piece of land, this or that group of houses, always with one idea: to find the right place for the achievement of what she had at heart.

She was well aware that circumstances would not be propitious; the relations between Church and the civil authorities had not yet been clarified. But she was moved by an urgency that would not be baffled for long. It was a grandiose plan. Her intention was to open a church, and attached to it an elementary school, a secondary school, a nursery school, and an oratory for official holidays.

To define and speed up the decision that she had taken there supervened some controversy with the administration of the Opera Pia Barolo which, in 1872, went so far as arbitrarily to insist on a reduction of the numbers of religious in the house that belonged to it in Via della Consolata. This seemed to be a warning from Providence. Having listened to the opinions of her assistants and consulted a number of people, she decided to acquire a site in the area of Borgo San Secondo. At that period the district was in the open countryside on the outskirts of Turin, 'a bleak and bare piece of land, almost uninhabited, with a few scattered shacks', in the words of the Annals. It was an area deficient in all services, unprovided with any ecclesiastical support, not yet endowed with a parish church—an ideal spot to shoulder with courage a work of genuine social improvement.

In the achievement of her enterprise Mother Enrichetta had at her side Canon Luigi Nasi, the ecclesiastical superior of the Institute and its generous benefactor. Another notable benefactor was don Pietro Ponte, the late foundress's confessor.

The funds needed to go ahead with the work were limited. A total of 40,000 lire is mentioned, invested at interest in one of the city's banks. One day, when the contracts for the buildings had already been signed, a rumour circulated that the bank was on the brink of failure. It was a piece of news that was frightening, if true.

Mother Enrichetta mentioned this to no-one so as not to alarm the community. She kept the distress to herself and, full of confidence, passed the whole night in chapel, in consultation with her 'good Daddy'. At one moment, as she raised her eyes to the altar, she heard rise up from the depths of her soul the words, 'Enrichetta, enough!' and she recognized the voice. Her worries melted away, to be replaced by an immeasurable peace. To a sister whom she met in the corridor she said with a smile, 'I have recovered what I had lost!'[8] That morning she betook herself to the bank and succeeded in laying hands on all that belonged to the Institute. So her capital was safe. In recognition of the grace obtained she was to provide that a lamp should be alight in perpetuity on the altar of St Ann; and that slender flame which still burns will be a reminder to future generations of how very present Providence is in the works accomplished in its name.

Construction started again and progressed. The walls of the great group of buildings began to take shape, and once the city had expanded so far, it was to be enclosed between Corso Re Umberto, Via Montevecchio, Via Massena and Via Legnano.

Before its completion in 1873, she acceded to the insistent requests of don Bosco, an intimate friend of the Turin Institute, to send a number of sisters to Mornese to initiate into the religious life the incipient congregation of the Daughters of Mary Auxiliatrix, founded by himself. The Annals of that year in fact supply the information thus: 'On the last Sunday of January we had the privilege of hearing a sermon by the very Reverend don John Bosco, founder and Superior of the Salesian Congregation. He took occasion to ask our venerable Mother General for the cooperation of our Institute in the foundation of the Daughters of Mary Auxiliatrix, who were under the same don Bosco. As this was a favourable opportunity to repay to others the charity that our dear Institute had received at the outset of its existence, our dearest Mother General, with the approval of her council, acceded to the request and sent to Mornese, cradle of the infant institute, the Reverend Sister Francesca, then her secretary and second assistant general, with our good Sister Angela as companion in her important mission'.

The enterprise at Mornese must have been negotiated at length, and as evidence of don Bosco's high regard for Mother Enrichetta a letter of 24 April 1871, recently discovered in the archive of the Sisters of St Ann, may be quoted: 'Reverend Mother, I deliver the Rule of our congregation into your hands in order that you should have the kindness to read it and see if it can be adapted to an institute of religious in the sense which I had the honour to explain to you in person. Begin with the third paragraph – the purpose of this institute, Daughters of Mary Immaculate—and afterwards remove or add as, in your wisdom, you think best with a view to founding an institute whose daughters will be genuine religious in the eyes of the Church, yet free citizens in the eyes of our civil society. These headings or articles of the Rule of St Ann which could be adapted I shall have much pleasure in so adapting. As soon as you think fit for us to have a talk, you can have me told so by one or other of our clerics or messengers who often turn up there. This is certainly a difficult sapling, but I believe that it will redound to the greater glory of God. And if we succeed in saving a soul or two, you will have had the greater part in it. God bless you and all your family of religious, and I commend myself and these pupils of mine to the charity of your holy prayers, and sign myself with gratitude as your Reverence's most obliged servant, John Bosco, priest.'

In the following year, 1876, at the request of Countess

Carlotta Callori, a nursery school and a needlework centre were opened at Vignale Monferrato, and a few months later another nursery school was opened at Monticelli in the province of Piacenza.

But all this vigorous work did not slow down the construction of the church and house that were rising in Borgo San Secondo in Turin. In early April 1877 all was completed and the building was solemnly opened. The first rector of the church in Via Massena was don Pietro Ponte, who at his own expense had offered to face in marble the high altar dedicated to the Sacred Heart.

The 'widow's mite' and Pope Leo XIII

On 7 February 1878 Pope Pius IX died. In the Catholic world it was a sorrowful and irreparable loss for all who had seen and believed in the venerable white-robed figure, whose heroism and suffering gave expression to Catholic intransigence in face of the situation brought about in Rome.

When Cardinal Gioacchino Pecci was elected as the successor of St Peter, taking the name of Leo XIII, Mother Enrichetta, who had been reconfirmed as Mother General in 1876, sent the Pope a letter of filial devotion and fervent homage. Not satisfied with her letter which she regarded as an insufficiently expressive act, she went to Rome in May with her two assistants, Sister Eufrasia and Sister Francesca.

On 11 May the three nuns were received in special audience by the Holy Father, and every detail was reported in a circular letter to the community, dated 28 May 1878: 'My dearest daughters, I am sure that I am giving you pleasure by letting you know of the happy issue of our journey to Rome. And to start with I rejoice to assure you that in our visits to various holy places I always had you in mind and commended you with fervour to the Holy Apostles, to St Ignatius and many other saints on whose tombs we had the opportunity to prostrate ourselves. For all and for each in particular I invoked the true spirit of our holy Institute and a generous fidelity to self-conquest. Now I come to details.

'As you, my dearest daughters, already know, on the sixth of this month we set out on our journey to Rome and arrived there safely on the evening of the seventh. The following day we went to pay our respects to our Cardinal Protector, who welcomed us with fatherly kindness and gave proof of his sincere affection and genuine attachment to our dear Institute. Then, when he understood that I greatly desired a private audience of the Holy Father, and as soon as might be, he told me that it was very difficult to obtain one and added that various deputations from abroad had had to wait as long as a fortnight before being admitted. Nonetheless he promised that if he were to go to the Vatican he would mention it to His Holiness; meanwhile, we should present our request, and in fact I presented it the next day. While the reply, granting us a public audience on Monday the 13th, was being prepared, our Cardinal Protector visited the Vatican, spoke to the Holy Father and obtained a change of permit, saying that his Holiness would receive us in private audience on the evening of the eleventh. This was indeed a singular favour, obtained in my opinion by the many prayers which my dear daughters offered with this intention. For this I feel a lively need to thank them with all my heart.

'Saturday, at half past four in the afternoon, his Eminence, our Protector, sent to fetch us in his carriage, and at five o'clock we were in the Vatican. At about six we had the high privilege of being introduced into the presence of the Holy Father, Leo XIII. After the usual genuflections, we knelt to kiss the holy foot, but he at once held out his hand to us and we kissed his apostolic ring. Then, seeing that we wished to perform the other act also, his Holiness said to us graciously: "So you want to kiss my foot as well?" and stretched it out towards us.

Next he made us stand up, and himself standing also he began in a tone at once majestic and charming a short speech that lasted about ten minutes.

'This was how his Holiness expressed himself: "My daughters, your Protector, Cardinal Caterini, spoke to me about you and told me that you wished to come to see me, and I at once gave my consent, because I thought that you, being nuns, might be able to speak words of consolation to me. I know that you are virtuous, that you do good, that there is a spirit of goodness in your Institute. Nonetheless, as representative of Jesus Christ, I cannot but exhort you always to increase in virtue, in the exact observance of your duties and your Rule, and in the perfect fulfilment of the holy vows that you have taken. You have abandoned everything to consecrate yourselves to God; you have chosen a way of privation and mortification, the better to assure your eternal salvation. Do not withdraw a sacrifice made of your own free choice, but seek to live in faithful harmony with the divine favours. With fidelity keep yourselves close to the Lord in prayer, in your inner spirit, in the constant union of your hearts with the divine Heart. Without this full and unwavering union with God it is impossible to fulfil your special duty, impossible to conform to the purpose for which you are consecrated to the service of God. All strength comes to us from remaining united with God, and it is for this reason that I so earnestly exhort you to give your minds to this union, in order to stand firm in the battles which come to you from our enemies. Be on guard, my daughters, against the snares of the devil and even more of those who go about his business. All too hard do they try to deprive our poor young people of religion and to instil them with anti-Catholic principles . . . This devilish spirit works its way in everywhere, even in monasteries and convents! Only last week in a monastery that I will not and must not name, there were serious disorders, I will not say actual apostasies, but believe

190

me, my heart was profoundly saddened". He said this with such feeling that it made us shed tears.

'Up to this point the Holy Father stood motionless, with his eyes closed, and not for a moment did we take the liberty of interrupting him. But when his long pause made us think that he had brought his exhortation to a close, we protested our will to do our best never to cause him any pain, committing ourselves ever more deeply to the exact performance of our duties and praying for the holy Church and for his Holiness whom we wished relieved of such griefs. We thanked him for having graciously consented to be our father. When he heard these words, he assumed an even more amiable air and with fatherly kindness turned to me and asked me what was the purpose of our Institute, how many houses we had and where, how many members we had and if there were any from Rome or its surroundings.

'After I had replied to all these questions I presented to him the address of our sisters and that of our pupils. Then I put a little packet into his hand with the words: "Your Holiness, here is the widow's mite, but how much more we would like to do!" I wanted to say more, but he did not give me the chance, saying at once with great friendliness: "Thank you; whatever they offer me is very welcome! Thank you and I accept it all the more warmly in that it is the outcome of sacrifices and privations. If a very rich man were to offer a large sum, it wouldn't make an impression because we would know that he could offer so much more; but you, poor nuns, have certainly no superfluity of money, especially in times like these, yet you think of coming to the help of the Vicar of Christ!" We could see that he was really moved. Finally we knelt to receive the apostolic blessing. I called for it on myself, on our dear Institute, on our good Father Superior, on our excellent Fr Testa, on don Ponte and don Casassa, and on our girls. Then I wanted to name also our poor Sister Anna, and his Holiness added: "Yes, so that by suffering she may acquire much merit".

'Next dear Mother Assistant spoke and the Holy Father broke in with the words: "Yes, I bless you, your Institute, your Superiors, your spiritual and temporal benefactors, your relatives and everyone whom you wish to name, all those who work together for the good of your houses, and you, Mother General, so that you may be able to fulfil satisfactorily all the duties attached to your office".

'He then raised his right hand, gave us his heartfelt blessing, and held it out for us to kiss. We then kissed his foot as well and, having thanked him for the favour granted to us, we left his apartment with our hearts much moved and filled with holy joy.

'I am confident, my dearest daughters, that the special blessing given by the Vicar of Christ to each one of us will produce its effect, and the holy words that he spoke to us, which I have reported to you word for word as far as possible, will bind us all the closer to the precise fulfilment of our duties . . . Goodbye, my dearest daughters; accept with my affectionate greetings those of the Mother Superior and of my assistant. Keep well, good and cheerful, and believe me your most loving mother, with a heart full to overflowing, Sister Maria Enrichetta'.

More fireworks for Mother Enrichetta
The visit to Rome left a deep longing to return in Mother Enrichetta's heart. Her brief stay had confirmed an idea that she had long cherished: a house of the Sisters of St Ann in the papal city. For this purpose she sent Sisters Eufrasia and Francesca to the capital to look for a suitable place. Their first efforts came to nothing, but the project was not abandoned.

In 1879 Mother Enrichetta was all absorbed in the thought of her 'Benjamins' in India. Already in 1876 she had despatched another three nuns to assist the mission.

Now she was seriously considering the possibility of sending another three and wanted to join them herself. In this way she would achieve an old aspiration of hers and bring comfort to those distant daughters.

Before speaking of the decision that she wanted to take, she prayed and asked advice. Once the decision, insofar as she held it to be God's will, was taken, she obtained the necessary permissions from Cardinal Caterini (the Institute's protector), from the Archbishop of Turin, Mgr Lorenzo Gastaldi, and from her council.

Meanwhile in June new elections fell due. She was unanimously reconfirmed in office. In face of this renewed sign of esteem she showed herself strangely resigned. This was also due to the bustle of preparations for the voyage, and above all to the many enterprises that she had set in motion.

As for the elections, we read in her letter of 9 June, 1879, to Fr Tofoni: 'I fixed the precious day of the Holy Trinity for getting in the votes. The elections took place with the utmost tranquillity; I was not aware of any fuss. As you already know, I did not require the sisters to come from their establishments—I sent them the circulars and voting papers—and I think this was for the best, at least this time. Doing it like this made it apparent that each one was at complete liberty to act as she thought best. Perhaps a vote or two may have gone astray, never mind! I maintain my confidence in all turning out well; for my own part anyhow I am more than certain that I shan't catch it from anyone! "Daddy" is too well disposed to me to deprive me, at such a moment, of so rich and productive a seam of merit!'

In the same letter there is a reference to the current search for a site in Rome: 'Who knows when the Roman house will be opened? It looks as if "dear Daddy" wants to play a game with us. It is painful to think how much vexation those two poor girls must be having, always on the go in search of the house we want. May God quickly console them, and, with them, me too!'

Notice of the voyage to be undertaken in October was sent round to all the houses. Great was the joy, above all at Secunderabad, where the community lit a votive lamp to the Blessed Sacrament during the whole period of waiting.

On 22 October 1879, after a brief visit to Castelfidardo and the sanctuary of Loreto—where she entrusted all her hopes to our Lady—she left with three companions for Venice. From there she was to set out for the East. In the city of the *Serenissima* they were given hospitality in the convent of the Sisters of Charity, founded by Bartolomea Capitanio. It was a happy coincidence, because five nuns of that Congregation were also on the point of leaving for India; in fact they were to travel together. At the moment of departure the group was joined by six sisters of the Order of Canossa, likewise bound for the missionary field.

On the morning of the 23rd, and with intense devotion, they heard Mass celebrated by the Patriarch of Venice in the monastic church of St Vincent, and after receiving his blessing, went on board for Alexandria. The voyage was without incident except for sea-sickness caused by a brief storm between Venice and Ancona. From Brindisi, where the ship stopped to take on fresh supplies, she wrote to Fr Tofoni on 26 October, 1879, as follows: 'Since the ship has stopped here in Brindisi it gives me a favourable opportunity to send my good Father news of myself and my fellow-travellers, because I am sure they will give him pleasure. These past two days three of us, including myself, suffered a lot from sea-sickness; indeed in two days I could not keep down more than a single cup of clear soup and just a little lemon. Sister Annetta, however, has not suffered at all so far and eats with a relish that is a pleasure to see. So she was able to act as nurse for us who had no wish at all to leave our cabins. Our dear father in heaven always thinks of everything and acts as a most loving superior. On our first night the sea was very rough and I think that is what has so upset all our stomachs. Today, however, I can say that I am well and we are all passably well. I write to you as best I can leaning on a wash basin, but my good Father will be just as pleased with this letter of mine. "Dear Daddy" and our "Mama" of Loreto have promised to keep me company and I am convinced that they are with us, but they don't make themselves felt as in the last journey that you know of. I stay very quiet, always ready to do God's will. We shall be accompanied as far as Suez by four missionary priests and ten sisters as well. From Suez onwards we four shall remain with Fr Eugenio Salvi who will conduct us all the way to Secunderabad to the house of our "Benjamins". But before we get there a good long time has to pass. God is with us: so, forward!'

On 5 November they arrived at Aden, and on the 12th at Bombay. Then still two days of journeying over the mainland to reach their destination.

At Bombay they were welcomed by the missionary Fr Malberti and by the Superior of the Indian houses, Mother Bonosa, along with Sister Margherita. The meeting was full of emotion. On 14 November they were at Secunderabad, and their welcome exceeded all expectations: solemn celebrations in which there took part Mgr Barbero, the missionary priests of the area, all the nuns, and the people. These latter showed the liveliest enthusiasm and competed to kiss the hand of a traveller from so far away. What struck Mother Enrichetta from the very first days was the human warmth of those Indians, their spontaneity in showing their feelings, the dignified speech of the older ones. Her quick perceptions discovered a new world, an unknown civilization from which she had much to learn.

An echo of the celebrations is to be heard in the article of a local English newspaper: 'Roman Catholic convent. Friday, 14 of the current month, November, will be regarded as a memorable day in the history of the Convent of St Ann at Secunderabad . . . The road was lined on both sides by children of European and indigenous convents. Halfway between the gateway and the sisters' house a second triumphal arch had been erected. Also the effect produced by the illumination of the convent and its surroundings by numerous Chinese lanterns in various colours was very fine. In the central arch of the upper colonnade of the house was displayed a splendid "Welcome!" in metal lit by gas-jets. The brass band of the Twenty-Eighth Regiment, graciously lent for the occasion, struck up with its instruments as soon as the Most Reverend Mother General had entered the cathedral, and continued to play throughout the evening, with short breaks, under the direction of its conductor, Moraes. A great number of people of every rank, every faith, every caste, had assembled to see the solemn reception which took place in one of the spacious rooms, decorated for the occasion. Here were read aloud well-turned addresses in English and Italian, and splendid pieces of music, both instrumental and for voices, were performed. A grand display of fireworks brought the evening's festivities to a close'.[9]

Such attentions to her personally were in sharp contrast to her shy, retiring spirit, even if she was convinced that the congratulations and honours were not for her, but for the Lord, for 'dear Daddy', who had in such an extraordinary way given ear to her vow to go out to the missions. 'How great is my need of humility, charity, sweetness and strength', she wrote from India on 26 November 1879; 'several times, in the midst of such grand celebrations, I had the feeling of being quite alone, with none but God. I know that "dear Daddy" is to be found here and within me, and I go forward in all quietness, here as in Italy, "dear good Daddy's" daughter, always wholly surrendered to him in all that concerns my, and still more his, Institute!'

Once rested from the journey, she set off, with
Mother Bonosa and Sister Margherita, for a health-resort
called Bolarum where the sisters had a very modest
house which they had named the 'Moncalieri of India'.
If the air there was less sultry and healthier, the poverty
was extreme. The convent and school were compressed
into a low house, with walls of mud, two rooms in all.
Emergency schoolrooms were in the nearby church of St
Francis Xavier and an open space roofed with a spread of
mats. The little community lived in the most absolute
poverty, in every way on a level with the inhabitants
except for their heroism and the witness of their apostolate.

She confided in Fr Tofoni: 'To see the spiritual and
temporal poverty of these natives, Oh! how it makes one
value the more the grace of having been born in a
Catholic country of Catholic parents. What pain it causes
to see such poverty without being able to mitigate it!'[10]
If the widespread poverty, an ancestral poverty, made
her suffer because she would have wished to do more,
and in her charity to go everywhere in that vast countryside, at least to stay with the children of the Bolarum
school was a great comfort to her. Among these children
she was transfigured; in their intelligent faces she saw the
face of 'good Daddy' whom she imagined far away, left
behind in Europe: 'I happened to be at Bolarum, in a
little mission house where our sisters run a school for
some forty boys and girls, almost all natives of the place.
What a consolation it is to see and hear those dear little
black faces saying their Christian prayers with such
devotion. That is really the site of my greatest satisfaction! . . . In the evening of the 2nd of this month I
stayed in church rather longer, and when I was with the
sisters at recreation they asked me if I had found my
"Daddy". I replied: "I know that he is here too, but I
failed to find him because he stopped on the beaches at
Venice". My reply gave them all a good laugh, and one

of them said with an air of astonishment: "Even you, Mother, no longer feel his presence in these parts; I thought it happened only to me!" This gave me an opening to tell them something of the precious surrender that we ought to make to God, and this left them encouraged to practise so dear a virtue. My "dear Daddy" gave ear to our discourse, and on the morrow when I was in church for Mass, he intimated that he had not stayed in Venice, but was here, close to me, in India'.[11]

On her return to Secunderabad she gave many lectures to the assembled community; her themes can be gathered from the Annals: humility, surrender to God, observance of the Rule, simplicity, charity, the all-ness of God and the nothingness of his creatures.

She had brought from Italy as a gift to her 'Benjamins' a glorious statue of the Immaculate Conception, and from Our Lady she obtained the grace to present at the baptismal font three neophytes who took the names of Enrichetta, Teresa and Giuseppina. A second grace was the consecration of two young Indian women who had been pupils of the sisters and intended to work permanently in the mission. Thus on 19 March, 1880, the first step was taken towards the foundation of a new Institute that arose of itself in the orbit of the Sisters of St Ann. It was to be called the Daughters of Our Lady of Sorrows.

The day of departure drew near, and before it she called all the nuns together at the convent in Secunderabad. This time the meeting was less festive than when she arrived. Sadness for the imminent parting was the expression on all faces. Many, the more senior, felt that they would never see her again, and she was prey to the same thought, certain never to return to India, an extraordinary land that had won her heart.

Her words of farewell are reported by one of the missionary sisters: 'I recommend great exactitude in the observance of the Rule and in your duties, because in the end this is what the Lord wants of us. This is how he wants to make us holy. Pay attention, all of you, to this because I have it much at heart. Included among your duties you will find also the one that is the greatest of all, holy charity and fraternal harmony. It is this precious harmony which makes religious houses flourish. Mutual sympathy is needed; we have to impress it firmly on our minds that we all have faults and that for this reason each one of us, even involuntarily, is a cross for the others to bear, for all that she possesses fine virtues. Let us show sympathy towards each other, and let us stand firmly united. To do so requires humility and great generosity of mind . . . accordingly, my dears, great charity and great humility!'[12]

As she embraced the daughters whom she was leaving behind, she handed to each an image of the crucified Christ, and on every one she had written with her own hand the same words: 'My dear daughter, as we look on Jesus, crucified for love of us, shall we have the heart to deny him any sacrifice?'

On 1 April, 1880, she embarked on the return journey in the company of Sister Felicita, who was returning to Italy with her, Mother Bonosa and Sister Margherita who were going some of the way, and Fr Valentino, a mission priest. From Bombay she would again take the steamship to bring her back to Europe. Her last words to the two sisters who were staying on have been handed down by long tradition: 'Carry your crosses together; it is this, nothing else, that is God's will!'[13]

During the voyage she suffered terribly from sea-sickness, aggravated further by the Lenten fast which she imposed on herself. After twenty days she reached Brindisi and from there went on by train to Castelfidardo, to avoid sea-sickness certainly, but above all to let Sister Felicita embrace her aged parents.

She was at the end of her strength, and the long

exhausting train journey, in trains of that period, seems to have worsened her condition.

The Mother Superior of Castelfidardo, learning by telegram of the unexpected visit of the Mother General, went with several of her sisters to the station at Osimo to receive her. When she saw her descend from the string of smoky carriages, she was struck dumb with surprise—so pale, aged and tired did the Mother General seem. At some points Sister Felicita seemed almost to want to hold her up. But her smile and her unfailing warm cordiality soon obliterated the first impression.

She stayed for a week in the Marches. The short rest did her good; and the long hours spent in silence as she sat in the convent's little garden overlooking the valley below gave her back life and vigour. The visit of her spiritual father, don Tofoni, who came on purpose from Turin, was most welcome. They went to Loreto together to thank 'Mama'.

In the service of God it is not the wallet that counts
On 29 April 1880 Mother Enrichetta returned to Turin, arriving in the evening. Tired though she was, she could not withdraw from the welcome prepared for her with such affection and joy.

As always on entering one of the houses, the first stop was in the chapel. The whole community followed her and together they all sang a *Te Deum*.

In the afternoon of Saturday, 1 May, her happy return was celebrated with a dramatic recital organized by the pupils; a large audience, which included important guests, was present. It is curious to recall the subject of the much-applauded performance—a performance to be repeated not infrequently in the various houses of the Institute. It was inspired by the just-completed visit to India, a melodrama in which Satan, no less, is brought onto the stage; with snares and deceptions he battles against the Mother General as she is on the point of departure for India; the invincible opponent of the unleashed forces of evil is the archangel Raphael, on whose day, 24 October, Mother Enrichetta had embarked for the distant missions. There was a large cast of actors, patient and careful production, costumes supplied and sewn by ladies of the sisters' acquaintance, and pieces of music composed by Fr Giuseppe Anfossi.

Recovered from her fatigues, she took up the threads of her wonted life. In June 1880 don Pellegrino Tofoni was appointed Bishop of Assisi. She was his spiritual daughter, and signed herself as such in her letters written to strengthen him for the new and heavy charge: 'Courage, my best of fathers; do not be dismayed by the sublimity of the cross to which God subjects you. As the kind father that he is, he will always be with you to encourage, comfort and guide you. Remain like a child in his fatherly arms, and you will see how the new bishop of Assisi will be assisted and enlightened in the very difficult task that his bishopric brings him. God, only God in all things and for ever!'

The complete text of the letter from which the above extract, dated 17 June 1880, is taken, supplies some details which throw into relief her spirit of penitence: 'I have almost, not quite, acquired a taste for the consideration and comforts in which, through necessity, I acquiesced in the first days after my arrival, trying to consider myself. But after some time and at the present moment I do so through self-gratification. How willingly this animal adapts itself to better treatment! However I shall see to it that I get it back to its original state, since at present I feel as I did before, the pain in my shoulder has gone, and I still don't know if it was induced by a touch of rheumatism or by some muscular debility. At the moment I am under treatment, which consists in ointments and poultices. I shall see how it goes. If it does not pass, I shall keep it as a precious souvenir of my journey to India. It is a small matter, however;

nothing to make a fuss about. I am still using the mattress. Perhaps I discarded it too soon; I did without it just for one night, but took it back again at once as my poor old bones were not yet able to find rest on a palliasse alone. Now, however, I am much better, and for a few days have been getting up at the community's regular hour. The old animal grumbles a bit but comes to no harm. It will really have to adapt itself and get on with it'.

This same letter lets us know that the projected house in Rome was already something more than a mere project. Several months before, in fact, the sisters who had been sent to reconnoitre the capital had rented a house in Via Gioberti, small and modest but capable of accommodating a number of elementary classes and the beginnings of a nursery. At Turin they referred to it affectionately as 'our little niche in Rome'. Rather than a house it was a start, the substantial hope of a very different programme that would become fact as soon as possible. To convert hope into reality, many important people in the ecclesiastical world of Rome were giving their support—people who were in a position to know and respect the Sisters of St Ann. Among them was Cardinal Luigi Oreglia, titular of Santo Stefano, who wanted the sisters from Turin in Pieve Fosciana, near Castelnuovo di Garfagnana. Scarcely had one 'niche' been opened than thought was already being given to something else elsewhere, with courage and trust in Providence, whose active presence was met with day after day.

In Rome, for example, it was difficult to make progress. The house, small though it was, with the indispensable minimum, was in great need. Sister Francesa, the Superior, found herself one morning with only eight pence in the money-box which out of devotion she always kept under the picture of St Ann. The good nun who had been Mother Enrichetta's general assistant and secretary was not dismayed. She was accustomed to such shortages and knew very well that the works of God do not get done by keeping an eye on the wallet. She went into church, prayed, and entrusted her account books to the Lord: the very same day the money to pay the butcher and the baker turned up unexpectedly.

The year 1880 ended with various deaths that saddened the Institute. On 18 September, feast of Our Lady of Sorrows, Mgr Barbero died suddenly at Chudderghaut in India. It was a blow for the 'Benjamins' who lost an irreplaceable fatherly support. The Mother General was deeply grieved. She had met him not long before and knew his generosity to the depths. She remembered his words when, in asking her to send her daughters to India, he had added: 'Remember, Mother, so long as there is a loaf of bread for the bishop, there will be one for the missionaries too, so don't worry'.

Less than a month after this grievous loss the old Cardinal Protector, Prospero Caterini, passed away, to be succeeded in this charge by Cardinal Raffaello Monaco La Valletta.

Meanwhile the project of a new foundation in the valley of Garfagnana went ahead briskly. The house was ready, built at Pieve Fosciana by the Lady Isabella Turriani Raffaelli. After the first exploratory visits carried out by Sister Francesca and Sister Leonina, the business seemed well on the way to completion. The place and the inhabitants of the village made an excellent impression. We read in the Annals: 'The building is workable, the half-public chapel very fine, the people poor but normally healthy, the climate excellent, the site picturesque—in a valley framed by a ring of the encircling Appennines, rich in chestnut woods and medicinal springs, abounding in game, fish and mushrooms'. Obviously poetry had taken over the writer's hand, because in fact life in the Garfagnana, a harsh land and difficult to cultivate despite the abundance of water, was anything but romantic: houses climbing up on the backbone of the Appennines, roads of pounded earth for the passage of mules, villages that had lived for centuries in their silence, far from historical change, farther still from any sort of progress. The inhabitants were well disposed, willing, honest, but most of them compelled to emigrate to America to escape the inexorable poverty that closed in on them like a vice. They went as recruits to join the ranks of the makers of plaster figures, well known in the district of Lucca, who in New York as elsewhere bring a breath of Italian art into the new world.

Towards the end of 1883, when the house had already been provisionally opened, Mother Enrichetta made the journey to Pieve Fosciana and was received with great enthusiasm by the whole population. She was fifty-four years old and the journey was tremendously exhausting for her. Her effort, however, was repayed by the success achieved and, when she got back to Turin, a new task had been officially undertaken.

The following year, 1884, was the golden jubilee of the foundation of the Sisters of St Ann. The anniversary, which fell on 10 December, was to be commemorated in liturgical and civil ceremonies. Great preparations were made for the day and all the Mothers Superior were invited to the Mother House by circular letter.

The festivities were preceded by a solemn triduum, concluded on the eve with illuminations in the courtyard of Via della Consolata, and, on the morrow, they began with pontifical High Mass in chapel sung by Mgr Giovanni Cagliero, the newly-appointed bishop of Magida, Vicar Apostolic in Patagonia. In the afternoon there was a party for friends and benefactors, during which the Mother General was presented with a splendid book with an embroidered velvet binding in which every house, even the most distant, had its own page. In the evening the company was enlivened by a short topical comedy entitled *Charity Conquers*. When the performance was over, Cardinal Gaetano Alimonda, the recently appointed archbishop of Turin, arrived and imparted the eucharistic blessing to all present as well as transmitting to them the blessing of the Holy Father.

The 10 December 1884 came to an end. It had been a day of joy and thanksgiving. The outlook for the future seemed rich in ever bolder enterprises.

Notes

1.   From the letter to Tofoni of 12 November 1867.
2.   To Tofoni, 14 February 1868.
3.   *Ibid.*
4.   *Ibid.*
5.   Gastaldi, *op. cit.*, p. 282 quotes a sentence from Sister Bonosa's letter: 'If God inspired her [Mother Enrichetta] to direct her [Sister Bonosa] to those remote countries, she was ready to respond to the slightest hint: she was at the disposal of a Mother's complete freedom of action, because at all costs she wanted to be completely her daughter'.
6.   To Tofoni, 13 December 1870.
7.   To Tofoni, 21 November 1871.
8.   *VI testis, Rev. Sis. Maria Severina Pravettoni, Proc.*, p. 536.
9.   Gastaldi, *op. cit.*, p. 320-21.
10.   To Tofoni, 26 November 1879.
11.   To Tofoni, 11 May 1880.
12.   Gastaldi, *op. cit.*, p. 334-36.
13.   *Ibid.*

VIII Love dwindles when it ceases to increase

God's own slaveys

From the windows of the moving train the view of the country-side was enchanting: the country in spring, the fields still fresh from the plough, the dark earth upturned by the deep furrows, the scattered cottages, the trees becoming tinted with colour, the blue mountains in the distance.

In the compartment, two nuns: one more elderly, in her fifties; the other very young, a novice. It was still dark when they left Turin and by now it was morning. The journey was long, unending, with all those stops and the jolting on the rails.

Not a hint of impatience: Mother Enrichetta spoke seldom and her eyes were half-closed throughout the whole journey. She was absorbed in prayer. From time to time she gazed at the landscape. Her thoughts were elsewhere, on the far side of the mountain-chain of the Appennines that engulfed the train in tunnel after tunnel. She was on the way to Rome to negotiate the purchase of a house for her nuns, an important business which she entrusted to her 'good Daddy'. The young woman sitting near her missed nothing that the journey offered. She thought that she was asleep and abstained

206

from the least noise in order not to wake her. Then, tired of so prolonged a silence, she put a question or two to her.

'No, I'm not asleep; I'm talking to my good Father; with my eyes half-closed like this I can see him. The beauties of nature that I glimpse in the distance speak to me of him, and the view enhances my meditation'. Then, pointing to the surrounding countryside, she reminded the girl that it is the Lord who encompasses us in such magnificent scenery in order that we may remember him and do better. 'When I see his works, I shut my eyes and come close to him'.

The puffing train proceeded on its way. By evening, on 13 March 1885, they reached the recently built Termini station in Rome. There to meet them were Sister Francesca and Sister Leonina.

The prolonged negotiations to draw up the contract began. She was quite by herself because the two sisters were engaged in the schools in Via Gioberti, and the inexperienced novice was of very little help to her, though full of good will. Permits, licences, appointments, endless hanging around in the waiting-rooms of offices: the self-consistent temper of a genuine Piedmontese, all of a piece, was sorely tried by the Roman bureaucracy. Despite her ceaselessly multiplying engagements she did not neglect prayer; it was prayer that sustained her and kept her from despair about the many unforeseen difficulties. Her energies revived and acquired meaning in the hours that she spent near the altar.

Every morning she was off to the basilica of Santa Maria Maggiore, and on her knees in the Cappella Borghese recited the rosary—the fifteen decades. Likewise, when she could, she went to perform the pious exercise of the Scala Santa. But St Peter's in the Vatican remained the haven of her choice despite its distance from where she was living. Here, with her arms about the Confessio, she felt herself to be authentically Roman.

For the moment the little community in the capital was very restricted: four nuns in all, including the Mother General and the novice who came with her. Hence a family feeling, no pretensions, scarcely the bare minimum. Mother Enrichetta often helped in the kitchen because she wanted her daughters who ran the school to find everything ready.

The negotiations for the purchase of the property had their ups and downs. The matter was commended to St Joseph, although he seemed 'to turn a deaf ear', as the sisters humorously observed.

Mother Enrichetta stayed in Rome for almost five months. Novena followed novena for the successful issue of the mission in the various houses of the Institute. There was every need not to be faint-hearted.

Finally, on 14 May 1885, a telegram could be sent to Turin with the long-awaited news. The purchase was agreed, and the house, in the words of the Annals, 'was very fine, a first-rate building in Via Buonarroti'.[1] On 20 June the contract was signed and attested by the Notary Public; the legal costs were paid and the keys handed over.

Meanwhile in Via della Consolata in Turin, as the six-year period of Mother Enrichetta's generalship was expiring, the sisters decided to sign a petition to the Holy Father that her name should not be excluded from among those eligible for the responsibility which she alone was capable of carrying forward. The petition was sent in great secrecy, with the approval of the Archbishop's Curia.

In Rome, meanwhile, the removal and the adaptation had to be thought of, and this was an even more exhausting undertaking, especially as the summer heat was close at hand; it was an overwhelming labour faced with extraordinary enthusiasm and limited means. The funds of the Institutes supplied all or a high proportion, without concern for the future which belongs to Providence.

The removal, and the fitting out of the new house were no small burden. In those days of hard work, during which in addition the school in Via Gioberti had to continue in regular operation, the sisters made every effort, so much so that Mother Enrichetta, always at work too, called them affectionately 'God's own slaveys'.

The Annals report thus: 'The venerable Mother made short work of organizing the new house: she made the best reception room into the chapel, the best suite of rooms into the fee-paying boarding school and day school. The free schools were to find room for the 150 children who attended at Via Gioberti in addition to the new intake. The mansards and attics were assigned as lodging for the sisters'.[2]

To save money the furniture was sent from Turin, and while arranging it the novice found a crucifix in a drawer. She picked it up with joy and took it to show to Mother Enrichetta who was always on the spot where her daughters were at work. At the sight the Mother General took the crucifix in her hands, clasped it to her breast, and kissing it with passionate love said: 'This time Jesus is with us!' and it was a real consolation for them all.

In all the turmoil due to the change, Mother Enrichetta was not only the soul of the community but also its courage and its carefree cheerfulness. She was always ready to burst into amusing sallies, and when they felt more than usually fatigued she struck up some song or other to give a lift to morale. She never backed down in face of any obstacle. She helped to carry the furniture, she scrubbed the floors and did the cooking. She seemed rejuvenated.

One day the young novice, worried that such toils could do the Mother harm, spoke to the secretary who had recently arrived from Turin. The secretary mentioned the anxiety to Mother Enrichetta, only to get the following answer: 'Let us remember that we came to Rome to work and acquire merit!'

On 13 July, by favour of the Cardinal Protector Monaco La Valletta, there arrived an unlooked for invitation to a private audience of the Pope for the following day. At that moment Mother Enrichetta was in the kitchen washing up with the other sisters. Crossing herself in a large gesture she exhorted them all to give thanks to God. After some minutes of thought about the great joy of meeting the Holy Father, she came out with these words: 'Grand people put on special clothes for a visit to the Vatican, but we, the brides of Christ, do not make this fuss. Tomorrow the Pope will receive us in the very same habit in which we work in the kitchen. We shall have only to shake off the dust, give ourselves a brush, pull our sleeves down, and there we all are ready in a trice. Lucky us!'[3]

The paradox of the dark night of the soul
The audience was fixed for 14 July 1885, at five o'clock in the afternoon. At that hour in summer the sun still strikes pretty hot in Rome. The carriage, sent by the Cardinal Protector, called at the entrance to the detached house in Via Buonarroti, at that time on the outskirts of the city, near the tree-lined avenue that leads from Santa Maria Maggiore to St John Lateran. From the Esquiline to the Cortile di San Damaso in the Vatican is a long drive. The Mother General; the Superior of the new house, Sister Francesca; the secretary from Piedmont, Sister Pellegrina; and the young novice, took their places in the carriage.

When they alighted they were excited. The novice scarcely had time, intimidated by such grandeur, to raise her eyes to the colonnades of the Vatican. Then they mounted the grand staircase that leads to the Sala Clementina. The overpowering frescoes, the varieties of marble, the uniforms of the Swiss Guards: there was everything to admire. Through room after room, accompanied by an attendant in crimson apparel, they drew near to the place appointed for the audience.

Leo XIII came forward to greet Mother Enrichetta on the threshold of his study door. He said he knew her, remembered her, esteemed her highly. To the question how many years she had been General, she replied in all simplicity: 'Holy Father, I have been pulling this cart for twenty-four years', and he, looking at her benevolently, said: 'Twenty-four years . . . well, your daughters want you to continue as Mother. They put their request to the Pope and he has given his consent. So it is God's will and you must have patience!' She knew nothing of it and gave consent by silence.

As the audience proceeded, they got to speak of the basic importance of a good novice-mistress. At this point Sister Francesca introduced the novice, and Leo XIII asked: 'Are you a novice? Well now, remember that what you do now is done for ever. If you are fervent in your novitiate, you will also be so after your profession and you will do very well'. Sister Francesca with her exuberant temperament went on: 'In a few months' time she will make her profession', and the Pope, turning towards the young woman, added: 'Do you know what it means to make your profession? You have to consecrate yourself wholly to God and work for him alone. You will make yourself holy, satisfy your superiors and be helpful to your neighbour'.[4]

With the assurance of a special blessing on the work of the Institute and the Roman house, the nuns took their leave, kissing the hand of St Peter's successor.

Having in this way got to know of her confirmation as Mother General, on 16 July she wrote this letter to all her distant daughters: 'Precisely here, in the Holy City, I have had to make avowal of my resignation to the will of God, *fiat,* manifested by the majority of votes cast for my poor self; I am thus obliged to bow my head and to shoulder for another six years the heavy burden from which I would certainly have wished to be relieved. But since God has disposed otherwise, I neither can nor wish to say no. So, while I resign myself, I feel a debt of gratitude for your affection and for the trust that you put in me. I assure you of my most lively desire to help you and always to show myself a true mother towards every one of you.

'In this connexion I feel the need to ask your pardon and forgiveness if I have sometimes in the past offended you, and I assure you that it was never my intention, but rather the result of human weakness, without my will having any part in it at all. Trusting to your known kindness that everything will be already forgotten, I take courage to hope that you will always wish to help me with your prayers and make it a duty to lighten my heavy burden by your compliance. This, however, does not exempt me from having to apply compulsion rather than sweetness from time to time, solely for your own true good. In that case you, lovers of perfection as you are, will not wish to lay it at my door.

'My dearest daughters, I commend to you mutual charity, which ought to be the characteristic virtue of our dear Institute. It is so pleasing to Jesus that his brides should love one another with a true love and form one single heart and one single soul! Certainly to succeed in this continual watchfulness over ourselves is needed; we have to know how to repress certain impulses of impatience, how to show indulgence to others' weaknesses and always be ready to tolerate and excuse them. This is the true means of attracting an abundance of divine blessings to us, to our labours and to our entire Institute. This is the consolation that I hope for from my dear daughters whom I know all to be animated by a noble spirit and a keen desire for sanctification.

'It is also a consolation to me to know that my present good assistants have been re-elected. They will help me to bear my cross and will know very well how to lighten it by their sagacity and the sincere attachment that both have to the Institute.

'On Tuesday evening, 14 of this month, I had the happy privilege of kissing the Holy Father's foot. I already had doubts about obtaining such a grace, but the good God willed to grant me this comfort, and it brought me such encouragement to see what an interest the Vicar of Christ takes in our humble Institute. From him I brought back a special blessing on myself, on each one of my dear daughters, on the girls entrusted to us, on our spiritual and temporal benefactors, in short on all who belong to us. Blessed be God for everything!

'Moreover will not our dear mother St Ann herself wish also to concern herself that all of us unitedly begin a new life in perfect conformity with the Rule that we profess? I have no doubts on that score, convinced as I am of the firm undertaking of every one always to honour her, but more pertinently in this novena of hers which will be concluded by the renewal of our holy vows. Let us all compete to prepare ourselves thoroughly well for this solemn act; let us pray for each other so that all of us may find ourselves eventually one day reunited to sing the hymn of everlasting gratitude to God for the graces that he has showered on us, and most signally for that of our religious vocation.

'Here, then, my dearest daughters, I leave you, imploring a special blessing from the Blessed Trinity on you for your comfort and sanctification, to the glory of God and to the consolation of your most loving mother, Sister Maria Enrichetta'.

Before leaving Rome she had the satisfaction of obtaining the permission required to reserve the Sacrament in the chapel in Via Buonarroti. She confided to Sister Francesca: 'Now Jesus is with us; let us keep him good company!'

On 23 July, after ascending the Scala Santa yet again, she left Rome for Turin.

During the return journey it never even distantly

crossed her mind that she had accomplished something truly great. Soon she would have been General of the Institute for twenty-five years, and what progress it had made! Mother Enrichetta, however, did not measure the distance covered by the number of houses founded or by the steady increase of vocations. That was only an outward sign, a mark of undoubted vitality; but the more genuine vitality that really counted was the degree of change in the heart of every community. The Institute had got over its crisis and was on the march towards the future.

When she was back in Via della Consolata her perpetual preoccupations became more pressing, even threatening. The Indian missions required more nuns; relations with the Opera Pia Barolo became more strained; the possession of the house at Carmagnola, after the death of Canon Ariccio in 1884, was disputed by his heirs, and the continuance of the retreat house of the Immaculate Conception, already doing well, was called in question. There was an abundance of problems and questions to resolve, enough to undermine a much stronger constitution. The General was serene and untroubled; she would not let herself be overwhelmed by events, but looked with confidence beyond them, beyond the vicissitudes which at times could seem to block her path. She continued to speak of her 'good Daddy', of the Blessed Trinity, of her mother St Ann who together would smooth out all difficulties and put them to rights.

'I hope for the best, against all hope', was her usual reply to those who brought this or that snag to her notice. She was capable of instilling great confidence and courage in her daughters, even when the profoundest disillusion stirred in her heart.

Her most surprising trait was her constancy in action, in undertaking projects beyond her strength with an ardour that had a dash of the foolhardy about it. And strength she found in her union with the supernatural;

she explains it in a letter: 'My prayer is silence; it is to fix the mind's eye on God, which his goodness so affects that, seeing nothing, I see, and, hearing nothing, I understand and grasp the situation with such assurance that not the slightest doubt remains on what to do'.[5]

On 1 October 1885 Ariccio's heirs finally came to an agreement. The house at Carmagnola became the Institute's property; it was a foundation destined to accomplish great things.

The 'conquest' of the south

For the twenty-fifth anniversary of her generalship on 28 July 1886 there was a programme of solemn celebration: religious ceremonies, a triduum, a concert, and in the evening fireworks in the court-yard of the convent. To mark the occasion sisters, benefactors, and present and former pupils offered their guest of honour a statue of St Ann, which was placed in the common-room of the professed nuns, and a second statue in gilt bronze of St Peter enthroned, after the admirable image in St Peter's, Rome, which was placed in the convent entrance.

Telegrams and letters of congratulation poured in. Mgr Valentino Bigi, apostolic missionary and Vicar General of Hyderabad in India, wrote: 'I have just heard this evening in the convent of your "Benjamins" that on the next feast of St Ann will be celebrated the "silver wedding", the twenty-fifth anniversary of your election as Mother Superior General of the Order of St Ann and of Providence. Twenty-five years of such solicitude are equivalent in merit to fifty of profession in the same order'.

A few days after that unforgettable 28 July a prelate of Turin cathedral proposed to the Mother General to accept the supervision of Santonoceto College at Acireale. This was a complex institution consisting of a school for upper and middle class girls, an orphanage for the poor,

215

a weekly fee-paying boarding school, and a nursery school. In those days Sicily was tremendously distant, even farther away than it is today; far removed from Piedmont not only in mileage but in attitudes of mind, habits and customs. At that period to talk to the Piedmontese about Sicily was much the same as talking of a country that simply could not belong to Italy. Government officials went there reluctantly, but might well return as enthusiasts, enamoured for ever of that incomparable province. This is the fate of northerners, so attached to their fogs, who at times speak ill of the south simply because they do not know it.

Mother Enrichetta hesitated, asked for time before replying, and asked for the prayers of all the houses. God's will was not slow to show itself, and she allowed no delay in carrying it out. Indeed she was remaining faithful to her mode of action as expressed in a letter to a sister: 'To will what God wills, as he wills it and as long as he wills it'. On 17 October 1886 five St Ann's nuns, with her secretary Sister Pellegrina as superior, went off to Sicily.

About the same time there reached Turin a formal request from Mgr Pietro Caprotti, Barbero's successor, to open a school at Chudderghaut in India. The unexpected request provoked a wave of enthusiasm for the missions. Many were eager to go and the applications piled up on the Mother General's desk, although she had not yet come to a decision. At the session of the Institute's council on 3 October she outlined the missionary bishop's plan. Opinion was more than positive; acceptance was unanimous, and the names of the nuns to send overseas were decided on—Sisters Eletta, Natalina, Delibera, Silvana and Pasqualina, a novice of scarcely four months' standing.

Mother Enrichetta accompanied their departure as far as Marseilles. It was an act of motherly love, regard and esteem for the sacrifice made in the name of an ideal

216

which was love. They left Turin on 18 November 1886. A month later the new 'Benjamins' reached Madras by sea and so on to Secunderabad.

After the Christmas festivities of 1886 Mother Enrichetta went off to Sicily. It was two days' journey by train. She was accompanied by seven nuns intended for service there and by her second assistant, Sister Maria Pia.

The stay at Acireale lasted for three weeks. Her welcome was quite out of the ordinary and for the first time she came in contact with the generosity and exuberance of those southern regions. The Santonoceto college was a superb achievement: the building was spacious and of the highest standard, surrounded by a magnificent garden, in an enchanting landscape. What was more important, the community made a harmonious group, was esteemed by the inhabitants, and appreciated and assisted by the civil administration, owners of the property.

On the way back to Turin she made short stays at Rome, Bagnorea and Pieve Fosciana in the Garfagnana. Everywhere she found her daughters' morale very high, generously dedicated to the education of youth. In the spring of 1887, encouraged by all that she had been able to see and hear on her various visits, she opened a nursery school at Druento, a small town in the province of Turin, then a modest agricultural centre with a few hundred inhabitants. About the same time she opened a second one at Borgo San Bernardo and yet another at Mazzè near Ivres. The funds required for this last foundation had been offered by Anna de Scavenius, an unmarried Danish lady and a convert from Protestantism to the Catholic Church.

Everything and nothing
While the Institute's affairs made progress in Italy, no less success was achieved in India. On 13 January 1890 Mgr Pietro Caprotti's project was realized and the

Catholic school at Chudderghaut was inaugurated with the title of 'School of the Most Holy Rosary'. As for the staff of nuns, three sisters from the house at Secunderabad were sent at the first stage, but it was only a provisional solution: very soon the need for additional missionaries arose. Once again, after sounding her assistants, the Mother General gave her consent, and on 2 December 1890 four novices and one professed nun left Venice for India. It was Sister Eufrasia who accompanied them to the harbour this time as Mother Enrichetta was in Rome to negotiate the final acceptance of a house at Narni, where Cesare Boccanera had shortly before been elected bishop. He had been parish priest of Santa Maria Maggiore under whose jurisdiction the schools in Via Gioberti had been placed. He had come to know the nuns of the 'niche in Rome' and learnt to appreciate their value. Now he wanted them established permanently in his new diocese and was ready to face any sacrifice to get his way.

When the negotiations for the new house were completed—as early as 1881 she had sent several sisters there—the Mother General waited in Rome for Sister Eufrasia's arrival from Venice, with whom she had intended to make the return journey to Turin. But the repeated insistence that they wanted her in Sicily made them change their minds. After asking her 'good Daddy's' advice she was persuaded that she could not say 'no' to the call of her distant daughters. In the company of her secretary, Sister Valentina, she faced the long train journey. Her reception was, as ever, festive, affectionate, heartfelt. She stayed for almost four weeks at Acireale and untiringly found means to visit people, foundations, persons in authority. Unforgettable was her meeting with the bishop who counted it a blessing to have acquired for his diocese these good Piedmontese nuns, as he familiarly called them. Her humility, her sagacity and her reserve in speaking so little of herself and her works made a deep impression on the prelate, who envisaged and hoped for further schemes for the Institute. Many of his projects, such as the establishment of a large novice house, could not be carried out because of financial stringency. The projects boiled down to accepting a modest building for a school and an oratory for feast days at Aci Santa Lucia, a village not far from Acireale.

Mother Enrichetta had intended to return to Rome before the Christmas festivities of 1890, but she was compelled to prolong her stay at Acireale because of torrential rain at the time which flooded the railway lines at several places. On 8 January 1891, advised by many people against the train journey in view of the persistence of bad weather, she took ship at Messina about four o'clock in the afternoon. Torrents of rain fell and the sea was rough. The time-table indicated arrival at Naples at 10 a.m. the following day; instead *The Tiger*—such was the name to be read on the steamship's bows—was to reach its destination six hours late.

As soon as anchor was weighed and the crossing begun, a terribly violent storm broke loose. The ship was knocked about and sucked down by the angry waves that broke about it. This caused Mother Enrichetta great suffering from sea-sickness and she had constantly to get up from her bunk. Sitting was bad enough, lying down was worse. If she went onto the deck to get a little fresh air the wind thrust her against the cabins. Tottering, and supported by the faithful Sister Valentina who also felt ill, she got some relief by leaning on the taffrail at the stern. But the violent lurches of the boat caused her severe jolts. In the midst of the elements' rage she kept calm and tried to inspire her companion with courage, although she was at the end of her strength.

She arrived at Naples utterly worn out and was for long to feel the effects of the stormy passage—so much so that the doctors were perhaps right to connect them with the origin of the illness that was insidiously to undermine her.

By being six hours late she had to stop in Naples until 10 p.m., a long and exhausting wait punctuated by periods in the waiting-room or in some nearby church. For, having missed the connexion that had been planned, she had to wait for the next train. This was yet another unforeseen circumstance that put her patience and more than decrepit vitality to a severe strain. A propos of trains, it should be pointed out that the Mother General always preferred third class, and her reply to a nun who advised her to go second, if not first, to reduce her fatigue, was: 'Remember that we are poor and travel like the poor.'

When she arrived at the Termini station towards six in the morning of the following day, 10 January 1891, the community of Via Buonarroti was in a state of great anxiety. To take a whole day for the journey from Naples to Rome!

After a few days' rest, and despite the many who advised her against it, she then set off for Bagnorea. The same love for her daughters that had impelled her to Sicily now carried her into northern Latium. She hoped that the weather would improve, but at Montefiascone the mail-coach on which she was a passenger was forced to stop on account of ice and snow. To push on would have been a rash undertaking, and she waited three days for it to clear, uncertain whether to continue or to admit defeat and return to Rome. During these days she and her companion were guests of the Mimmi family, benefactors and well acquainted with the Institute.

Just as she was resigning herself to giving up the trip, as no driver would take it on himself to defy the state of the roads in that terrible winter, there turned up unexpectedly a carriage sent by the superior of Bagnorea, who refused to forgo the privilege of having the General even for a short time under her roof. On the evening of

17 January, an evening deep in freezing snow, she was welcomed by that community with affection and respect. After suffering so much from the cold, the sight of a blazing fire was attractive and captivating. Yet, as every time that she entered a religious house, her first steps took her into the chapel. She knelt down, numb with cold and with her feet soaking, but on the altar a fire was alight that had no need of flames or fuel to generate warmth. Her prayer rose in spontaneous gratitude, the breath of a soul that sees God continuously. She stayed on in that convent for more than a week, and as far as she could she gave an impression of having recovered and was quietly ready to listen to all of them.

On the return journey an accident to the horses of the mail-coach seriously endangered the lives of the passengers.

On 29 January she was back again in Rome and there received the news that the sisters present at the Chapter, taking advantage of her absence, had again presented a petition to the Holy Father that she should be put forward as eligible for another six-year period, as her term of office was due to expire. Still in Rome in February she received a visit from Mgr Caprotti who had been forced to leave the mission field for reasons of health. (Slightly improved in health he was to return to India on 28 July in the same year, after a stay in Via della Consolata at Turin, and to die at Yercaud in India in 1897). The meeting was extremely welcome to her. To speak of her 'Benjamins' and to hear news of them from their bishop was a tremendous comfort to her.

When she was back in the mother-house at the end of February, and the petition, sent in advance, had been approved, preparations were made for the Chapter in which the election would take place. On 23 June she wrote in a circular letter addressed to all the communities: 'His Eminence our Cardinal Protector, in his letter of the 7th of this month, informed me of the result of the elections conducted last month, and to my equal surprise and satisfaction reported the confirmation in office of my good assistants as well as my own. I have put "surprise" first since, in full awareness of my poor health, I really hoped to be relieved of the cross that has weighed on me for years. In second place I have mentioned "satisfaction" in the reconfirmation of my assistants, whose vigorous help and wise counsel have already served to such advantage in years past.

'Whatever may be my own estimate of my inadequacy and weakness, I feel in duty bound to thank both the electors and all of you, my dearest daughters, for the petition that you put forward to this end. I hope that the Lord before whom we so urgently laid the case will apportion grace to necessity, and by upholding our common good will see to it that our affairs always proceed according to his will and to his greater glory, to the edification of souls and the advancement of our dear and holy Institute. It is due to him alone that I guarantee, for myself and my good assistants, the illumination and counsel that are required for the proper fulfilment of the delicate and difficult assignment! Our glorious advocate and mother, St Ann, will intercede for us, and to her we shall address our prayers in full confidence. Is this not so, my dear daughters?

'Further, the better to ensure the success of our petitions, let us see to it that we combine action with prayer, holding ourselves as close as possible to the faithful and exact observance of the Rule and to that zeal in God's service which, without being accessible to our physical senses, stamps on even our slightest and most trivial actions an impress of generous love which makes them pleasing to God and most edifying to our neighbour.

'Again, in these times of widespread confusion, it is the strict duty of all who are consecrated to God to show themselves more reverent and faithful to him, because they have been so singularly favoured and filled to the brim with graces!

'Let us see to it, my dearest daughters, that Jesus should always have good reason to call himself satisfied with his brides, and find in them amends for the neglect and indifference in which he is left by the bulk of mankind, that he should delight to descend into the garden of our hearts and to find there the red roses of charity, the fragrance of white lilies, the sweet scent of the humble violet, and the ever attractive charm of the simple daisy. These four virtues ought particularly to be the mark of the Sisters of St Ann and I invoke them, my dearest daughters, on each of you as on myself, in heartfelt supplication to the Lord to grant grace and strength to all, that we may wish and know how to take advantage of all opportunities.

'Accept, with mine, the cordial greetings of my good assistants; persevere in your charitable prayers for me and believe me, so long as it may please God, your most loving **Mother**'.

'So long as it may please God': it is a veiled reference to the first symptoms of her inexorably worsening illness, a fleeting presentiment of the impending end, unsuspected by anyone.

In the same year, 1891, a new house was opened at San Giovanni Gemini, in the diocese of Girgenti: the Alessi orphanage, so called by the name of the owner of the building and surrounding land. She would have liked to get to Sicily for the inauguration, but her health would not allow it. For some time she had been feeling tired and old although she was only sixty-two. At the cost of great effort she fulfilled the obligations of community life. She suffered greatly, not so much from general weakness as from the constant sharp pains in her chest. She could have paid some attention to them, but she preferred not to talk to anyone about them and, conscientious in everything, to fulfil the many engagements that irked her even more than the pain.

She accepted her suffering from her 'good Daddy' in silence, without complaint. Long before, on 29 June 1871, she had written to one of her daughters who had asked her who her 'good Daddy' was. In a short note which, ever-thoughtful, she had had delivered, she explained: 'Everything and nothing! "Nothing" is incomprehensible in its malice and mischief. "Everything" is incomprehensible in its goodness and pity. Two beings separated from each other by an infinite distance; opposed to each other by differences of nature and of tendency. "Nothing" all agog for self-assertion and ostentation; "everything", for love of "nothing", humbles itself, empties itself to the point of self-annihilation. What a prodigy of grace! Fancy seeing the two approach, meet, intermingle, and form one single thing! . . . O immeasurable goodness of my God, the better I know you, the greater my wonder. The greater my wonder at you, the less I understand you and the deeper my perplexity. The great mystery of divine goodness? This is all that the daughter of her "dear Daddy" knows'.[6]

Trusting in that everything in which even the greatest suffering acquires meaning, Mother Enrichetta was ready to accept any gift whatsoever. Even disease and death.

Notes
1. Gastaldi, *op. cit.*, p. 362.
2. *Ibid.*
3. *Op. cit.*, p. 371.
4. *Op. cit.*, p. 372.
5. *Op. cit.*, p. 367.
6. *Op. cit.*, p. 374-376.

IX Death is at hand

The wind has lost its way
Tall gloomy cypresses darkened the sky. It was near to closing time at the cemetery and the two nuns left quickly. The sisters held the rosary tightly in their hands while their steps slipped in the gravel, damp from the falling drizzle.

Whenever possible Mother Enrichetta, accompanied by her secretary, went in the afternoon to the cemetery at Vanchiglia, beyond Dora; they were very brief and emotional visits. She went to visit her friends, she said. The thought of death did not leave her, but she was not troubled by it; on the contrary the theme of her conversation was happiness and hope, especially after she discovered how serious her illness was.

She was visited by Professor Lorenzo Bruno; he was kind but his diagnosis was exact and inescapable: a malignant cancer of the breast. It was possible to operate and he seriously considered surgery, but then, at the last moment, he decided against it because the illness was too advanced. For a long time Mother Enrichetta had kept secret the terrible pain which had tormented her since her trip to Sicily. When examined by more doctors, the verdict was the same; no one could offer any hope of recovery.

She was not worried by the gravity of her illness. She did not neglect her duties, but continued to work even when she was tired. Her whole life became one of joyful preparation for death, and the fact that the time was near did not frighten her. She waited confidently, as if she were receiving a gift from her good Father. By now her life was spent in thinking of eternity, and the grief around her showed that everyone knew that she would soon die. On 2 October 1892, in Via Massena, the chaplain died: don Petro Ponte, supporter, confidant and father, always sympathetic to the flourishing work in the San Secondo quarter. Between 2 January and 11 July 1893 she lost eight of her daughters: among them, Sister Rosalia, a cholera victim in India, Sister Veronica, novice-mistress, Sister Fedele, her friend from novitiate days and indefatigable head bursar of the Institute for twenty-nine years.

Her health declined relentlessly; but she did not wish anyone to worry about that. She was faithful until the end to every point of the Rule. One day Sister Eufrasia, who was looking after her, suggested that it was not advisable to get up in the morning as soon as the bell began ringing, but that she should rest more. She replied: 'If I stop to think for a few minutes, I will never get up again, because I feel such weakness in me that I certainly will not have the strength to overcome it if I do not get up immediately'.

The anguish caused by the reports she received from Secunderabad, where Sister Bonosa was also gravely ill, added to her physical pain. Likewise, the Superior of Castelfidardo was dying. It was these events that disheartened and saddened her. Indifferent to her own state, she wished to leave for the Marches, to take the consolation of a mother to her faraway daughters. She knew very well that she would not be supported over this exhausting journey; she listened disappointedly to all who wished well, but they could not, between the tears, make her admit that to do this would cost her more than ever.

Meanwhile the illness did not delay in changing her appearance drastically; many nights she was unable to sleep because of the pain but she would not disturb anyone. Only when she was no longer able to bear the intensity of the attack hour after hour did she call Sister Natalia, who brought her something from the infirmary, to relieve the pain.

All the nuns worried about her health and tried to be useful in some way, to prevent her from becoming too exhausted. In the community prayers were said for her recovery, but this request never seemed to be answered. The doctor confirmed that the cancer was incurable.

The month of September 1893 ended without hope. Resignation began to show on everyone's faces. Only Mother Enrichetta didn't seem to lose spirit. She was sustained by an extraordinary strength and in turn did not wish to see sadness in others. On the contrary, she appeared composed and full of high spirits, even ready to joke about her illness. She called the cancer that caused her swollen breast 'my burden', 'my precious gift'. She considered it very precious, like so many other gifts, no less precious, that she had had in her life from the good Father.

On 5 November 1893, as she did every so often, she wished to hold a meeting with her sisters. Her steps, once agile, prompt and quick like the wind, had become slow. The smallest movement caused her pain. Entering the council room she sat down, subduing the pain that tormented her; her face was pale and sickly; nevertheless, she still smiled on seeing her daughters assembled. She spoke calmly, choosing her words, and speaking carefully. Her theme was love, and everyone present that memorable day remembered the energy with which she articulated the final sentence: 'As long as I have breath, I recommend love to those I leave behind!' Her words were drowned by everyone's tears.

On the 19th of the same month she decided to attend another meeting, but before entering the room, even with her strength failing, she was accompanied to the chapel, where she prayed. She was so tired and bent by the concentration of prayer she already seemed much older. Then, acquiescing when she was supported, she went to the meeting in silence. In a clear, persuasive voice, she spoke of attachment to the Rule, the constant pledge of every nun who wished to grow in sanctity.

Before her birthday she went to visit the teachers and children. The pupils stood up to greet her; one of the girls recited a poem which the Mother followed attentively.

As she was leaving, a teacher asked for a blessing for herself and her class. The answer was 'Yes, yes, the Madonna blesses them all, all, and makes them holy'.[1]

Restricted to her room for long periods, she dedicated her time to sending out many letters. She spent whole afternoons dictating letters to her secretary and reading notes. In that way she could feel close to all her daughters and participate in their work carried out in the name of a great common ideal.

She seldom wrote herself: she was too easily tired, but she made an exception when replying to a missionary in India who asked for news of her health: 'Regarding my health, what can I say? The hour of God has come and it is necessary to carry out his will. If we enjoy good health for many years with gratitude to the Lord, we must also now make a good face of suffering, and be content that while we had leave to work for so long in his vineyard, he works in the same way on our bodies and souls with the hammer of sickness. Anything is good if it comes from his most blessed hands. However I will not fail to use the bottle of miraculous water which you have recommended to me, in case the Blessed Virgin of Huoch wishes me to be cured of my illness. I thank you

228

again for your sisterly kindness and in return I shall ask for a special blessing for you from the Lord'. First she signed the letter, and then she added some advice: 'Always show courage, my dear daughter; in difficulty I think that the Lord is a good father who will in his own time generously reward all the sacrifices made for his love'.

On 26 November, Sunday, she went down to the refectory to take part in the communal meal. The exertion of doing so tired her, as her strength was failing; nevertheless with a smile she told the nuns, who were afraid she would wear herself out, that she had decided to 'create a little festivity in the community'. When they had silently gathered around the table the Mother Superior intoned the blessing, which was continued by her neighbour, because she became choked by tears. The sight of her so weak and weighed down by suffering convinced them all that this would be the last time that she came down to join them.

She was given very little to eat but she tasted a little of it so as not to worry her companions, and she looked serenely at her daughters between one course and the next. Some were young, some old, and some were new novices. She knew them individually and no one had any secrets. Her door was always open to everyone. She knew that, in spite of their limitations, they remained faithful to their vocation, a blessed choice fulfilled in the name of love. Some were already close to perfection, others would be; all were pledged to the ascent to the summit, which was a constant desire in her life also, a life which was ending; this she did not delude herself about as she felt weaker and weaker all the time. But it was a life which left behind something living which would continue into the future. The Institute which she loved was a tangible reality, indestructible because the love for it would not perish. That love came from God not men; it was inspired in the novices, and increased in the elderly, as long as there were generous spirits, and generosity never disappears because it is the prerogative of youth, and youth is present in every epoch even if it is over-shadowed. Thoughts like these gave her courage and restored her will for the end which she felt near, with the progressive diminution of her strength.

After the frugal meal came recreation. She did not go out to the courtyard even though it was a marvellous day. She did not feel up to it and as she collapsed into a chair they suggested again and again that she should rest. She replied with a sigh: 'I have stayed on my feet for as long as possible, now I must resign myself to the fact that I am not able to any longer'.[2] Supported, almost carried, she went to her room.

Two days later she visited the doctor. The cancer was in a terrible condition: opening, it had formed a wound that was horrible to look at and even worse to endure. The pain became convulsive and it was absurd to hope any longer, even if everyone's prayers for a cure were multiplied.

The doctor asked why she wished to conceal this terrible development any longer. The reason she gave was that she could then work to the end, as she wished to cause the least possible trouble. The truth was different, and she confessed it, in a confidential moment, to one of her daughters: it was the great fear that once definitely confined to bed, she would not be able to go to chapel any more. She thought that she could not survive for long without taking the Eucharist daily.

On 1 December, she received communion. While she was absorbed in prayer, she turned round to the nun who attended her, inviting her to make her confession, because that was the wish of the good Father. The nurse was surprised at such an unexpected invitation as she had not taken communion for some time because too many doubts disturbed her peace of mind. The next day when, almost in tears, she thanked the Superior, the invalid embraced her happily.

One morning Professor Bruno made an urgent call. He was much admired in Turin and knew Mother Enrichetta well; he affectionately called her 'my daughter'. He was an old doctor. He had a solemn face with a large white beard. He had dedicated himself to science, and he was an unshakeable liberal with slight socialist sympathies. He had a very kind nature and was always ready to hurry to visit the poor, without ever claiming any honour, as he esteemed it a small thing in comparison to a life of healing.

The cancer had opened, and had been bleeding. It was necessary to lance it immediately. After this operation, the patient was better; she was even able to get up from time to time. She went to the chapel as much as possible, even if only for a short visit as she should not tire herself out. The nuns and teachers considered it an honour to accompany the Superior on her visits to the Sacrament. One time, a young novice asked her what the good Father would say to her on seeing her again after so long. The Superior looked at her, admiring this simplicity born of faith, and with equal simplicity replied: 'He will say nothing to me and he will not even be surprised to see me'.

Even though she was so weak and easily tired, she did not give up her discussions with her daughters. She asked for news of this and that house, wishing to be informed of every little detail, and her only anguish was the thing that she kept hidden. In spite of the pain, which rarely left her, she was always ready to receive all the people who wished to see her. She refused no one and, as always, she was composed and full of spirit and confidence.

She spent the quiet hour in prayer and reading: her favourite book was *My Imprisonment* by Silvio Pellico and she loved to talk about the author whom she had known and who had taught her French together with all the other nuns at the Institute. Sometimes her peaceful spirit was provoked by vivid memories to compare times past with the present, and the comparison was not without a trace of irony.

The story of death
The illness advanced uncontrollably, accomplishing its work of destruction with such violence that the decline was noticeable day by day. Mother Enrichetta tried to cause the least possible trouble. She gave in only to the comfort which the nuns provided in turn by sitting near to her bed through the night.

As Christmas approached, she asked if she could have a statue of the child Jesus which she had brought back from Sicily and to which she was very attached, on a chair near her pillow. Alone in her room during the mornings, while the songs of the children rang out outside the window, she would never tire of looking at the child Jesus.

At the end of December she received eight novices in her room who were to make their solemn vows in a few days. It was an occasion which gave her great joy, and when they came up close she spoke to them, her speech punctuated by long pauses which added weight to her words.

These words were recorded, or at least their essential sense was, and went thus: 'Humility, humility not only in things in general but in private. If you have virtue, you have everything. If you have humility you also have love and mutual understanding. In the future you will learn how to ignore certain expressions which injure our real love. We must be the pillars of the Institute as well as being good nuns: love any job because in this way whatever happens we will be the leaders. We must not make a great fuss over studying the love of God; this you know already if you love God . . . this you know . . . this you know. One must abandon oneself in the arms of

Jesus, to be generous and great. Do not act with a small heart . . . in practising virtue, my sisters, it is necessary to be truly great, then we will truly love the Lord! In meditation we must not look for consolation, but to do the will of God. Remain humble, you have the foundation, and never think that you have wasted time'.

On 1 January 1894, the eight nuns made their vows and returned to the Superior, who again had the strength to speak to great effect: 'Oh, what dear young brides! This morning I prayed a great deal for you in order that the Lord would give you the strength to love him. I hope for this, because I see you armed with so much good intention. Once you have begun it is necessary to go forwards always, even if you are discouraged. God is with us, even in the middle of the worst troubles. And if we never suffer, what would we have to compare Jesus to? You must abandon yourselves completely to the guidance of obedience. In whatever place we are, whether carrying the fuel, washing dishes, looking after the geese, like Vettigné, we always remain contented, because we know that we are fulfilling God's will and because of this, certainly, certainly God is with us. Where there is obedience, God is never absent. God, always God, we must look for God in all our actions. Never worrying, always confident! When Jesus's love is not apparent, do not be tempted to say that he has deserted us, on the contrary he is very close. I would suggest one thing more to you, have mutual understanding in your hearts. In other words, who is able to say she does not have faults? We all have some, so we must all sympathize. My dear sisters, remember always, humility, obedience, confidence are enlightened by God'.

During the illness, of all the many people who came to pay her a visit while she remained up, she remembered Maria Clotilde of Savoy, her friend and confidant. They had talked for about an hour. She returned a second time from Moncalieri, which had been reconstructed at great cost.

On 15 February, Sister Eufrasia wrote: 'I have noticed a decline. The fever rose very high; the stomach of the dear patient did not retain any food, the pain caused by the terrible illness developed into convulsions, which no medicine was able to provide adequate relief for'.

'Our blessed Mother draws near to the end of the pain from which she has suffered much violence, and she found comfort in invoking the name of Jesus, exhorting him to thank God for so much she wished for and did in him'.[3] To complete the destruction continuously wrought by the cancer, she suffered a stroke, which rendered her semi-conscious.

On the evening of the 16th the whole community of Via della Consolata accompanied the chaplain as he administered the last rites to the dying Superior. Many had tears in their eyes as they followed the ceremony kneeling in prayer around the bed. The patient had no strength: propped up on pillows, her arms crossed on her chest, she replied with difficulty to the priest.

The days, the hours passed without hope. Professor Bruni was nearby with every relief, but this was a moment in which medicine became useless. Her life ebbed slowly away, death advanced: it was the end. But it was also a beginning, of light and hope. How right he was when the kind old doctor said: 'She who has been your mother for many years is ready to die'.

On 19 February, the end seemed imminent; death had come to take her on the journey. It was six in the afternoon. She roused herself, in a lucid mood, from the drowsiness of sickness and the nuns asked for her blessing, a word to carry in their hearts for ever and to pass on to the generations to come. Mother Enrichetta opened her eyes, she looked around her and raised her hands, almost in an affectionate embrace to all, murmuring softly 'The Lord bless you!' There then followed a silent pause which seemed interminable after which she resumed: 'Remember, humility!'[4] She articulated the last word slowly so that it would be strongly impressed on those present.

From the expression on her face they understood that she wished to say more. She was tired from speaking and her idea was escaping with her departing life; she was able to say one more time, 'Humility'.

She spent the 20th sleeping; her breath was hardly perceptible. The nurse who attended her whispered in her ear and she seemed to respond, but perhaps it was an illusion.

At midday a telegram arrived announcing that the Holy Father prayed for a blessing for her. They read the message to the Mother but it was difficult to know if she had heard.

Before supper, the Archbishop of Turin arrived. He gave his blessing. There was no sign of a response. The coma continued and the moments of light in the shadows which implacably advanced were scarce.

Dawn of 21 February brought a final problem. Her breathing became very laboured and her obliviousness to her surroundings was worrying. Sister Eufrasia wrote: 'Since seven this morning she has not given much sign of seeing or feeling. It appeared that at certain moments she called someone to her, beckoning with her hand to the bottom of the bed, where we were waiting. Perhaps she was seeing her heavenly spouse or one of our sisters who had already passed into eternity?'

That morning of sorrow passed as usual in the house. At the correct moment the bell in the courtyard announced the beginning of classes. The school was strongly commited to staying open. The children came as usual, in spite of the sad circumstances. The teachers all had expressions of profound sorrow. The pupils understood, they perceived that something very serious was about to happen. The older ones knew that the Superior was ill, perhaps dying, so they whispered quietly among themselves, with great respect. But the thought of death, in the minds and also the imagination of children, took on the character of a story, a story which the adults did not have the courage to tell the children.

At midday, before going down to the refectory, the pupils went to the chapel to ask for the special favour which was so late in coming. The voice in the heart of the children followed the words spoken by the nuns who led them and their prayers were intermingled with tears.

Mother Enrichetta waited a little longer in her room for her life to expire; her face pale, eyes closed, unmoving. The chaplain, don Pietro Montefameglio, who attended her, described her death himself: 'She had sunk into unconsciousness, and she gave no further indication of feeling or of understanding, until she gently opened her eyes at a movement in the room, and her expression cheered up unexpectedly as she smiled joyfully, as if amused by a delightful and happy vision. Suddenly from the large group of weeping nuns who surrounded the bed came the unanimous cry: Mother, mother, bless us one more time! She raised her right hand which was by now almost lifeless and unmoveable, to make the blessing. Scarcely had a brief moment passed, I would say ten seconds, when she closed her eyes for ever to the light of this world and after a few moments yielded up her spirit. It was 3.35 on 21 February 1894'.

Notes
1. Gastaldi, *op. cit.,* p. 690.
2. *Op. cit.,* p. 693.
3. From Sister Eufrasia's circular letter of 24 February 1894.
4. *Ibid.*

Selected bibliography

Primary sources:
Autobiography of Mother Enrichetta
Diary (December 1865 to November 1866)
Correspondence (Letters to Monsignor Pelligrino Tofoni, from 1866 to 1880)
Annals of the Sisters of the Institute of St Ann and of Providence, and of the Sisters of St Ann
Memorie Storiche del Borgo Salsasio di Carmagnola (Carmagnola, 1930)

Secondary sources:
Gastaldi, P.P., *Umiltà e Grandezza* (Life of Sister Maria Enrichetta Dominici, Turin, 1926)
Morazzetti, S.P., *Vigilia Eroica* (Tivoli, 1951)
De Montis, G., *Nobiltà Vera* (Turin, 1950)
De Melun, A., *La Marchesa di Barolo* (Paris, 1869)
Pellico, S., *La Marchesa Giulia Falletti de Barolo Nata Colbert* (Turin, 1914)
Giacinto, R., *La Cappella Votiva della Madonna della Concezione nella Chiesa Parrocchiale di Carmagnola* (Turin, 1954)
Menochio, R., *Memorie Storiche della Città di Carmagnola* (Carmagnola, 1963)
Gervasio, R., *Storia Aneddotica Descrittiva di Torino,* Vol. 3 (Turin, 1974)